ESTATES IN LAND
AND FUTURE INTERESTS

Problems and Answers

ASPEN COURSEBOOK SERIES

ESTATES IN LAND AND FUTURE INTERESTS

Problems and Answers

Sixth Edition

JOHN MAKDISI
Professor of Law
St. Thomas University School of Law

DANIEL B. BOGART
Professor of Law and Donley and Marjorie Bollinger Chair
in Real Estate, Land Use, and Environmental Law
Chapman University School of Law

Wolters Kluwer
Law & Business

Printed in the United States of America.

1 2 3 4 5 6 7 8 9 0

ISBN 978-1-4548-4082-4

Library of Congress Cataloging-in-Publication Data

Makdisi, John, author.
    Estates in land and future interests : problems and answers / John Makdisi, Professor of Law, St. Thomas University School of Law; Daniel B. Bogart, Professor of Law and Donley and Marjorie Bollinger Chair in Real Estate, Land Use, and Environmental Law, Chapman University School of Law Wolters Kluwer Law & Business. — Sixth edition.
        pages cm. — (Aspen coursebook series)
    ISBN 978-1-4548-4082-4
    1. Future interests—United States—Problems, exercises, etc. 2. Estates (Law)—United States—Problems, exercises, etc. 3. Conveyancing—United States—Problems, exercises, etc. I. Bogart, Daniel B., 1960- author. II. Title.
    KF605.M35 2014
    346.7304'2—dc23
                                                                            2013042604

About Wolters Kluwer Law & Business

Wolters Kluwer Law & Business is a leading global provider of intelligent information and digital solutions for legal and business professionals in key specialty areas, and respected educational resources for professors and law students. Wolters Kluwer Law & Business connects legal and business professionals as well as those in the education market with timely, specialized authoritative content and information-enabled solutions to support success through productivity, accuracy and mobility.

Serving customers worldwide, Wolters Kluwer Law & Business products include those under the Aspen Publishers, CCH, Kluwer Law International, Loislaw, ftwilliam.com and MediRegs family of products.

CCH products have been a trusted resource since 1913, and are highly regarded resources for legal, securities, antitrust and trade regulation, government contracting, banking, pension, payroll, employment and labor, and healthcare reimbursement and compliance professionals.

Aspen Publishers products provide essential information to attorneys, business professionals and law students. Written by preeminent authorities, the product line offers analytical and practical information in a range of specialty practice areas from securities law and intellectual property to mergers and acquisitions and pension/benefits. Aspen's trusted legal education resources provide professors and students with high-quality, up-to-date and effective resources for successful instruction and study in all areas of the law.

Kluwer Law International products provide the global business community with reliable international legal information in English. Legal practitioners, corporate counsel and business executives around the world rely on Kluwer Law journals, looseleafs, books, and electronic products for comprehensive information in many areas of international legal practice.

Loislaw is a comprehensive online legal research product providing legal content to law firm practitioners of various specializations. Loislaw provides attorneys with the ability to quickly and efficiently find the necessary legal information they need, when and where they need it, by facilitating access to primary law as well as state-specific law, records, forms and treatises.

ftwilliam.com offers employee benefits professionals the highest quality plan documents (retirement, welfare and non-qualified) and government forms (5500/PBGC, 1099 and IRS) software at highly competitive prices.

MediRegs products provide integrated health care compliance content and software solutions for professionals in healthcare, higher education and life sciences, including professionals in accounting, law and consulting.

Wolters Kluwer Law & Business, a division of Wolters Kluwer, is headquartered in New York. Wolters Kluwer is a market-leading global information services company focused on professionals.

Summary of Contents

Contents

Preface

The goals of this book are to simplify a remarkably complex area of property law and to provide students with a chance to solidify their learning through practice. As a supplement to any casebook on property or wills, trusts, and estates, this book provides a skeletal, systematized account of the common law in its present form, interspersed with six hundred problems and answers to test one's ability to apply the rules to specific fact situations.

Many students find this area of law very difficult and challenging. Therefore, top priority has been given to organizing the rules in a way that is clear and concise. Coverage in this book does not include some of the more advanced topics in this area, such as an explanation of personal property rules (including per capita class gifts), equitable estates, marital estates, concurrent estates, lapse, trusts, adoption, the Rule in Clobberie's Case, or some of the more sophisticated or collateral rules for construction of ambiguous conveyances (including implied conditions of survivorship) or for perpetuities (including infectious invalidity and the validity of charitable gifts). It is our firm belief that the surest path to mastery of estates and future interests is to concentrate on the core of the subject as presented in this book, without too many digressions into ancillary areas.

What are estates in land and future interests? The rules governing this area stand as relics of the past, attempting to serve the needs of the present. Based on the vagaries of historical circumstance, these rules have developed piecemeal into a complicated structure. The arguments of antiquity no longer justify the intricate convolutions that hallmark this area of the law, but time is slow to remove them. Legislation has been enacted in many jurisdictions to simplify and improve the structure, but the common law rules that were a millennium in the making exert considerable control over this area. As a result, these rules continue to haunt the hallowed halls of our law schools, becoming the bane of every law student's existence.

Despite its legacy, however, this book avoids the historical approach. It focuses on an in-depth study of the rules as they exist here and now. Within the constricted confines of a fundamental property course, there is no time to do both well. An historical approach to estates and future interests is important for a thorough understanding, but it is best left for advanced courses. Premised on the idea that it is preferable to understand the "what" well, rather than to understand a whittled "what" and a hurried historical "how," this book adopts the present-day approach to ensure a firm foundation in the rules.

This sixth edition removes some of the material that appeared in the previous edition in order to increase the number of problems in the first six chapters by 50 percent. The deleted material includes the correlation chart at the beginning of the book; the section on recent modifications to the Rule Against Perpetuities (RAP) and the twenty-five questions corresponding to this section at the end of Chapter 6; the whole of Chapter 7, on powers of appointment; and the whole of the appendix on the fee tail. The problems in the first six chapters have been increased from four hundred to six hundred—with each chapter now containing one hundred problems.

This workbook is self-sufficient in explaining the rules of estates in land and future interests. More importantly, problem sets with fully explained answers are provided at the end of each of the chapters. Students have found these to be extremely valuable teaching tools because of the reinforcement they provide through the self-testing process. Those students who wish to further their understanding with other texts in this area may wish to consult Bergin and Haskell's *Preface to Estates in Land and Future Interests* and Moynihan's *Introduction to the Law of Real Property*.

Danny Bogart joined John Makdisi as a coauthor starting with the fourth edition of this book, and together they have made a great team. Danny Bogart would like to acknowledge the importance of the work of the late Jesse Dukeminier in Professor Bogart's development as a student of property law. John Makdisi would like to acknowledge the importance of the work of his teacher, the late Professor George Haskins, whose inspiration generated an excitement for this area of the law that has never waned.

November 2013

John Makdisi
Daniel Bogart

1

Classification of Estates

A. DEFINITIONS

Ownership of land is passed from one person to another by sale, gift, testate succession, or intestate succession. The first three are accomplished by an act of will on the part of a grantor and are each called a *conveyance* or *grant*. Intestate succession is accomplished by law and is called *inheritance*.

When land is passed successively through different people with each person passing it on to the next, each transfer is a conveyance of sole ownership in a present interest. When it is passed at one time to different people to enjoy together, it is a conveyance of joint ownership in a present interest. When it is passed at one time to different people, each to enjoy it successively over time, it is a conveyance of sole ownership in a present interest simultaneously with sole ownerships in future interests.

A conveyance *inter vivos* is a sale or a gift. A testamentary conveyance is a *will* (known more specifically as a *devise* when it concerns land). Intestate succession, or succession without a will, is not a conveyance. A *grantee* or *purchaser* (the term includes donee of a gift as well as buyer in a sale and devisee in a will) is one who takes an interest from a *grantor* by way of inter vivos or testamentary conveyance. An *heir* takes an interest from an *intestate* by way of inheritance (known also as *descent*). For the sake of convenience, a conveyance in this book should be understood as a conveyance inter vivos unless otherwise indicated to mean a testamentary conveyance.

There are different forms of joint ownership, including tenants in common, joint tenants, and tenants by the entirety. The definition of *tenant* in this context is not the same as that for tenant in the landlord-tenant relationship. The tenant who holds jointly is an owner who shares with other owners concurrently but is not subject to any other owner, whereas the tenant in the landlord-tenant relationship is an owner who is subject to the landlord. An owner who is not subject to another is the owner of a freehold estate. A tenant in the landlord-tenant relationship is the owner of a nonfreehold estate, which is dependent on the landlord's concurrent freehold estate. In common parlance, the tenant is not even considered an owner. The landlord is considered the owner, and the tenant is considered the holder of a right to possess.

The *nonfreehold estates* are a *term of years*, a *periodic tenancy*, and a *tenancy at will*. A term of years has the potential of lasting for a fixed period of time and is created by any words indicating such. For example, when an owner O conveys "to A subject to a term of ten years in B," O conveys a freehold estate to A and a nonfreehold estate (called a term of years) to B.

The *freehold estates* are a *fee simple* and a *life estate*. There is a third type of freehold estate called a *fee tail*, which is changed by statute in virtually every state into some form of life estate and/or fee simple. Therefore, fee tail estates are not discussed in this book.

In most of the conveyances discussed in this book, it is assumed that the grantor owns the whole estate (present interest in a fee simple estate) in the property he or she conveys. When the grantor owns less than the whole estate (such as a present interest in a life estate or a future interest in a fee simple estate), the grantor's interest and estate will be specified in the discussion of the conveyance. Of course, if the grantor owns less than a present interest in fee simple absolute, the grantor can convey no more than the estate the grantor has.

B. CATEGORIES

(1) A *fee simple* has the potential of infinite duration and is created by the words "to A and her heirs" or merely by the words "to A" (although problems may arise on rare occasions if the words "and her heirs" are not used). The fee simple estate is the longest in duration of the two estates; it is infinite. It can be inherited by anyone specified in the intestate succession laws, but it is important to note that a conveyance "to A and her heirs" is a conveyance to A alone. The words "and her heirs" merely classify the estate that A receives as a fee simple and do not give the heirs any interest. Variations on the words in the conveyance, such as "to A and her heirs on her father's side," do not prevent or restrict the creation of a fee simple, and the estate is still inheritable by anyone specified in the intestate succession laws despite the attempted restriction.

(2) A *life estate* has the potential of lasting until the death of the purchaser or another designated person or persons. An estate measured by the life or lives of another person or persons is called, more specifically, a *life estate pur autre vie*. A life estate is created by the words "to A for life" or "to A for the life of B."

Each of these two estates may be conveyed by its owner to another person by sale or gift. The fee simple and the life estate pur autre vie are devisable (may be conveyed by will) or inheritable (may pass to one's heirs as determined by the intestate succession laws); the life estate is not devisable or inheritable because it ends on the death of its owner. When the grantor of a fee simple or a life estate pur autre vie conveys all her estate, her heirs lose the opportunity to inherit it, and it becomes inheritable by the heirs of the new owner.

Thus, when O conveys "to A and her heirs," and A turns around and conveys her fee simple estate to B, A's heirs (who were never grantees of O) lose the chance to inherit the estate from A when she dies. When O conveys "to A for the life of X," and A then conveys her life estate pur autre vie to B before X's death, A's heirs lose the chance to inherit the estate from A when A dies.

What is the nature of the estate conveyed to B in each of the conveyances described in the paragraph above? When O conveys "to A and her heirs," and A turns around and conveys her fee simple estate to B, B takes a fee simple estate inheritable by his heirs. When O conveys "to A for the life of X," and A then conveys her life estate pur autre vie to B, B takes a life estate pur autre vie measured by the life of X and inheritable by B's heirs.

One more definition: In a conveyance, *words of purchase* identify the grantee, also known as the purchaser; *words of limitation* identify the estate that the grantee takes. For example, when O conveys "to A and his heirs," O conveys a fee simple absolute to A. The words of purchase are "to A," and the words of limitation are "and his heirs." When O conveys "to A for life," O conveys a life estate to A. The words of purchase are "to A," and the words of limitation are "for life."

C. SUBCATEGORIES

Each of the freehold estates may be subdivided further into four subcategories. The first subcategory contains no condition that limits the duration of the estate. The other three subcategories contain a condition that, if it occurs, cuts short or gives the grantor the power to cut short the estate. This condition is called a *condition subsequent* (to be distinguished from a *condition precedent*, which is explained in Chapter 2 in connection with the vesting of future interests). The four subcategories of each freehold estate are as follows:

(1) An *absolute* estate characterizes an estate without a condition subsequent. The two absolute estates are the *fee simple absolute* ("to A and her heirs" or "to A") and the *life estate* ("to A for life").

(2) An estate *determinable* characterizes an estate with a condition subsequent that, if it occurs, automatically cuts shorts the estate in favor of the grantor. The two estates determinable are the *fee simple determinable* ("to A as long as A does not divorce") and the *life estate determinable* ("to A for life as long as A does not divorce").

(3) An estate *subject to condition subsequent* characterizes an estate with a condition subsequent that, if it occurs, gives the grantor the

power to retake the estate. In this subcategory the condition subsequent does not automatically cut short the estate until the grantor exercises his option to retake the estate either by making an entry or by bringing an action to recover the land. The two estates subject to condition subsequent are the *fee simple subject to condition subsequent* ("to A, but if A divorces, O may reenter") and the *life estate subject to condition subsequent* ("to A for life, but if A divorces, O may reenter").

(4)   An estate *subject to executory limitation* characterizes an estate with a condition subsequent that, if it occurs, cuts short the estate in favor of a grantee. The two estates subject to executory limitation are the *fee simple subject to executory limitation* ("to A, but if A divorces, then to B" or "to A as long as A does not divorce; otherwise to B") and the *life estate subject to executory limitation* ("to A for life, but if A divorces, then to B" or "to A for life as long as A does not divorce; otherwise to B").

An estate subject to condition subsequent differs from an estate determinable by the fact that the former is cut short on the reentry or action to reenter by the grantor after the occurrence of the condition subsequent, while the latter terminates automatically in favor of the grantor when it is cut short by the condition subsequent. There may be some difficulty, however, in distinguishing between these two estates. An estate is identified as one or the other by the intent of the parties, which in some conveyances may be expressed only in the language of the condition subsequent. Words of *condition*, such as "provided that," "on condition that," "if," "but if," and "provided, however," connote an estate subject to condition subsequent. Words of *duration*, such as "during," "until," "so long as," "as long as," and "while," connote an estate determinable. Since in an estate subject to condition subsequent the grantor has a power of termination but does not automatically receive a present interest on the happening of the condition subsequent, words indicating this power, such as "the grantor shall have the right to reenter," also help indicate (and sometimes are required to indicate) the estate. Since the intention of the parties controls, an ambiguity may be clarified by looking to the circumstances of the transaction.

The difficulty that exists in distinguishing between an estate subject to condition subsequent and an estate determinable does not exist in identifying an estate subject to executory limitation. The first two estates are followed by an estate in the grantor, while the estate subject to executory limitation is followed by an estate in another grantee. There is no need to use special words of condition or of duration. Words of either type may be used, and the estate will automatically terminate on the happening of the condition subsequent in favor of the estate in the other grantee.

In addition to the freehold estates, the nonfreehold estate called a *term of years* may be cut short by a condition subsequent as well. When the condition subsequent occurs, this estate terminates automatically in favor of the landlord. It is called a *determinable term of years*, but it should not be confused with a freehold estate that is determinable. The nonfreehold estate in the tenant is concurrent with the freehold estate in the landlord until the former is cut short by the condition subsequent, and then the landlord's freehold estate, which has been a present interest all along, continues alone. An example of the determinable term of years is "to *A* for ten years as long as *A* does not divorce." *O*, the grantor, retains a present interest in fee simple absolute while *A* holds a determinable term of years. When *A* divorces or the ten years have passed, whichever is sooner, the nonfreehold estate ends and the freehold estate continues without the nonfreehold estate. Compare with an example of a fee simple determinable, such as "to *A* and her heirs as long as *A* does not divorce." The freehold estate that is determinable stands alone until it is cut short by the condition subsequent, and then another freehold estate takes over at that point in time. This concept is explained more fully in Chapter 2.

Problem Set I

The problems in this section ask for a description of an estate. The answers for estate are:

A. term of years
B. term of years determinable
C. life estate
D. life estate pur autre vie
E. life estate determinable
F. life estate subject to condition subsequent
G. life estate subject to executory limitation
H. fee simple absolute
I. fee simple determinable
J. fee simple subject to condition subsequent
K. fee simple subject to executory limitation
L. none
M. none of the above is correct

Problems

O conveys Blackacre "to Arthur and his heirs."

1. What is Arthur's estate?
2. What is the estate of Arthur's heirs?

O conveys Blackacre "to Arthur for life." Arthur then conveys his interest "to Barbara."

3. What is Barbara's estate?
4. If Barbara were to die after Arthur's conveyance but before the death of Arthur, what is the estate of Barbara's heirs?
5. If Arthur were to die after Arthur's conveyance but before the death of Barbara, what is Barbara's estate?

O conveys "to A for ten years."

    6. What is A's estate?

O conveys "to John and his heirs until Abby graduates from law school, then to David and his heirs."

    7. What is John's estate?

O conveys "to A to have and to hold during the life of B."

    8. What is A's estate?

O conveys "to A for forty-nine years or until the land lies fallow, whichever is first."

    9. What is A's estate?

O conveys "to A and her heirs on her mother's side."

    10. What is A's estate?

O conveys "to A for life, but if A divorces, then to O."

    11. What is A's estate?

O conveys "to A and his heirs as long as this old house remains standing, then to O."

    12. What is A's estate?

O conveys "to A, but if A makes this property something other than a residence, then to B for ten years."

    13. What is A's estate?

O conveys "to A for life, but if A gets married, then to B."

    14. What is A's estate?

O conveys "to the heirs of A."

    15. What is the estate of the heirs of A?

O conveys "to A for life as long as the house on the property remains standing." After the conveyance, A dies and leaves all her property "to B" in her will. The house is still standing on the property.

    16. What is B's estate?

O conveys Blackacre "to A for life." A then gives Blackacre "to B and her heirs" as a gift.

    17. What is B's estate?

O gives Blackacre as a gift "to A for life as long as she maintains the property; otherwise it is to revert to O."

    18. What is A's estate?

O conveys "to A and his heirs." Then A conveys "to B and her heirs."

    19. What is the estate of B's heirs?

O conveys "to A for the life of B." Then A dies, leaving B as her only heir.

    20. What is B's estate?

O conveys "to A, but if A divorces, then the property is to go back to O." O reenters the property even though A has not divorced.

    21. What is A's estate after O's reentry?

O conveys "to A, but if A divorces, then the property is to go back to O." A divorces, but O has not yet reentered the property.

    22. What is A's estate?

O conveys "to A as long as A does not divorce, then the property is to go back to O." A divorces, but O has not yet reentered the property.

    23. What is A's estate?

O conveys "to A for life." A then conveys "to B for ten years."

    24. What is B's estate?

O conveys "to A and her heirs, but if A divorces, then B shall have the right to reenter and retake the property as of his own estate."

    25. What is A's estate?
    26. If A divorces and B does not reenter the property, what is A's estate?

O conveys "to A for life to have during the time the property is used as a farm, then to B subject to a term of ten years in C."

    27. What is A's estate?
    28. If A stops using the property as a farm, what is B's estate?
    29. If A stops using the property as a farm, what is C's estate?

O dies while his mother is alive and in his will he gives "to my heirs on my father's side for the life of my mother."

    30.   What is the estate of the heirs on the mother's side?
    31.   What is the estate of the heirs on the father's side?

O conveys Blackacre "to *A* and her heirs." *A* then conveys Blackacre "to *B* for life." *B* then dies and leaves Blackacre in his will "to *C*."

    32.   What is *C*'s estate?

O conveys Blackacre "to *A* and her heirs to have while the house remains standing on the property; otherwise Blackacre shall revert to *O*."

    33.   What is *A*'s estate?
    34.   If a fire destroys the house on the property, what is *O*'s estate?

O conveys Blackacre "to *A* for life." *A* then conveys Blackacre "to *B* so long as the property is not used as a tavern."

    35.   What is *B*'s estate?
    36.   If *A* is still alive when the property is used as a tavern, what is *B*'s estate?
    37.   If *A* dies and the property is still not used as a tavern, what is *B*'s estate?

O conveys "to *A* provided that the old oak tree on the property remains standing for the next ten years; otherwise *B* shall have the right to enter the property."

    38.   What is *A*'s estate?
    39.   If the old oak tree falls in three years and *B* does not enter the property, what is *A*'s estate?

O conveys "to *A* provided that the old oak tree on the property remains standing for the next ten years; otherwise *O* shall have the right to enter the property."

    40.   What is *A*'s estate?
    41.   If the old oak tree falls in three years and *O* does not enter the property, what is *A*'s estate?

O conveys "to *A* so long as the old oak tree on the property does not fall within the next ten years; otherwise to *B*."

    42.   What is *A*'s estate?
    43.   If the old oak tree falls in three years and *B* does not enter the property, what is *A*'s estate?

O conveys "to *A* so long as the old oak tree on the property does not fall within the next ten years; otherwise to *O*."

44. What is *A*'s estate?
45. If the old oak tree falls in twelve years, what is *A*'s estate?

O conveys Blackacre "to *A* and his heirs." *A* dies without leaving any will.

46. What is the estate of *A*'s heirs?

O conveys Blackacre "to *A* for the life of *X*." *A* then conveys "to *B*." Then *A* dies, leaving *C* as her only heir. Then *B* dies, leaving *D* as his only heir. *X* is still alive.

47. After *A*'s death and before *B*'s death, what is *B*'s estate?
48. After *A*'s death and before *B*'s death, what is *C*'s estate?
49. After *B*'s death, what is *D*'s estate?

O conveys Blackacre "to *A* for the life of *X*." *A* then conveys "to *B* for twenty years." Then *A* dies, leaving *C* as her only heir. Then *B* dies, leaving *D* as his only heir. *X* is still alive.

50. After *A*'s death and before *B*'s death, what is *B*'s estate?
51. After *A*'s death and before *B*'s death, what is *C*'s estate?
52. After *B*'s death, what is *D*'s estate?

O conveys "to *A* for life during the time the Empire State Building remains standing." *A* conveys "to *B* for the life of *B*."

53. What is *A*'s estate before *A* conveys to *B*?
54. What is *B*'s estate after *A* conveys to *B*?

O conveys "to *A* on condition that *A* never goes to business school."

55. What is *A*'s estate?
56. If *A* goes to business school and then dies, what is the estate of *A*'s heirs upon her death?

O conveys Blackacre "to *A* for life if *A* never goes to law school."

57. What is *A*'s estate?
58. If *A* dies without going to law school, what is the estate of *A*'s heirs?

O conveys Blackacre "to *A*." Then *A* conveys Blackacre "to *B*." Then *B* conveys Blackacre "to *C* for life until the next president of the United States is elected." Then *C* conveys Blackacre "to *D* for fifteen years."

59. What is *C*'s estate?
60. What is *D*'s estate?

O conveys "to *A* for life." Then *A* conveys "to *B* for the life of *C*."

61. What is *B*'s estate?

62. If *B* then dies, what is the estate of *B*'s heirs?

A and *B* are both presently confined to wheelchairs. *O* conveys "to *A* for life while *A* remains confined to a wheelchair." Then *A* conveys "to *B* for life while *B* remains confined to a wheelchair."

63. What is *B*'s estate?
64. If, one year later, *A* is no longer confined to a wheelchair, what is *B*'s estate?

Orville, a widower, conveys "to my son Stephen for life provided that Stephen puts a red rose on his mother's grave every year." Then Stephen conveys "to my brother Arthur."

65. What is Arthur's estate?
66. If, in the year following Stephen's conveyance, Arthur puts the rose on the mother's grave instead of Stephen, what is Arthur's estate?

O conveys "to *A* for life." Then *A* conveys "to *B* for ten years." Three years later *A* dies.

67. What is *B*'s estate?

O conveys Blackacre "to *A* for the life of *X* provided, however, that *A* never gets married; otherwise to *O*." Then *A* conveys Blackacre "to *B*." Then *B* conveys Blackacre "to *C*."

68. What is *C*'s estate?

O conveys Blackacre "to *A* if *A* does not divorce; otherwise to *O*." Then *A*, who was married at the time of the conveyance, divorces. Then *A* conveys Blackacre "to *B* for life."

69. What is *B*'s estate?

O conveys "to *A* for life." Then *A* conveys "to *B* and his heirs." Then *B* conveys "to *C* for life." Then *C* conveys "to *D*."

70. What is *D*'s estate?
71. If *B* dies, what is *D*'s estate?

O conveys "to *A* until the old oak tree on the property falls." *A* then conveys "to *B* for five years." *B* then conveys "to *C* for life."

72. What is *A*'s estate?
73. What is *C*'s estate?

O conveys "to *A* provided, however, that *A* never takes drugs." Then *A* conveys "to *B* for life."

74. What is *B*'s estate?
75. If *A* then dies without ever having taken drugs, what is *B*'s estate?

O conveys "to *A* on condition that *A* never commits a felony or until *A* goes to prison, whichever is sooner."

76. What is *A*'s estate?
77. If *A* commits a felony but does not go to prison, what is *A*'s estate?
78. If *A* goes to prison but does not commit a felony, what is *A*'s estate?

O conveys "to *A* as long as the property is used as a residence by *X*, then to *B*." Then, one year later, *A* conveys "to *C*."

79. What is *C*'s estate?
80. If *A* dies and the property is still being used as a residence by *X*, what is *C*'s estate?
81. If *X* dies and the property is still being used as a residence, what is *C*'s estate?

O conveys Blackacre "to *A* for life to hold while *A* never leaves the country."

82. What is *A*'s estate?

O conveys "to *A* for ten years, but if the property is not maintained, then *A* shall lose it." Then *A* conveys "to *B* for the life of *X*."

83. What is *B*'s estate?
84. What is *O*'s estate?

O conveys "to *A* so long as *A* never divorces." Then *A* conveys "to *B* as long as *B* never divorces." Then *B* conveys "to *C* until *C* divorces." Then *A*, *B*, and *C* die together in a car crash. None of them left a will.

85. What is the estate of *C*'s heirs?

O conveys "to *A* for life on condition that *A* never smokes; otherwise to *B* for life on condition that *B* never smokes; otherwise to *C*."

86. What is *A*'s estate?
87. If *A* smokes, what is *B*'s estate?
88. If both *A* and *B* smoke, what is *C*'s estate?

O conveys "to *A* provided, however, that *A* never smokes; otherwise to *B* during the time cigarettes continue to be manufactured in the United States."

89. What is *A*'s estate?
90. If *A* dies without smoking, what is *A*'s heirs' estate?
91. If *A* smokes, what is *B*'s estate?

O conveys "to *A* while *A* continues to live in Arizona." Then *A* conveys "to *B* for ten years."

> 92. What is *A*'s estate?
> 93. What is *B*'s estate?
> 94. If *A* stops living in Arizona, what is *B*'s estate?
> 95. If *A* stops living in Arizona, what is *O*'s estate?

O conveys "to *A* for the life of the survivor of *A* and *B*."

> 96. What is *A*'s estate?

O conveys "to *A* for the joint lives of *A* and *B*."

> 97. What is *A*'s estate?

O conveys "to *A* for life." Then *A* conveys "to *B* for the life of *C*." Then *B* conveys "to *D*." Then *D* conveys "to *E* for the life of *F*."

> 98. What is *E*'s estate?
> 99. If *C* dies, what is *E*'s estate?

O conveys "to *A* and *B*."

> 100. What is *A*'s estate?

Answers

1. *H. Fee simple absolute.* The words "to Arthur" are words of purchase. The words "and his heirs" are words of limitation that designate Arthur's estate as a fee simple absolute.
2. *L. None.* "And his heirs" are words of limitation; they give no estate to the heirs.
3. *D. Life estate pur autre vie. O* conveys a life estate to Arthur. Arthur's estate when it is transferred to Barbara continues to be measured by Arthur's life.
4. *D. Life estate pur autre vie.* Barbara's estate is measured by Arthur's life. Since a life estate pur autre vie is inheritable, this estate is inherited by Barbara's heirs.
5. *L. None.* Barbara's estate is measured by Arthur's life. When Arthur dies, the estate ends.
6. *A. Term of years. O* retains a present interest in fee simple absolute. In essence, *O* as landlord has given a lease to *A* as tenant.
7. *K. Fee simple subject to executory limitation.* It does not matter whether words of condition or words of duration are used in the condition subsequent.
8. *D. Life estate pur autre vie. B*'s life measures the duration of *A*'s estate. If *A* dies without transferring her estate, *A*'s heirs inherit the estate, which continues to last until the death of *B*.

9. *B. Term of years determinable.* The duration of the estate is limited to forty-nine years and may be terminated before that time by a condition ("until the land lies fallow"). It is a nonfreehold estate. *O* retains a present interest in fee simple absolute subject to this term of years.

10. *H. Fee simple absolute.* Attempted restrictions of the words of limitation for a fee simple estate have no legal effect.

11. *F. Life estate subject to condition subsequent.* The "but if" language in the condition, coupled with the fact that the condition is followed by an estate in the grantor, creates this estate.

12. *I. Fee simple determinable.* The "as long as" language in the condition, coupled with the fact that the condition is followed by an estate in the grantor, creates this estate.

13. *H. Fee simple absolute.* The "but if" condition is not designed to cut short *A*'s freehold estate. If it occurs, it will cut short *A*'s possession to give *B* a term of ten years, and *A*'s freehold estate will continue to exist concurrently with the nonfreehold estate in *B*.

14. *G. Life estate subject to executory limitation.* Regardless of the language used in the condition, the mere fact that the occurrence of the condition will cut short *A*'s estate in favor of a grantee creates this estate.

15. *H. Fee simple absolute.* "To the heirs of *A*" are words of purchase. There are no words of limitation. Therefore, the estate is a fee simple. Note the difference between this conveyance and the conveyance "to *A* and her heirs," where the words "and her heirs" are words of limitation.

16. *L. None.* When *A* died, her life estate determinable ended.

17. *D. Life estate pur autre vie.* *A* had only a life estate. Despite the words of limitation indicating a fee simple in *A*'s conveyance, *A* can only convey what she has.

18. *E. Life estate determinable.* The "as long as" language in the condition, coupled with the fact that the occurrence of the condition will cut short *A*'s estate in favor of the grantor, creates this estate. The language indicating that the property will revert to *O* is consistent with this classification. If the language were that *O* would have a right to reenter the property, then it could be argued that the estate would be a life estate subject to condition subsequent.

19. *L. None.* The first conveyance gives *A* a fee simple absolute. The second conveyance gives *B* a fee simple absolute. Although *B*'s estate is inheritable by *B*'s heirs, it is not an estate that they presently own. The words "and her heirs" are words of limitation.

20. *C. Life estate.* *O*'s conveyance gives *A* a life estate pur autre vie. When *A* dies, her estate is inherited by *B*. Since *B* now has a life estate measured by his own life, he has a life estate.

21. *J. Fee simple subject to condition subsequent.* The "but if" language in the condition, coupled with the fact that the condition is followed by an estate in the grantor, creates this estate. The fact that *O* has reentered before the occurrence of the condition does not affect *A*'s ownership. *O* is a trespasser. *O*'s reentry must occur after the condition, not before.

22. *J. Fee simple subject to condition subsequent*. The condition has occurred, but the fact that *O* has not reentered keeps the ownership in *A*'s hands.

23. *L. None*. The "as long as" language in the condition, coupled with the fact that the condition is followed by an estate in the grantor, creates this estate. When the condition occurs, the estate is automatically terminated in favor of the grantor even without her reentry.

24. *B. Term of years determinable*. *A*'s life estate limits *B*'s term of years so that if *A* dies before the ten years have passed, the term of years terminates.

25. *K. Fee simple subject to executory limitation*. The "but if" condition is designed to cut short *A*'s freehold estate. If it occurs, it will cut short *A*'s freehold estate in favor of *B*.

26. *L. None*. The right of reentry language is ineffective to create a right of reentry in a grantee. When the condition occurs, *A*'s estate is terminated automatically, whether or not *B* chooses to reenter.

27. *G. Life estate subject to executory limitation*. The "during" condition is designed to cut short *A*'s freehold estate in favor of *B* if the property is not used as a farm.

28. *H. Fee simple absolute*. There are no words of limitation accompanying the words of purchase "to *B*" and no condition that can be used to cut off *B*'s estate.

29. *A. Term of years*. *C* gets a nonfreehold estate that runs concurrently with *B*'s freehold estate.

30. *L. None*. The words "to my heirs on my father's side" are words of purchase, and therefore the designation excludes the heirs on the mother's side.

31. *D. Life estate pur autre vie*. The words of limitation are "for the life of my mother."

32. *L. None*. *B* had only a life estate and therefore, upon her death, did not have Blackacre to give.

33. *I. Fee simple determinable*. The durational "while" condition, if violated, cuts short *A*'s freehold estate in favor of the grantor, *O*.

34. *H. Fee simple absolute*. *A*'s estate is cut short in favor of the grantor, *O*. *O*'s estate, on the other hand, has no conditions that can be used to cut it short, thus making it absolute.

35. *M. None of the above is correct*. *A* had only a life estate to convey. When she conveyed it, she gave a life estate pur autre vie. *A* conveyed it with a durational condition subsequent that does not specify who gets the estate after the condition subsequent has happened. Therefore, if the condition happens, it will revert automatically to the grantor, *A*. Remember that the language of the condition, expressed in the words "so long as," is important to determine whether *B* gets an estate subject to condition subsequent or an estate determinable. Both estates have conditions subsequent, but only one uses the term "condition subsequent" in its name. Since the language of the condition is durational, the estate is an estate determinable. Therefore, *B* has a life estate pur autre vie determinable.

36. *L. None.* The occurrence of the condition subsequent automatically terminates *B*'s estate.

37. *L. None. B*'s life estate pur autre vie can last only while *A* is alive.

38. *K. Fee simple subject to executory limitation.* The condition subsequent, starting with the words "provided that," stands ready to cut short *A*'s estate in favor of a grantee if it happens.

39. *L. None.* The words giving *B* a right to enter do not have any legal effect other than to express a right of *B*'s ownership. Even though *B* has not entered, when the condition happens, *A* automatically loses her estate in the property.

40. *J. Fee simple subject to condition subsequent.* The condition subsequent, starting with the words "provided that," stands ready to cut short *A*'s estate in favor of *O* if it happens and *O* enters. The particular type of fee simple is determined by the fact that the words of the condition are "words of condition" and not "words of duration."

41. *J. Fee simple subject to condition subsequent.* The words giving *O* a right to enter express the legal effect of the fee simple subject to condition subsequent in *A*. The fee simple is not lost until both the condition subsequent occurs and the entry takes place. Because it has not yet taken place, *A* retains the fee simple subject to condition subsequent.

42. *K. Fee simple subject to executory limitation.* The condition subsequent, starting with the words "so long as," stands ready to cut short *A*'s estate in favor of a grantee if it happens. Note that the classification of the words of the condition as "words of condition" or "words of duration" is not relevant when dealing with an estate subject to executory limitation.

43. *L. None. B* does not have to enter the property to own the property in fee simple absolute when the condition happens.

44. *I. Fee simple determinable.* The condition subsequent, starting with the words "so long as," stands ready to cut short *A*'s estate in favor of *O* if it happens. The particular type of fee simple is determined by the fact that the words of the condition are "words of duration" and not "words of condition."

45. *H. Fee simple absolute.* The condition cannot be broken. Therefore, it disappears.

46. *H. Fee simple absolute.* When *O* conveys Blackacre, *A* gets a fee simple absolute. When *A* dies intestate, his heirs inherit Blackacre. Note that it was not until *A* died that the heirs took any estate.

47. *D. Life estate pur autre vie. O*'s conveyance gives *A* a life estate pur autre vie, measured by the life of *X*. *A*'s conveyance gives *B* the same life estate pur autre vie, measured by the life of *X*. *A*'s death has no legal effect on this conveyance because *A* no longer owns Blackacre.

48. *L. None. C* has nothing to inherit.

49. *D. Life estate pur autre vie. D* inherits *B*'s estate upon *B*'s death.

50. *B. Term of years determinable. O*'s conveyance gives *A* a life estate pur autre vie, measured by the life of *X*. *A*'s conveyance gives *B* a nonfreehold estate while *A* retains the freehold. The condition

subsequent making *B*'s estate determinable is *X*'s death. *A*'s death does not change what *B* has.

51. *D. Life estate pur autre vie.* When *A* dies, *C* inherits *A*'s life estate pur autre vie.

52. *B. Term of years determinable.* *D* inherits *B*'s estate upon *B*'s death.

53. *E. Life estate determinable.* The word "during" indicates a durational condition subsequent, and this fact, coupled with the fact that the condition is followed by an estate in the grantor, makes the life estate one that is determinable.

54. *M. None of the above is correct.* When *A* conveys to *B*, *B* gets *A*'s estate limited to *B*'s life. Therefore, it is a life estate pur autre vie determinable. The life that defines this life estate is the first to die as between *A* and *B*.

55. *J. Fee simple subject to condition subsequent.* The words "on condition that" indicate a conditional condition subsequent. If *A* goes to business school, the condition is broken, and the estate will terminate upon the entry of O.

56. *J. Fee simple subject to condition subsequent.* The estate is not over until O makes an entry or brings an action to recover the land. The heirs receive by intestate succession the same estate as *A* held, but will lose it upon O's entry or action to recover the land.

57. *F. Life estate subject to condition subsequent.* The word "if" indicates a conditional condition subsequent. If *A* goes to law school, the estate is cut short by the happening of the condition subsequent and the entry of O.

58. *L. None.* If *A* never goes to law school, the estate terminates at *A*'s death because it is a life estate.

59. *E. Life estate determinable.* The word "until" indicates a durational condition subsequent. The conveyance of the nonfreehold term of years to *D* does not change the nature of *C*'s freehold estate.

60. *B. Term of years determinable.* *D*'s term of years is limited by two conditions subsequent, the end of *C*'s life and the election of the next president.

61. *D. Life estate pur autre vie.* The life that defines this life estate is the first to die as between *A* and *C*.

62. *D. Life estate pur autre vie.* The heirs inherit *B*'s life estate pur autre vie, since neither *A* nor *C* is dead.

63. *M. None of the above is correct.* *B* has a life estate pur autre vie determinable. The life that defines this life estate is the first to die as between *A* and *B*. The "while" condition is durational, and *B* has two of these conditions limiting his estate. If either *A* or *B* were no longer to be confined to a wheelchair, then the estate would end.

64. *L. None.* One of the limiting conditions has occurred.

65. *M. None of the above is correct.* Orville conveyed a life estate subject to condition subsequent to Stephen, since the words of the condition, "provided that," are conditional language. Stephen then conveyed a life estate pur autre vie subject to condition subsequent to Arthur. Arthur's life estate is measured by Stephen's life.

66. *M. None of the above is correct.* The condition requires Stephen to put the rose on his mother's grave. The condition is broken, but

Stephen has not yet exercised his right of entry. Therefore, Arthur still has a life estate pur autre vie subject to condition subsequent. Arthur will have nothing after Stephen exercises his right of entry.

67. *L. None.* B's estate can last no longer than the estate of his grantor. Therefore, when A conveyed a term of years to B it was determinable, and the condition subsequent, A's death, has happened, thus terminating B's term of years.

68. *M. None of the above is correct.* The words of the condition, "provided, however," are conditional language, and the condition is followed by an estate in the grantor. Therefore, A received a life estate pur autre vie subject to condition subsequent. C has the same estate as A had.

69. *F. Life estate subject to condition subsequent.* O conveys a fee simple subject to condition subsequent to A, since the condition starts with "if," which is conditional language, and the condition is followed by an estate in the grantor. The condition is broken when A divorces, but O does not exercise his right of entry. Therefore, A still has an estate to convey to B, which he does but limits it to B's life.

70. *D. Life estate pur autre vie.* O conveys to A a life estate. A conveys to B a life estate pur autre vie. Even though the words of limitation, "and his heirs," indicate a fee simple, A does not have anything more to give than his own life estate. B's life estate pur autre vie is measured by A's life. B conveys to C a life estate pur autre vie, now measured by the life of either A or C, whoever is the sooner to die. C conveys this life estate pur autre vie to D. Again, although the words of limitation are absent, thus indicating a fee simple, C does not have anything more to give than her life estate pur autre vie. D's life estate pur autre vie is measured by the life of either A or C, whoever is the sooner to die.

71. *D. Life estate pur autre vie.* Because B's life is not one of the measuring lives, B's death has no effect.

72. *I. Fee simple determinable.* The condition starts with "until," which is durational language, and the condition, if it happens, cuts short the estate in favor of the grantor. A's conveyance of a nonfreehold term of years does not take away her freehold fee simple determinable estate.

73. *B. Term of years determinable.* A conveyed to B a term of years determinable, the condition subsequent being the old oak tree falling. B could convey no more than this estate. Because he conveyed an estate limited by C's life, the term of years is now determinable with two conditions subsequent, the occurrence of either one of which will terminate B's estate. The two conditions subsequent on B's estate are C's dying and the old oak tree falling.

74. *F. Life estate subject to condition subsequent.* The words of the condition, "provided, however," are conditional language. O conveys to A a fee simple subject to condition subsequent, and A conveys to B a life estate subject to the same condition.

75. *C. Life estate.* When A dies, the condition will never happen, and it disappears.

76. *M. None of the above is correct. A* has a fee simple that has two conditions, one conditional and the other durational. One could call this a fee simple subject to condition subsequent and determinable.

77. *M. None of the above is correct.* This is still a fee simple subject to condition subsequent and determinable. Although the condition subsequent is broken, the estate is not yet over because the grantor, *O*, has not yet entered the property.

78. *L. None.* Once the durational condition is broken, the estate is cut short, and *A* is left with nothing.

79. *M. None of the above is correct. O* conveys to *A* a life estate pur autre vie subject to executory limitation because the estate has a condition subsequent that will be violated and will cut short the estate either at *X*'s death (thus making the estate a life estate pur autre vie) or sooner (thus making the estate subject to executory limitation). *A* conveys this same estate to *C*. Note that if *X* dies while still using the property as a residence, the estate is considered terminated by the ending of the life estate rather than the cutting short of the condition. The importance of this distinction will become apparent in later chapters.

80. *M. None of the above is correct.* The condition is not affected by *A*'s death.

81. *L. None.* The condition has occurred.

82. *E. Life estate determinable.* The condition is durational and is followed by an estate in the grantor.

83. *B. Term of years determinable. O* conveyed to *A* a term of years determinable. The conditional "but if" condition does not make this a term of years subject to condition subsequent because there is no such estate. Then *A* conveyed this estate to *B* with the restriction that it last only for the life of *X*. There can be no life estate in a term of years. Therefore, two conditions limit *B*'s term of years determinable: the maintenance of the property and *X* not dying.

84. *H. Fee simple absolute. O*'s conveyance of a term of years does not change his ownership of a fee simple absolute.

85. *H. Fee simple absolute. O* conveys a fee simple determinable to *A*. *A* then conveys this fee simple determinable to *B* and adds a durational condition. *B* then conveys this fee simple determinable to *C* and adds a durational condition. *C* then has a fee simple determinable with three conditions subsequent. After the deaths of *A*, *B*, and *C*, none of the conditions can happen, so they disappear. *C*'s heirs inherit a fee simple absolute.

86. *G. Life estate subject to executory limitation.* The condition subsequent, if it occurs, will cut short the estate in favor of a grantee, *B*.

87. *G. Life estate subject to executory limitation.* The condition subsequent in *A*'s estate has occurred, and the estate is cut short in favor of *B*. The condition subsequent in *B*'s estate, if it occurs, will cut short the estate in favor of a grantee, *C*.

88. *H. Fee simple absolute.* Both conditions subsequent have occurred, thus cutting short the estates in *A* and *B*. *C*'s estate has no condition subsequent on it.

89. *K. Fee simple subject to executory limitation.* The condition subsequent, if it occurs, will cut short the estate in favor of a grantee, *B*.

90. *H. Fee simple absolute.* The condition subsequent in *A*'s estate can no longer be broken, so it disappears, leaving an absolute estate to be inherited by *A*'s heirs.

91. *I. Fee simple determinable.* When the condition subsequent in *A*'s estate is broken, *B* takes his estate, which is determinable because it has a condition subsequent with durational language and, if broken, will cut short *B*'s estate in favor of the grantor, *O*.

92. *E. Life estate determinable.* The condition subsequent is durational and cuts off *A*'s estate in favor of the grantor, *O*, if it is broken. This makes the estate determinable. It must be broken no later than *A*'s death, when it will be impossible for *A* to continue living in Arizona. This makes the estate a life estate. This estate is not affected by the conveyance of the nonfreehold term of years to *B*. Note that if *A* dies while still living in Arizona, the estate is considered terminated by the ending of the life estate rather than the cutting short of the condition. The importance of this distinction will become apparent in later chapters.

93. *B. Term of years determinable.* This estate exists concurrently with *A*'s estate. Its condition subsequent is the failure of *A* to live in Arizona.

94. *L. None.* Because *A* cannot convey more than *A* has, *A*'s conveyance gave him a term of years determinable, and the condition subsequent has occurred.

95. *H. Fee simple absolute.* The termination of *A*'s estate is in favor of *O*, who retakes his fee simple absolute.

96. *D. Life estate pur autre vie.* The measuring life is the person who is the last to die as between *A* and *B*.

97. *D. Life estate pur autre vie.* The measuring life is the person who is the first to die as between *A* and *B*.

98. *D. Life estate pur autre vie.* The measuring life is the first person to die as between *A*, *C*, and *F*.

99. *L. None.*

100. *H. Fee simple absolute.* It is shared with *B* in joint ownership.

2

Classification of Future Interests

A. DEFINITIONS

Ownership is measured in terms of time when it is divided and conveyed at one time as two or more successive ownerships called a *present interest* and *future interests*. These interests are created and exist together, but they are enjoyed seriatim over time. For example, an owner of a fee simple estate, *O*, at one time may convey his ownership in land to two grantees *A* and *B* by using one deed to grant to *A* an ownership for the rest of *A*'s life and to *B* an ownership after *A* is dead (i.e., "to *A* for life, then to *B* and his heirs"). By this one conveyance *O* has divided his ownership between *A* and *B* so that *A* now has a present interest and *B* now has a future interest. *A* owns an interest now that can be enjoyed immediately, while *B* owns an interest now that can be enjoyed only in the future.

The term *interest* refers to when an ownership begins to be enjoyed. The term *estate* refers to when an ownership ends being enjoyed. In the conveyance above, *O* conveys to *A* an ownership for the rest of *A*'s life. *A*'s ownership is a present interest because its enjoyment begins immediately, and it is a life estate because it ends on *A*'s death. *A*'s present interest is vested in possession because it can be enjoyed now. *B*'s ownership is a future interest because it begins on *A*'s death, and it is a fee simple absolute estate because it has no end point. *B*'s future interest is not vested in possession, although, as we discuss later in this chapter, it is vested in interest.

There is at least one owner for every piece of land that is owned who will have a present interest and at least one owner (possibly the same owner) who will have a fee simple absolute. In the example above, even though *B* will die or convey his property away at some point, his estate will continue to exist in another owner or owners. For example, if *B* makes a conveyance of his future interest in fee simple "to *X* for life, then to *Y* for life, and then to *Z*," each one receives a future interest. *X* and *Y* each receive a life estate, and Z receives a fee simple estate. A full listing of every interest and estate in the property would be: present interest in a life estate in *A*, future interest in a life estate in *X*, future interest in a life estate in *Y*, and future interest in a fee simple absolute in *Z*. Should it happen that no heir exists to take an estate when its owner dies, it would escheat to the state, but this rare event would occur only if there were no heirs of the intestate under the intestate succession laws.

This measurement of ownership in terms of time, whereby one transfer creates several ownerships enjoyed successively over time, may be difficult to grasp at first. To be clear, it is important to understand that *O*'s one conveyance now of a present interest to *A* in a life estate and a future interest to *B* in a fee simple estate does not have the same effect as *O*'s conveyance now of only a present interest to *A* in a life estate with the *intention* of conveying a present interest in a fee simple estate to *B* when *A* dies. *O* cannot revoke a future interest conveyed to *B*, but *O* can change his intention to convey. Also, if *B* dies before his future interest becomes a present interest, his heirs will inherit his future interest; but his heirs cannot inherit *O*'s good intention. *B* owns property the moment that he receives a future interest from *O*; he owns no property if *O* merely has an intention to convey him an interest. (There are tax consequences as well.)

After *O*'s conveyance "to *A* for life, then to *B* and his heirs," *B* cannot own the property after he dies or transfers it, but his right to enjoy the property forever means that when he dies or transfers it, it continues in either his heirs or transferees. When *A* dies and her estate terminates, *B*'s future interest transforms into a present interest. If *B* is alive at the time of *A*'s death and has not otherwise disposed of his interest, *B* has an immediate right upon *A*'s death to enjoy the property. If *B* dies before *A*'s death and has not otherwise disposed of his interest, *B*'s future interest descends to his heirs by intestate succession and later, on *A*'s death, it becomes a present interest in his heirs.

In the example above, *B*'s future interest follows the *natural termination* of the preceding estate in *A*. The natural termination of an estate occurs for a life estate when the life estate ends upon the death of the life that determines the length of time for the estate. A fee simple absolute, on the other hand, has the potential of infinite duration and cannot terminate naturally. *A*'s life estate can terminate naturally; *B*'s fee simple cannot.

A future interest may also follow the *unnatural termination* of a preceding estate when the preceding estate is terminated by court action or a condition subsequent. This type of termination is often termed a forfeiture. Court action may occur because the court finds a violation of the law such as the fact that a life tenant is committing waste of the property. For example, where *O* conveys "to *A* for life, then to *B* and his heirs," and thereafter *A* wastes the property, a court may decree her life estate forfeited. *B*'s future interest would transform at that time into a present interest because of the unnatural termination of *A*'s life estate. The forfeiture of *A*'s life estate for waste is an unnatural termination because it occurs before the time of natural termination that is *A*'s death.

A more frequent cause of forfeiture (or unnatural termination) is the occurrence of a condition subsequent. These conditions are discussed in Chapter 1 for three subcategories of life estates and three subcategories of fee simples. When a condition subsequent cuts short a preceding estate, the estate terminates in favor of a future interest. In other words, the future interest replaces the estate that is cut short. If the preceding estate is created in a *grantee*, the future interest *shifts* from the preceding estate; if the preceding estate is in the *grantor*, the future interest *springs* from the preceding estate. For example, where O conveys "to A and his heirs, but if A divorces, then to B," B's future interest *shifts* from the preceding estate in A on the happening of the condition subsequent of A's divorce that cuts short A's preceding estate. Where O conveys "to B if and when A divorces," O has left a present interest in herself (because B cannot take a present interest until A divorces) and given B a future interest. B's future interest *springs* from the preceding estate in O on the happening of the condition subsequent of A's divorce, which cuts short O's preceding estate. (Note that O owns the preceding estate because O's conveyance has not designated anyone to take a present interest, and therefore the present interest remains in O. This is discussed as the No Gap in Seisin Rule in Chapter 4.)

A future interest may be part of a number of interests, all of which shift or spring from a preceding estate cut short by a condition subsequent. For example, where O conveys "to A and her heirs, but if A divorces, then to B for life, and then to C," O conveys a present interest to A in fee simple subject to executory limitation, a future interest (prepared to shift from A's estate on the happening of the condition subsequent of A's divorce) to B in a life estate, and a future interest (which, along with the future interest in B, is prepared to shift from A's estate on A's divorce) to C in a fee simple absolute. Note that from the original present interest in fee simple absolute, O has created two separate lines of conveyances. There is no natural connection between the estate of A on the one hand and the estates of B and C on the other. If the condition subsequent occurs (that is, A divorces), A's estate is cut short and replaced by the estates of B and C. Then B would have a present interest in a life estate, and C would have a future interest in a fee simple absolute.

Likewise, where O conveys "to A for life, then to B and his heirs as long as B does not divorce, but if B divorces, then to C for life, and then to D," O conveys a present interest to A in a life estate, a future interest (following the termination of A's life estate) to B in fee simple subject to executory limitation, a future interest (prepared to shift from B's estate on the happening of the condition subsequent of B's divorce) to C in a life estate, and a future interest (which, along with the future interest in C, is prepared to shift from B's estate on B's divorce) to D in fee simple absolute. Note again that from the original present interest in fee simple absolute, O has created two separate lines of conveyances. There is no natural connection between the estates of A and B on the one hand and the estates of C and D on the other. If the condition subsequent occurs (that is, B divorces), B's estate is cut short and replaced by the estates of C and D. Then the ownerships in the land become naturally connected: A continues to hold a present interest in a life estate, C has a future interest (following the termination of A's life estate) in a life estate, and D has a future interest (following the termination of A's life estate and C's life estate) in a fee simple absolute.

An example of a conveyance with more than one future interest springing from a preceding estate cut short by a condition subsequent is where O conveys "if and when X divorces, to A for life, then to B for life, then to C." In this conveyance O gives no present interest since all interests are dependent on the occurrence of *X*'s divorce. Therefore, *O* retains a present interest in fee simple subject to executory limitation. *O* does give a future interest (which springs from the grantor's estate) to *A* in a life estate, a future interest (which springs from the grantor's estate) to *B* in a life estate, and a future interest (which springs from the grantor's estate) to *C* in fee simple absolute. If *X* dies without having divorced, the condition cannot be satisfied, thus destroying the interests in *A*, *B*, and *C*. If *X* divorces, then the condition is satisfied and *O* loses her present interest in fee simple subject to executory limitation, while *A*'s interest transforms into a present interest in a life estate, *B*'s interest transforms into a future interest in a life estate, and *C*'s interest transforms into a future interest in a fee simple absolute.

B. CATEGORIES

1. *Future Interests in a Grantee*

Future interests in a grantee are called remainders or executory interests:

(1) A ***remainder*** follows the natural termination of all preceding life estates. Thus, if *O* conveys "to *A* for life, then to *B* for life, then to *C*," *B* has a remainder that follows the termination of *A*'s life estate, and *C* has a remainder that follows the termination of both *A*'s life estate and *B*'s life estate. The subcategories of remainders are discussed further below.

(2) An ***executory interest*** shifts or springs from a preceding estate cut short by a condition subsequent. Thus, if *O* conveys "to *A* and her heirs, but if *A* divorces, then to *B*," *A* has a present interest in fee simple subject to executory limitation, and *B* has an executory interest in fee simple absolute. Likewise, if *O* conveys "to *A* for life, then to *B*, but if at any time *X* divorces, then to *C*," *A* has a present interest in a life estate subject to executory limitation, *B* has a remainder in fee simple subject to executory limitation (remainder following the termination of the life estate and not following the occurrence of the condition subsequent), and *C* has an executory interest in fee simple absolute. Note that if *X* divorces, both *A*'s and *B*'s estates are cut short, and *C*'s executory interest is transformed into a present interest in fee simple absolute. If *A* dies without *X* having yet divorced, *A*'s life estate subject to executory limitation terminates naturally, and *B*'s remainder transforms into a present interest in fee simple subject to executory limitation. If *X* should then divorce, *B*'s fee simple subject to executory limitation is cut short, and *C*'s executory interest is transformed into a present interest in fee simple absolute.

An executory interest also may be part of a number of interests, all of which together shift or spring from a preceding estate cut short by a condition subsequent and each of which is called an executory interest. Thus, if *O* conveys "to *A* and her heirs, as long as *A* does not divorce; otherwise then to *B* for life, then to *C*," *A* has a present interest in fee simple subject to executory limitation, *B* has an executory interest in a life estate, and *C* has an executory interest in fee simple absolute. These executory interests shift from *A*'s fee simple subject to executory limitation. If *A* divorces, *B*'s interest transforms into a present interest in a life estate, and *C*'s interest transforms into a remainder in fee simple absolute.

An executory interest may spring from a preceding estate cut short by a condition subsequent. One of the defining characteristics of a springing interest is that the preceding estate is owned by *O*. For example, when *O* conveys "if and when *X* divorces, to *A* for life, then to *B* for life, then to *C*," *O*, by not designating a present interest, leaves his own present interest in fee simple as the present interest in fee simple of his conveyance and then limits his estate with a condition subsequent in order to give springing executory interests to *A*, *B*, and *C*. *O* has a present interest in fee simple subject to executory limitation, *A* has an executory interest in a life estate, *B* has an executory interest in a life estate, and *C* has an executory interest in fee simple absolute.

2.   *Future Interests in a Grantor*

Future interests in a grantor are called *reversionary interests*. They are interests in the grantor's original estate retained by the grantor. There are three types of reversionary interests:

(1)   A *possibility of reverter* *always* shifts from an estate determinable or follows an executory interest in a life estate. It shifts from an estate determinable in the example where *O* conveys "to *A* and her heirs as long as *A* does not divorce, then to *O*." *A* has a present interest in fee simple determinable, and *O* has a possibility of reverter in fee simple absolute. It follows an executory interest in a life estate where *O* conveys "to *A* and her heirs as long as *A* does not divorce, then to *B* for life, then to *O*," *A* has a present interest in fee simple subject to executory limitation, *B* has an executory interest in a life estate (which shifts from *A*'s fee simple subject to executory limitation), and *O* has a possibility of reverter in fee simple absolute (which, together with *B*'s executory interest, shifts from *A*'s fee simple subject to executory limitation). Also, when *O* conveys "if and when *X* divorces, to *A* for life, then to *O*," *O* has a present interest in fee simple subject to executory limitation, *A* has an executory interest in a life estate (springing from the fee simple subject to executory limitation in *O*); and *O* has a possibility of reverter in fee simple absolute (springing, together with the executory interest in *A*, from the fee simple subject to executory limitation in *O*). If *X* divorces after this last conveyance, *A*'s executory interest transforms into a present interest in a life estate

and *O*'s possibility of reverter transforms into a reversion (see below) in *O* in fee simple absolute.

(2) A *right of reentry*, also called a *power of termination*, *always* shifts from an estate subject to condition subsequent, as in the example "to *A* and her heirs, but if *A* divorces, then back to *O*." *A* has a present interest in fee simple subject to condition subsequent, and *O* has a right of reentry in fee simple absolute. Note that the difference between the right of reentry here and the possibility of reverter above is in the language of the condition. The right of reentry immediately follows a conditional "but if" condition; the possibility of reverter immediately follows a durational "as long as" condition. This is explained in Chapter 1 with reference to the estate subject to condition subsequent and the estate determinable.

(3) A *reversion* stands ready to take at any time the preceding estates in grantees terminate other than by a condition subsequent, as in the example "to *A* for life, then to *O*." *A* has a present interest in a life estate, and *O* has a reversion in fee simple absolute. Note that a reversion may be coupled with a possibility of reverter, which cuts short the same life estate that the reversion follows. When this happens, the two interests are considered together as a reversion, as in the example "to *A* for life as long as *A* does not divorce, then to *O*." *O*'s interest can transform into a present interest on *A*'s death or even sooner on *A*'s divorce. *A* has a present interest in a life estate determinable, and *O* has a reversion in fee simple absolute.

C. SUBCATEGORIES OF REMAINDERS

Executory interests and the three reversionary interests have no subcategories. Remainders, on the other hand, are further divided into *vested* and *contingent* remainders according to whether they are subject to a condition precedent. A contingent remainder is subject to a condition precedent; a vested remainder is not. "Vested" in the context of a remainder, which is a future interest, means "vested in interest" and refers to the fact that the future interest is not subject to a condition precedent. A present interest is also not subject to a condition precedent. Vested in the context of a present interest means "vested in possession."

1. Contingent Remainder

A *condition precedent* is a condition that must occur before a future interest will be allowed to become a present interest. This is actually true of a condition subsequent as well, since a condition subsequent must occur before a reversionary interest or an executory interest can become a present interest. The difference between a condition precedent and a condition subsequent, however, is that a condition precedent does not cut short a preceding estate. For example, in the conveyance "to A for life, then to B if B gets married," the condition precedent of B's marriage must occur if B's remainder is to take as a present interest. B's remainder is a contingent remainder. If B gets married, A's life estate is not cut short. A's life estate continues to exist even though the condition has occurred. The occurrence of the condition precedent transforms B's remainder from a contingent remainder into a *vested remainder* because the remainder is no longer subject to a condition precedent but rather stands ready to take at any time the preceding life estate terminates. The occurrence of the condition precedent allows B's remainder to become a present interest only when A's life estate terminates.

There are three ways in which a remainder may be subject to a condition precedent. It may be a remainder (1) in an unborn person ("to A for life, then to B's children," where B has no children at the time of the conveyance), (2) in an unascertained person ("to A for life, then to B's heirs," since B's heirs cannot be ascertained until B's death), or (3) subject to some other condition precedent ("to A for life, then to B if B gets married").

Alternative contingent remainders occur when two contingent remainders follow an estate and the condition precedent for one is the opposite of the condition precedent for the other. For example, where O conveys "to A for life, then to B if A divorces, and to C if A does not divorce," B and C have alternative contingent remainders. If A divorces, then B's remainder becomes a vested remainder that ultimately becomes a present interest on A's death; C's remainder is destroyed by failure of its condition precedent. If A does not divorce (i.e., she lives her whole life without getting a divorce), then C's remainder becomes a present interest on A's death; B's remainder is destroyed by the failure of its condition precedent. Note in this latter case that C's contingent remainder does not become a vested remainder before becoming a present interest because the condition precedent of A's not divorcing can only be satisfied on A's death (since A might divorce at any time before her death) and A's death terminates the preceding life estate.

When a remainder is given to a person "or" her children, the word "or" is usually construed as disjunctive, giving alternative contingent remainders to the person and to her children. The condition precedent, which is implied, is survivorship. For example, where O conveys "to A for life, then to B or her children," the condition precedent to B's contingent remainder is B's survivorship of A's death; the condition precedent to the children's contingent remainder is the failure of B to survive A. The same analysis would apply if the conveyance read "to A for life, then to B or her heirs" or "to A for life, then to B or her issue." In these last two examples, the words "her heirs" and "her issue" are words of purchase, not words of limitation.

Note that when a contingent remainder exists in the examples above, there is always the possibility that the condition precedent may not occur. If it does not occur, there is a gap after the termination of the preceding life estate. This gap is filled with a reversion in the grantor. Thus, where O conveys "to A for life, then to B if B gets married," B's contingent remainder that follows A's life estate is supported by a reversion in O that follows A's life estate. In more detail, A has a present interest in a life estate, B has a contingent remainder in fee simple absolute, and O has a reversion in fee simple absolute. If the condition precedent on B's contingent remainder is satisfied, then B's interest transforms into a vested remainder following A's life estate, and O's reversion is divested. (Note that the reversion is divested without O's fee simple absolute being cut short by a condition subsequent since the reversion is merely a gap filler that disappears if the condition precedent occurs.) If the condition precedent on B's contingent remainder is not satisfied, then B's interest is destroyed by the failure of the condition precedent and O's reversion remains to become a present interest when A's life estate terminates.

Also, in the example of the alternative contingent remainders above, A's life estate is followed not only by the two alternative contingent remainders in B and C but also by a reversion in fee simple absolute in O, the vested interest that supports the two contingent remainders. This does not seem logical because it would seem that the failure of one condition precedent means that the other condition precedent will be satisfied. There does not seem to be any situation in which both contingent remainders would fail; however, there is the possibility that A may forfeit her life estate by committing waste on the property, leaving A still alive but not divorced. In this situation neither condition precedent would be satisfied; yet there must be someone to take an interest in the property. Therefore, O's reversion exists to support both alternative contingent remainders. (Note that even if you might devise alternative contingent remainders such that one had to take on the termination of the preceding estates, the Backup Rule, explained in Chapter 4, requires that a contingent remainder always be supported by a vested interest.)

2.   *Vested Remainder*

A vested remainder follows a life estate and has no condition precedent. Note that a vested remainder may be coupled with an executory interest in the same person, when the executory interest cuts short the same life estate that the vested remainder follows. When this happens, the two interests are considered together as a vested remainder, as in the example "to A for life as long as A does not divorce; otherwise to B." B's interest can transform into a present interest upon A's death or even sooner upon A's divorce. A has a present interest in a life estate subject to executory limitation, and B has a vested remainder in fee simple absolute. This coupling is similar to that of the reversion discussed above.

There are three types of vested remainders. The first two are determined by the nature of their estates. The third involves an interest in a class.

(1)   An *indefeasibly vested remainder* is one whose estate is absolute, such as in the conveyance "to A for life, then to B." B has an indefeasibly vested remainder in fee simple absolute.

(2)   A *vested remainder subject to (complete) divestment* is one whose estate is determinable, or subject to condition subsequent, or subject to executory limitation. For example, in the conveyance "to A for life, then to B and her heirs, but if B divorces, then to C," B has a vested remainder subject to divestment in a fee simple subject to executory limitation.

(3) A *vested remainder subject to open*, otherwise known as a *vested remainder subject to partial divestment*, is one wherein the grantee may be joined by one or more other persons to share equally in the interest. Of course, to ensure the vested nature of this remainder, the grantee must be born, must be ascertained, and must have an interest that is not subject to any other condition precedent. In the conveyance "to *A* for life, then to the children of *B*," the children of *B* have a contingent remainder if *B* has no children because the grantees of the remainder are all unborn. If *B* has one child *X*, *X* has a vested remainder because *X* is born and ascertained and *X*'s interest is not subject to a condition precedent. *X*'s vested remainder is also subject to open because *B* is alive and may have other children who will be born. If and when other children are born during the time they all hold future interests, *X*'s remainder will "open" to include each child as it is born, and that child will share the vested remainder subject to open. Vested remainders subject to open are described more thoroughly in Chapter 3.

To conclude this chapter, it is helpful to review the classification scheme that has been discussed so far to identify interests and estates in land.

D. SUMMARY: DICHOTOMOUS KEY FOR IDENTIFICATION PROCEDURE

(1) For each person who takes an estate through a conveyance you must ask what is his *interest* and what is his *estate* (in that order). You must always *separate* between these two!

(2) Under *interest*, is it *present* or *future*? If it is present, there is nothing further to ask about the interest.

(3) Under *future interest*, is it in the *grantor* or in the *grantee*?

(4) Under *future interest in the grantor*, is it a *reversion, possibility of reverter*, or *right of reentry*? Remember that a possibility of reverter *always* immediately follows the condition subsequent of an estate determinable and *can* follow an executory interest in a life estate; a right of reentry *always* immediately follows the condition subsequent of an estate subject to condition subsequent.

(5) Under *future interest in the grantee*, is it a *remainder* or an *executory interest*? The answer to this question depends on whether or not it stands ready to follow the natural termination of a life estate. If it does, it is a remainder; if not, it is an executory interest. Remember that an executory interest *always* immediately follows the condition subsequent of an estate subject to executory limitation and *can* follow an executory interest in a life estate.

(6) Under *remainder*, is it *vested* or *contingent*? The answer to this question depends on whether it is in an unborn person, in an unascertained person, or subject to a condition precedent. If it is, it is a contingent remainder.

(7) Under *vested remainder*, is it *indefeasibly vested*, or *vested subject to divestment*, or *vested subject to open*? If it is vested subject to divestment, there is a condition subsequent that stands ready to cut off the estate. Note that a vested remainder in fee simple subject to executory limitation (or determinable or subject to condition subsequent) is a more complete description of a vested remainder subject to divestment.

(8) Under *estate*, is it *freehold* or *nonfreehold*?

(9) Under *freehold estate*, is it a *fee simple* or a *life estate*?

(10) Under each *freehold estate*, is it *absolute, subject to executory limitation, subject to condition subsequent,* or *determinable*? Note that each of the last three contains a condition subsequent even though the term "condition subsequent" appears in the name of only one.

CHART FOR IDENTIFICATION OF INTERESTS AND ESTATES

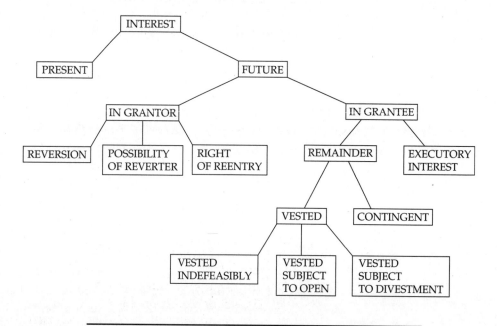

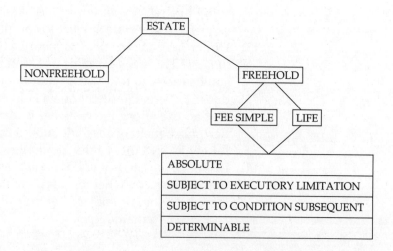

CHART OF INSEPARABLE CONNECTIONS

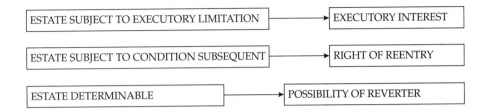

Problem Set II

The problems in this section ask for a description of an interest or an estate. The answers for interest are:

    A. present interest
    B. executory interest
    C. reversion
    D. contingent remainder
    E. right of reentry
    F. vested remainder
    G. possibility of reverter
    H. vested remainder subject to open
    I. none
    J. none of the above is correct

The answers for estate are:

    A. term of years
    B. term of years determinable
    C. life estate
    D. life estate pur autre vie
    E. life estate determinable
    F. life estate subject to condition subsequent
    G. life estate subject to executory limitation
    H. fee simple absolute
    I. fee simple determinable
    J. fee simple subject to condition subsequent
    K. fee simple subject to executory limitation
    L. none
    M. none of the above is correct

Problems

O conveys Blackacre "to Arthur for life." Arthur then conveys his interest "to Barbara."

    101. What is *O*'s interest?

O conveys "to *A* and her heirs, but if the old oak tree falls, *O* may enter and take the property as of his former estate."

    102.   What is *A*'s estate?

    103.   What is *O*'s interest?

O conveys "to *A* for life, but if the old oak tree falls, *O* may enter and take the property as of his former estate."

    104.   What is *O*'s interest?

    105.   If the old oak tree falls after *O*'s conveyance but before *A*'s death, what is *O*'s interest?

    106.   If the old oak tree does not fall after the conveyance by the time *A* dies, what is *O*'s interest upon *A*'s death?

O conveys "to *A* for life, then to *B* and her heirs, but if *A* divorces, then, on the divorce, to *C*."

    107.   What is *A*'s estate?

    108.   What is *C*'s estate?

O conveys "to *A* for life, then to *B*, with both estates to continue only as long as *C* does not get married."

    109.   What is *A*'s estate?

    110.   What is *B*'s interest?

    111.   What is *O*'s interest?

O conveys "to Arthur and his heirs, but if Arthur uses the property for agricultural purposes, to Bob for life."

    112.   What is Arthur's estate?

    113.   What is Bob's interest?

    114.   What is *O*'s interest?

O conveys "to *A* for life, then to *B* if *B* survives *A*, then to *C* if *B* does not survive *A*."

    115.   What is *C*'s interest?

    116.   What is *O*'s interest?

    117.   If *B* dies before *A*, what is *C*'s interest?

    118.   If *B* dies before *A*, what is *O*'s estate?

O conveys "to *A* for life, then to *B* for life if *B* gets married."

    119.   What is *B*'s interest?

    120.   What is *B*'s estate?

    121.   If *B* gets married, what is *O*'s interest?

O conveys Blackacre "to *A* for life, then to *B* for life, but if Blackacre is not maintained as a farm, then to *O*."

    122. What is *B*'s estate?
    123. What is *O*'s interest?

O conveys "to *A* and her heirs, but if *B* gets married, then, on his marriage, to *B* for life, then to *C* and his heirs."

    124. What is *B*'s interest?
    125. What is *C*'s interest?

O conveys "to *A* for life, then to *B* if *B* gets married, but if *B* does not have a son by the time of *A*'s death, then to *C*." *B* has never been married or had children.

    126. What is *B*'s interest?
    127. What is *B*'s estate?
    128. What is *C*'s interest?
    129. If *B* gets married, what is *B*'s interest?
    130. If *B* has a son after he gets married, what is *B*'s estate?
    131. If *A* dies after *B* gets married but before *B* has a son, what is *C*'s interest?

O conveys "to *A* for life, then to *B* if *B* gets married, but if *B* does not have a son, then to *C*." Then *B* gets married. Then *A* dies.

    132. What is *B*'s estate?

O conveys "to *A* for life, then, if *B* gets married, to *B* and his heirs as long as *B* never divorces." *B* has never married.

    133. What is *B*'s interest?
    134. What is *O*'s interest?
    135. If *B* gets married, what is his estate?

O conveys "to *A* for life or until he has a son."

    136. What is *A*'s estate?
    137. What is *O*'s interest?

O conveys "to *A* and her heirs, but if *A* does not enter law school, then the property shall revert to *O*."

    138. What is *A*'s estate?

O conveys "to *A* if *A* gets married." *A* is not married at the time of the conveyance.

139. What is *A*'s interest?
140. What is *O*'s estate?

O conveys "to *A* if *A* does not get married." *A* is not married at the time of the conveyance.

141. What is *A*'s interest?
142. What is *O*'s interest?

O conveys "to *A* and his heirs until *A* gets married, then to *B* for life, then to *O*, but if *B* gets married, then *B*'s estate to be cut short in favor of *C*."

143. What is *A*'s estate?
144. What is *B*'s estate
145. What is *O*'s interest?
146. What is *O*'s estate?

O conveys "to *A* for life, then to *B* for life, then to *C* and his heirs if *C* gets married, but if *C* does not get married, then to *D* as long as the old oak tree remains standing."

147. What is *D*'s interest?

O conveys "to *A* for life, then to *B* for life, then to *C*'s children." *C* is alive and has one child, *X*, at the time of the conveyance.

148. What is *X*'s interest?
149. If *C* then bears another child, *Y*, what is *Y*'s interest?
150. What is *O*'s interest?

O conveys "to *A* and her heirs, but if *A* divorces, then to *B* for life, then to *C* for life, then to *D*'s heirs."

151. What is *A*'s estate?
152. What is *C*'s estate?
153. What is the interest of *D*'s heirs?
154. What is *O*'s interest?
155. If *A* divorces, what is the interest of *D*'s heirs?

O, owning a vested remainder in a life estate, conveys "to *A* and her heirs, but if *A* divorces, then to *B*."

156. What is *A*'s interest?
157. What is *B*'s interest?

O conveys "to *A* for life, then to *B* or her children." *B* has no children.

158. What is the interest of *B*'s children?
159. If *B* has a child *X*, what is *X*'s interest?
160. If *B* dies after *X* is born and while *A* is still alive, what is *X*'s interest?

O conveys "to *A* for life, then to *B* or to *C*'s children." *C* has one child, *Z*.

    161.   What is *Z*'s interest?
    162.   If *B* dies while *A* is still alive, what is *Z*'s interest?

O conveys "to *A* for life, then to *B* for life, then to *C*, but only if and when all three have graduated from law school." None of the three has graduated from law school.

    163.   What is *A*'s interest?
    164.   If all three graduate from law school, what is *C*'s interest?

O conveys "to *A* for life, then to *B* for the life of *C*." Then *A* dies. Then *B* dies and leaves no heirs.

    165.   What is *O*'s interest?

O conveys "to *A* for life as long as the property is preserved as a wildlife area, then to *B* as long as the property is preserved as a wildlife area."

    166.   What is *B*'s interest?
    167.   What is *O*'s interest?

O conveys "to *A* for life, then to *B*, but if ever another hurricane of the magnitude of Andrew hits Miami, then to *O*." *O* then conveys any interest he has in the property "to *C*." Then a hurricane of the magnitude of Andrew hits Miami.

    168.   What is *C*'s interest?

O conveys "to *A* for life, then to *B* for life if *B* learns how to play the piano, then to *C* for life if *C* learns how to play the trombone."

    169.   What is *C*'s interest?
    170.   What is *O*'s interest?

O conveys "to *A* for life, then to *B*, but if *B* gets married, then, in place of *B*, to *C* for life, then to *D* as long as *D* does not get married." Then *B* and *D* marry each other. Then *C* conveys any interest she has in the property "to *F*." Then *O* conveys any interest he has in the property "to *G*."

    171.   What is *F*'s estate?
    172.   What is *G*'s interest?

O conveys "to *A* and his heirs, but if *B* gets married, then to *B*, and if *B* does not get married, then to *C*."

    173.   What is *C*'s interest?
    174.   If *B* dies without getting married, what is *C*'s interest?

O conveys "to *A* and his heirs during the time the old oak tree on the property remains standing."

175. What is *A*'s estate?
176. What is *O*'s interest?
177. If *O* conveys his interest to *B*, what is *A*'s estate?

O conveys "to *A*, but if *A* uses the property for nonagricultural purposes, then to *O*, but if *O* uses the property for nonagricultural purposes, then to *B* as long as *B* uses the property for agricultural purposes."

178. What is *A*'s interest?
179. What is *A*'s estate?
180. What is *O*'s interest?
181. What is *O*'s estate?
182. What is *B*'s interest?
183. What is *B*'s estate?

O conveys "to *A* for life, then to *B* for life, then to *C* if *C* gets married." *C* is not married at the time of the conveyance. Then *A* dies. Then *O* conveys any interest she has in the property to *D*.

184. What is *B*'s interest?
185. What is *C*'s interest?
186. What is *D*'s interest?
187. What is *D*'s estate?

O conveys "to *A* for life, then to *B* for ten years."

188. What is *B*'s estate?
189. What is *O*'s interest?

O conveys "to *A* for ten years, but if *A* gets married, then to *B*."

190. What is *A*'s estate?
191. What is *B*'s interest?

O conveys "to *A* for life, then to *B* for life if *B* gets married, then to *C* for life if *C* gets married." At the time of the conveyance, *B* and *C* are not married.

192. What is *C*'s interest?
193. What is *O*'s interest?
194. If *C* gets married, what is *C*'s interest?
195. If *C* gets married, what is *O*'s interest?

O conveys "to *A* for life, then to *B* for life, then to *C* for the life of *D*, but if *E* gets married at any time after this conveyance, then to *F*."

196. What is *B*'s estate?
197. What is *C*'s estate?
198. What is *F*'s interest?
199. If *D* then dies, what is *C*'s estate?
200. If after *D* dies *E* gets married, what is *F*'s interest?

Answers

101. *C. Reversion. O* conveyed a life estate to Arthur and left a reversion in herself. The reversion is not affected by the transfer of Arthur's life estate to Barbara as a life estate pur autre vie.

102. *J. Fee simple subject to condition subsequent.* The words of limitation for the fee simple estate are "and her heirs." The condition subsequent uses words of condition ("but if") and is confirmed by the "may enter and take" language. If words of duration had been used without the entry language, *A* would have had a fee simple determinable.

103. *E. Right of reentry.* This interest always follows an estate subject to condition subsequent. *O*'s estate is a fee simple absolute.

104. *J. None of the above is correct. O*'s reversion after *A*'s life estate subject to condition subsequent is coupled with a right of reentry upon the happening of the condition subsequent. Since the latter requires the exercise of an option to enter by *O* and the former does not, the two cannot be considered together as a reversion. *O*'s interest is a reversion coupled with a right of reentry.

105. *J. None of the above is correct. O*'s reversion after *A*'s life estate is still coupled with a right of reentry even though the condition subsequent has occurred. *O* has not yet exercised his right of reentry.

106. *A. Present interest.* Although the condition subsequent did not occur to cut short *A*'s life estate, the life estate terminated at *A*'s death.

107. *G. Life estate subject to executory limitation.* The condition subsequent (*A*'s divorce) cuts short both *A*'s life estate subject to executory limitation and *B*'s fee simple subject to executory limitation.

108. *H. Fee simple absolute.*

109. *E. Life estate determinable.* The condition subsequent uses words of duration ("as long as"), and there is no grantee designated to take on the happening of the condition subsequent.

110. *F. Vested remainder* in fee simple determinable. *B*'s interest stands ready to follow the natural termination of the preceding life estate in *A* without any condition precedent that needs to be satisfied for it to take.

111. *G. Possibility of reverter* in fee simple absolute. When there is no grantee designated to take on the happening of a condition subsequent that is durational rather than conditional, the grantor retains a possibility of reverter. When the condition subsequent occurs, it will cut short *A*'s life estate determinable and *B*'s fee simple determinable, and the possibility of reverter will transform into a present interest in *O*.

112. *K. Fee simple subject to executory limitation.* The condition subsequent is followed by an interest in a grantee.

113. *B. Executory interest* in a life estate.

114. *G. Possibility of reverter* in a fee simple absolute following Bob's executory interest in a life estate.

115. *D. Contingent remainder* in fee simple absolute. *B* and *C* have alternative contingent remainders because each interest is accompanied by a condition precedent that is the opposite of the other.

116. *C. Reversion* in fee simple absolute. The reversion supports both contingent remainders.

117. *F. Vested remainder* in fee simple absolute. The condition precedent to *B*'s interest will never happen and therefore *B*'s contingent remainder is destroyed. The condition precedent to *C*'s interest has just happened and therefore *C*'s contingent remainder transforms into a vested remainder to await the termination of *A*'s life estate.

118. *L. None.* *O*'s reversion in fee simple absolute is divested by the happening of the condition precedent.

119. *D. Contingent remainder* in a life estate. The condition "if *B* gets married" is a condition precedent to *B*'s interest; it is not a condition subsequent to *A*'s estate nor to *B*'s estate because it does not read to cut off either one.

120. *C. Life estate.*

121. *C. Reversion* in fee simple absolute. Before *B* got married, *O* had a reversion following *A*'s life estate. The transformation of *B*'s contingent remainder to a vested remainder upon the happening of the condition precedent pushes *O*'s reversion to follow *B*'s life estate.

122. *F. Life estate subject to condition subsequent.* The condition subsequent is the failure to maintain Blackacre as a farm.

123. *J. None of the above is correct.* *O* has a right of reentry ready to cut short both life estates subject to condition subsequent, and *O* also has a reversion ready to follow their natural termination. Since the former requires the exercise of an option to enter by *O*, it is appropriate to call *O*'s interest a reversion coupled with a right of reentry (rather than just a reversion).

124. *B. Executory interest* in a life estate. The condition subsequent of *B*'s getting married is precedent to *B*'s interest and subsequent to *A*'s fee simple estate. It cuts off *A*'s estate if it occurs. Therefore, both *B* and *C* have executory interests. If the condition happens, *B*'s executory interest transforms into a present interest in a life estate and *C*'s executory interest transforms into a vested remainder in fee simple absolute.

125. *B. Executory interest* in fee simple absolute. *C*'s executory interest and *B*'s executory interest together shift from *A*'s fee simple subject to executory limitation on the happening of the condition subsequent (*B*'s marriage).

126. *D. Contingent remainder.* The condition precedent is *B*'s marriage. *O*'s reversion following *A*'s present interest in a life estate supports the contingent remainder.

127. *K. Fee simple subject to executory limitation.* The condition subsequent in this estate is the cutting-off condition starting with "but if."

128. *B. Executory interest* in fee simple absolute. The condition subsequent (the "but if" condition) in *B*'s estate precedes *C*'s interest. It has the effect of a condition precedent to *C*'s interest but is not called a condition precedent.

129. *F. Vested remainder* in fee simple subject to executory limitation. The contingent remainder transforms into a vested remainder

upon the happening of the condition, and O's reversion is divested.

130. *H. Fee simple absolute. B* still has a vested remainder since A's life estate is not over, but his estate is no longer subject to executory limitation. The condition subsequent cannot happen, and therefore the condition subsequent as well as C's interest disappear.

131. *A. Present interest* in fee simple absolute. Upon A's death, C's executory interest cuts short B's fee simple subject to executory limitation by the happening of the condition subsequent, and C takes a vested remainder in fee simple absolute, which instantaneously transforms into a present interest because of the termination of A's life estate. (If you are wondering what happens if A dies before B gets married, there is a special rule to govern this situation called the Destructibility of Contingent Remainders Rule, which is discussed in Chapter 5.)

132. *K. Fee simple subject to executory limitation.* When B gets married, his contingent remainder in fee simple subject to executory limitation transforms into a vested remainder. When A dies, B's vested remainder transforms into a present interest. The condition subsequent (B not having a son) can still occur. So B's fee simple is still subject to executory limitation, and C has an executory interest in fee simple absolute.

133. *D. Contingent remainder* in fee simple determinable. The condition "if B gets married" is precedent to B's remainder. The condition "as long as B never divorces" is subsequent to B's estate.

134. *J. None of the above is correct. O* has a reversion and a possibility of reverter. They cannot be coupled together as a reversion because each follows a different estate. The reversion follows A's life estate and the possibility of reverter follows B's fee simple determinable.

135. *I. Fee simple determinable.* The condition precedent has been satisfied, so B's contingent remainder transforms into a vested remainder. The condition subsequent has not been broken, so B's estate remains the same.

136. *E. Life estate determinable.* The condition subsequent is A's having a son.

137. *C. Reversion* in fee simple absolute. O has a possibility of reverter that cuts short A's life estate determinable upon the happening of the condition subsequent, and O also has a reversion that follows A's life estate determinable upon the natural termination of that estate. The two are coupled into one.

138. *J. Fee simple subject to condition subsequent.* The condition subsequent is introduced by words of condition indicating an intent to create a right of reentry (power of termination) in the grantor, O.

139. *B. Executory interest* in fee simple absolute. The condition must be satisfied before A may take his interest. The undesignated present interest is O's original present interest in fee simple, which the condition, as a condition subsequent, limits in order to give a springing executory interest to A.

140. *K. Fee simple subject to executory limitation.*

141. *A. Present interest* in fee simple subject to condition subsequent. The nature of the condition in this conveyance is uncertain. Is it precedent to *A*'s interest or subsequent to *A*'s estate? If the condition were a condition precedent, then *A* would not be able to take this interest until the condition were satisfied, which is at her death. This interpretation of the condition does not make sense because *O* seems to have intended the estate for *A* to enjoy, albeit subject to a condition, so the condition must be a condition subsequent, cutting off the estate if it is broken. The fee simple estate is "subject to condition subsequent" because the condition uses conditional language ("if").

142. *E. Right of reentry*, which always follows an estate subject to condition subsequent.

143. *K. Fee simple subject to executory limitation. A*'s fee simple is limited by a condition subsequent in favor of a grantee, *B*, who has an executory interest.

144. *G. Life estate subject to executory limitation. B*'s life estate is limited by a condition subsequent in favor of a grantee, *C*, who has an executory interest in fee simple absolute.

145. *G. Possibility of reverter. O*'s interest follows *B*'s executory interest.

146. *K. Fee simple subject to executory limitation.* The condition subsequent involving *B*'s marriage, if it occurs, will cut off *B*'s life estate and every estate that follows it.

147. *D. Contingent remainder* in fee simple determinable. *A* has a present interest in a life estate. *B* has a vested remainder in a life estate. *C* has a contingent remainder in fee simple absolute. *D* has a contingent remainder in fee simple determinable. *O* retains a reversion in fee simple absolute following *B*'s life estate and also retains a possibility of reverter in fee simple absolute following *D*'s fee simple determinable. *C* and *D* have alternative contingent remainders. Even though the "but if" condition sounds like it is cutting off the preceding estate in favor of *D*, this condition is the reverse of the first "if" condition and is treated like the first condition as a condition precedent to its respective interest.

148. *H. Vested remainder subject to open. X*'s interest is vested because *X* is born and ascertained and her interest is not subject to any condition precedent.

149. *H. Vested remainder subject to open. Y*'s interest transforms from an executory interest into the vested remainder subject to open held by *X*. *Y*'s interest is now vested because *Y* is born and ascertained and her interest is not subject to any condition precedent.

150. *I. None.*

151. *K. Fee simple subject to executory limitation.* The condition subsequent (*A*'s divorcing) is followed by an interest in a grantee.

152. *C. Life estate. C* has an executory interest. It follows *B*'s executory interest in a life estate.

153. *B. Executory interest* in fee simple absolute. This executory interest is not only dependent on the condition subsequent of *A*'s divorce, but it is also subject to the condition precedent of the heirs being ascertained. They will be ascertained upon *D*'s death.

154.   *G. Possibility of reverter*. The executory interest in *D*'s heirs follows *C*'s life estate, but if *A* divorces and *B* and *C* die and *D* is still alive, *D*'s heirs will not be ascertained, and yet there is no other designated taker of the property. This gap in the conveyance is filled by *O*, who retains a possibility of reverter following *C*'s executory interest.

155.   *D. Contingent remainder* in fee simple absolute. Upon the divorce, *B*'s interest transforms into a present interest in a life estate, *C*'s interest transforms into a vested remainder in a life estate, the interest of *D*'s heirs transforms into a contingent remainder (following *C*'s life estate) in fee simple absolute, and *O*'s interest transforms into a reversion in fee simple absolute following *C*'s life estate and supporting the contingent remainder in fee simple absolute in *D*'s heirs.

156.   *F. Vested remainder* in a life estate pur autre vie subject to executory limitation. *A* receives part of *O*'s vested remainder in a life estate; it has an added condition subsequent which is *A*'s divorce. Thus, *A*'s estate will end either on the death of *O* or on *A*'s divorce, whichever occurs first.

157.   *B. Executory interest* in a life estate pur autre vie. *O* cannot convey more than he had; hence the life estate for the life of *O*.

158.   *D. Contingent remainder* in fee simple absolute. The word "or" is construed as disjunctive, giving alternative contingent remainders to *B* and to her children. The condition precedent, which is implied for *B*'s interest, is *B*'s survivorship of *A*'s death. The condition precedent, which is implied for the children's interest, is *B*'s failure to survive *A*'s death.

159.   *D. Contingent remainder* in fee simple absolute. Even though *X* has been born and ascertained, *X*'s interest is still subject to the condition precedent of *B*'s failure to survive *A*'s death. Therefore, *X* still shares the contingent remainder with *B*'s children.

160.   *F. Vested remainder* in fee simple absolute. The condition precedent to the children's interest has been satisfied, and *X*'s contingent remainder transforms into a vested remainder. It is not a vested remainder subject to open because upon *B*'s death no other children can be born because *B* is dead.

161.   *D. Contingent remainder* in fee simple absolute. Even though *Z* has been born and ascertained, *Z*'s interest is still subject to the condition precedent of *B*'s failure to survive *A*'s death. *Z* shares the contingent remainder with *C*'s children. It is an alternative contingent remainder to *B*'s contingent remainder.

162.   *H. Vested remainder subject to open*. The condition precedent to the children's interest has been satisfied, and *X*'s contingent remainder transforms into a vested remainder. It is subject to open because *C* may have more children, who, upon birth while *A* is still alive, will share *X*'s vested remainder. Note that a complete explanation of how this conveyance works must wait for the discussion in Chapter 3.

163.   *B. Executory interest* in a life estate. The condition subsequent that precedes *A*'s interest is all three graduating from law school. In the

meantime, *O* has a present interest in fee simple subject to executory limitation. *B* and *C* also have executory interests.

164. *F. Vested remainder* in fee simple absolute. Once the condition subsequent has occurred, *O*'s fee simple subject to executory limitation is divested and the grantees' executory interests transform into three vested interests. *A* has a present interest in a life estate, and *B* has a vested remainder in a life estate.

165. *C. Reversion*. When *A* dies, *B*'s vested remainder in a life estate pur autre vie transforms into a present interest. When *B* dies and leaves no heirs, his interest escheats to the state. The state now holds a present interest in a life estate pur autre vie, followed by *O*'s reversion in fee simple absolute.

166. *F. Vested remainder* in fee simple determinable. *A* has a present interest in a life estate subject to executory limitation. *B* has an executory interest coupled with a vested remainder, which together are called a vested remainder.

167. *G. Possibility of reverter* in fee simple absolute, following the second condition subsequent, which stands ready to cut short *B*'s fee simple determinable.

168. *E. Right of reentry* in fee simple absolute. *O*'s conveyance leaves in himself a right of reentry following the condition subsequent, because the condition uses the conditional language "but if," which makes *A*'s and *B*'s estates "subject to condition subsequent." When *O* conveys to *C*, he conveys what he has. Note that a right of reentry cannot be created in a grantee, but it can be conveyed to a grantee after it is created in the grantor. The right of reentry still exists because *C* has not yet exercised it.

169. *D. Contingent remainder* in a life estate. *B* has a contingent remainder in a life estate, followed by *C*'s contingent remainder. These two contingent remainders are not alternative.

170. *C. Reversion*. *O* has a reversion following *A*'s life estate and supporting the two contingent remainders. This reversion is prepared to take if both of the contingent remainders fail to vest.

171. *D. Life estate pur autre vie*. At the time of the conveyance, *A* has a present interest in a life estate, *B* has a vested remainder in fee simple subject to executory limitation, *C* has an executory interest in a life estate, *D* has an executory interest in fee simple determinable, and *O* has a possibility of reverter in fee simple absolute. The marriage transforms these interests so that they become a present interest in a life estate in *A*, a vested remainder in a life estate in *C*, and a reversion in fee simple absolute in *O*. *C*'s conveyance gives *F* a vested remainder in a life estate for the life of *C*.

172. *C. Reversion* in fee simple absolute.

173. *B. Executory interest* in fee simple absolute. *B* and *C* have what look like alternative contingent remainders, but they do not. Remainders follow life estates, and *A* has a fee simple subject to executory limitation. The two conditions are subsequent to *A*'s estate. The condition of *B*'s marriage, if it happens, will cut short *A*'s estate in favor of *B*'s executory interest, and the condition of *B*'s failure to marry, if it happens, will cut short *A*'s estate in favor of *C*'s executory interest.

174. *A. Present interest* in fee simple absolute. The condition subsequent preceding *C*'s interest has occurred, and *A*'s estate is cut short in favor of *C*'s interest. *B*'s interest disappears, not because *B* is dead but rather because the condition subsequent preceding *B*'s interest will never happen.

175. *I. Fee simple determinable.* The condition subsequent to *A*'s estate is durational, and it is followed by an interest in the grantor.

176. *G. Possibility of reverter*, which always follows an estate determinable.

177. *I. Fee simple determinable.* The condition subsequent to *A*'s estate is durational, and at its creation, it was followed by an interest in the grantor. The fact that the grantor conveys his interest to *B* does not change the interest. *B* now has a possibility of reverter.

178. *A. Present interest.*

179. *J. Fee simple subject to condition subsequent.* The condition subsequent to *A*'s estate uses the words "but if" and therefore is conditional, and it is followed by an interest in the grantor.

180. *J. None of the above is correct.* Following *A*'s fee simple subject to condition subsequent, *O* has a right of reentry. Following *B*'s fee simple determinable, *O* has a possibility of reverter.

181. *M. None of the above is correct.* *O*'s estate for the right of reentry is a fee simple subject to executory limitation. *O*'s estate for the possibility of reverter is a fee simple absolute.

182. *B. Executory interest* following *O*'s fee simple subject to executory limitation.

183. *I. Fee simple determinable.* The condition subsequent to *B*'s estate is durational, and it is followed by an interest in the grantor.

184. *A. Present interest* in a life estate. After *A*'s death, *B*'s vested remainder transforms into a present interest.

185. *D. Contingent remainder* in fee simple absolute. The "if" condition does not make sense as a cutting-off condition, and therefore it is not a condition subsequent but rather a condition precedent.

186. *C. Reversion.* At the time of the conveyance *O* retains a reversion, which supports the contingent remainder. This reversion is then conveyed to *D*.

187. *H. Fee simple absolute.* The "if" condition is not a condition subsequent but rather a condition precedent. If the condition (*C* getting married) occurs, it will not cut short *D*'s estate, and therefore *D* has a fee simple absolute. Nevertheless, *D*'s reversion will be divested, and *C*'s contingent remainder will become a vested remainder at that time.

188. *A. Term of years.* This ownership is a future interest designated to transform into a present interest when *A* dies. There is no name for this future interest because the ownership is a nonfreehold estate.

189. *C. Reversion* in fee simple absolute following *A*'s life estate. A term of years does not affect the future interests of freehold estates. The conveyance would be the same if it said "to *A* for life, then to *O*, whose estate is subject to a term of ten years in *B*."

190. *B. Term of years determinable.* The "but if" condition cuts off the term of years. There is no nonfreehold estate called a term of years subject to condition subsequent. Therefore, this nonfreehold estate is called determinable.

191. *B. Executory interest* in fee simple absolute. *B*'s estate has no words of limitation, and therefore it is a fee simple absolute, which is a freehold estate. Because it is not conveyed to *B* as a present interest, it is a future interest following the happening of a condition. So by her conveyance, *O* retains a present interest in fee simple subject to executory limitation, and *B* gets an executory interest following the condition subsequent to *O*'s estate. Note that *O*'s fee simple *subject to* executory limitation is also *subject to* a term of years determinable in *A*, but the first "subject to" is part of the name of *O*'s freehold estate, whereas the second "subject to" refers to the possessory aspect of *O*'s estate being in a nonfreehold estate for the time the term runs.

192. *D. Contingent remainder* in a life estate following *B*'s contingent remainder in a life estate.

193. *C. Reversion* in fee simple absolute following *A*'s present interest in a life estate and supporting the contingent remainders in *B* and *C*.

194. *F. Vested remainder* in a life estate following *A*'s present interest in a life estate and supporting *B*'s contingent remainder.

195. *C. Reversion* in fee simple absolute following *C*'s vested remainder in a life estate and supporting *B*'s contingent remainder.

196. *G. Life estate subject to executory limitation*. The condition subsequent on this estate is *E* getting married.

197. *M. None of the above is correct. C* has a life estate pur autre vie subject to executory limitation. The condition subsequent on this estate is *E* getting married.

198. *B. Executory interest* in fee simple absolute following the condition subsequent on the other estates.

199. *L. None. C*'s life estate is measured by the life of *D*.

200. *A. Present interest* in fee simple absolute. The condition subsequent has occurred and has cut short all the other estates.

3

Class Interests

A. INCLUSION

All the people who are designated to share in an interest are considered a *class*. A class consists of a group, such as children, nephews, or parents. For example, where O conveys "to the children of A," A's children are a class. A class may even consist of a group within a group, such as one's grandchildren by one's oldest daughter. Thus, where A has two daughters, B and C, and O conveys "to A for life, then to A's grandchildren by A's oldest daughter, B," A takes a present interest in a life estate, and A's grandchildren to be born to B, are designated to take a contingent remainder in fee simple absolute. A's grandchildren to be born to B are a class. When the members of the class are born, the first takes a vested remainder that subsequently "opens" to be shared with the other members of the class as each is born.

A person becomes a member of a class at the moment of conception, as long as that person is later born alive. Thus, where O conveys "to A's children" at a time when A is pregnant with twins and has one child, X, who is already born, the class is A's children, whoever they are or might be in the future, but the members of the class at the time of conveyance are the two twins (as long as they are later born alive) and X. If, six months later, one of the twins is born alive and the other dies before birth, then the twin who is born alive continues to be considered a member of the class from the time of the conveyance, while the twin who dies before birth is considered never to have been a member of the class.

In describing the members of a class designated in a conveyance, one should be careful to distinguish a characteristic of a class from a condition precedent (defined broadly to include a condition subsequent that acts as a condition precedent to the interest that follows). Although the literature on this subject is scanty, the cases seem to indicate that a characteristic of a class member, such as filial relationship or sex, defines the class, while an event, such as birth or the attainment of a certain age, poses a condition precedent to the vesting or distribution of a class member's interest. In the example above, the twin that is later born alive must satisfy the condition precedent of birth before her interest will become vested. At the time of the conveyance, both the child that is born and the twin that is later born alive are members of the class, but the child that is born has a vested present interest and the twin that is later born alive has an executory interest until she is born.

Another example is the conveyance "to A for life, then to A's children who reach twenty-one." If A is pregnant with triplets and already has one child, X, at the time of the conveyance, the class is A's children, whoever they are or might be in the future, but the members of the class at the time of conveyance are the three triplets (as long as they are later born alive) and X. If, six months later, two of the triplets are born alive and the other dies before birth, then the triplets that are born alive continue to be considered members of the class from the time of the conveyance, while the triplet that dies before birth is considered never to have been a member of the class. If one of the remaining triplets dies before reaching the age of twenty-one, then this triplet's membership in the class ceases on his death, although, contrary to the first triplet who died before birth, this triplet is still considered to have been a member of the class. When the third triplet reaches the age of twenty-one, her interest vests. The condition precedent to vesting is reaching the age of twenty-one, but remember that each of the triplets at least had to be born to be considered a member of the class. Thus, there was one triplet who is considered never to have been a member of the class, there was one who is considered to have been a member but whose interest never vested, and there is a third who is considered to be a member of the class and whose interest has vested.

Class members will hold two different interests when one is vested and the other is contingent. In the example of the twins above ("to A's children" and A is pregnant with twins and has one child, X, who is already born), the vested interest is held at the time of conveyance by X. X has a "present interest subject to open" to let in other members of the class who may be born after the conveyance. More exactly, X has a present interest subject to open in a fee simple subject to executory limitation. The condition subsequent that provides the executory limitation only partially divests the vested interest (i.e., partially cuts short the fee simple subject to executory limitation) when it happens. The condition subsequent is the birth of any member of the class so that the newly born member takes a share in the vested interest and cuts down proportionally, but never eliminates, the shares of the members already holding the vested interest. The contingent interest, held by the child who is not born at the time of the conveyance but will be born later, is an executory interest in a fee simple absolute. When the child is born, the executory interest transforms into the present interest already held by X, and both X and the newly born child share the present interest together.

The distinction between that which defines a class and that which is a condition precedent to the vesting or to the distribution of an interest of a class member may be illustrated by another example. Where O conveys "to the children of B who are female and who reach the age of twenty-one," the class is the daughters of *B, not* the daughters of *B* who are twenty-one and older. At the time of this conveyance the daughters of *B* who are twenty-one and older are members of the class and hold a vested present interest subject to open in a fee simple subject to executory limitation. The daughters of *B* who are conceived (later to be born alive) and who are born and under age twenty-one are members of the class, but they must satisfy the condition precedent of reaching age twenty-one before their interest will become vested. The latter have an executory interest in a fee simple absolute. The daughters of *B* who are not yet conceived, or who are conceived but will not be born alive, at the time of the conveyance are not members of the class. When they are conceived, if the class is still open to receiving members under the rules of exclusion described below, they become members of the class at the point of conception if they are later born alive.

Where *O* conveys "to *A* for life, then to the children of *B*," the children of *B* are a class. If no children of *B* have yet been conceived, there are no members of the class at the time of the conveyance, but the children of *B* are said to have a contingent remainder in fee simple absolute. If a child of *B* is conceived (later to be born alive), that child becomes a member of the class of *B*'s children at the time of conception, but this child in gestation still holds a contingent remainder in a fee simple absolute. When the child is born, she satisfies the condition precedent of birth, and her contingent remainder becomes a vested remainder subject to open in a fee simple subject to executory limitation. The interest of the other children, conceived or not, who are not yet born is transformed from a contingent remainder to an executory interest in a fee simple absolute. The condition subsequent that stands ready to partially cut short the estate of the child who is now born (that is, to open the vested remainder of the child who is now born) is the birth of any other child to *B*. On the birth of another child, that child's share in the executory interest transforms into a share in the vested remainder subject to open that is held by the first child who was born, while the rest of the children who are not yet born continue to hold the executory interest.

Note one aberration from the logic of these rules that originates from a case decided by the House of Lords in the seventeenth century: In a conveyance "to *A* for life, remainder to *A*'s first son and his heirs," if *A* has a son conceived but not born at the termination of *A*'s life estate and the son is later born alive, the law creates the fiction that the child is considered born at the moment of *A*'s death in order to avoid a reversion in the grantor to fill the gap between the death of *A* and the birth of *A*'s first son. The purpose to avoid a reversion is accomplished by giving retroactively to the child who is born a vested present interest for the time he was in gestation. The child's interest is considered vested from the moment of his conception and thus vested on *A*'s death, but this retroactive classification does not occur until and only if the child is born alive. Until the child is actually born alive, the child has a contingent interest. Thus, in a conveyance "to *A*'s children," if *A*'s first child is conceived at the time of the conveyance, the child is considered to have been born at the moment of the conveyance when he is later born alive. Also, in a conveyance "to *A* for life, then to the children of *B*," if *B*'s first child is conceived at the time of *A*'s death, the child is considered to have been born at the moment of *A*'s death when he is later born alive. The fiction of birth creates a vested interest in the child in gestation; however, distribution of the child's interest most likely will be postponed until birth.

B. EXCLUSION

1. *Class Closing Rules*

Not all people in a class are entitled to become "members" of the class. A class "opens" to accept new members on their conception (if they are later born alive), and a class may also "close" to prevent new people in the class from becoming members. Thus, a class may be defined as the children of *A*, and, if the class closes after two children are born to *A*, then any children conceived by *A* after the class closes are not members of the class and do not take any share with the members of the class. The people in a class must be conceived (later to be born) before the class closes if they are to be qualified as members of the class.

A class "closes," so that no more people may be admitted to the class, on the happening of one of two events, *whichever is sooner*:

(1) natural closing
(2) time determined by the Rule of Convenience

A **natural closing** occurs *on an event that is said to prevent the further creation of members of a class*. This event closes the class naturally because it is said there are no other people who can become members of the class. Thus, where *O* conveys "to *A* for life, then to the children of *B*," the class of *B*'s children will close naturally if and when *B* dies before *A*'s death, since *B*'s death is said to prevent any further children from being conceived. Practically, *B* may have more children after her death through artificial insemination or other artificial methods that produce birth after the death of a parent, but these methods are not considered in this calculation. On the other hand, note that the class is not considered naturally closed before *B*'s death even if *B* reaches the ripe old age of 110 and is physically incapable of having children, because the law conclusively presumes the fiction that any person who is alive is capable of having children.

A closing at a time determined by the **Rule of Convenience** occurs *when the time designated in a conveyance for distribution to a class has arrived, and at that time there exists some member of the class (or one who has inherited, bought, or otherwise received the interest of some member of the class) who is entitled to take distribution*. This event closes the class artificially because there may still be people conceived at a later point in time who might have become members of the class were it not for this closing. The closing of the class determines the maximum membership of the class because any person who has not become a member by that time will be barred from membership. By setting the maximum membership, the closing of the class also determines the minimum share of each class member. This determination is a matter of convenience to the member who has become, and those members who will become, entitled to distribution. They know at least the minimum amount of their share. It will never decrease, although it may grow if the class decreases for failure of a member to satisfy a condition precedent.

For example, where *O* conveys "to *A* for life, then one year later to the children of *B*," *A* has a present interest in a life estate, *O* has a reversion in fee simple subject to executory limitation (note that O has a fee simple and not a term of years, as is explained in the discussion of the No Gap in Seisin Rule in Chapter 4), and the children of B have an executory interest in fee simple absolute. The class of B's children will close under the Rule of Convenience if B has at least one child and is still alive (i.e., no natural closing yet) when one year passes after A's death, because the time for distribution designated in the conveyance is one year after A's death and there is a member of the class entitled to take distribution. Note that there is a member of the class entitled to take distribution in this case even if the child is in gestation, as long as he or she is later born alive.

In the example above, if B has a child who sells his share of the executory interest to X before one year passes after A dies, B may or may not have more children. If B has them on or before one year following A's death, they will become members of the class and will take their shares of the executory interest. At the point that one year passes after A's death, regardless of whether B has had more than one child, the class of B's children will close under the Rule of Convenience, since the time for distribution designated in the conveyance has arrived and X has received the interest of some member of the class and is entitled to take distribution.

Likewise, where O conveys "to A for life, then one year later to the children of B who reach twenty-one," A has a present interest in a life estate, O has a reversion in fee simple subject to executory limitation, and the children of B have an executory interest in fee simple absolute. The class of B's children will close under the Rule of Convenience if B is alive and at least one year has passed from A's death and at least one child has reached twenty-one, because the time for distribution designated in the conveyance is the later time of one year after A's death or the attainment of age twenty-one by one of the children.

Note that the time for distribution does not occur until all conditions have been satisfied in order to give distribution, *except that the condition of birth need not be satisfied*. This means that in some cases the time for distribution will arrive and there will be no member of the class to take because no member has been born or conceived later to be born. In such a case, the Rule of Convenience will not close the class. In the last example above, however, the age requirement, which is a condition that must be satisfied to reach the time for distribution, requires birth. Therefore, if and when the time for distribution arrives in the example above, there will necessarily be a member of the class entitled to take distribution or at least someone who holds the interest of a member of the class who is entitled to take distribution.

The maximum membership of the class in the last example above will be determined at the time of distribution to be all of B's children who are born or conceived (as long as they are later born alive). Therefore, the minimum share of each member also will be known. If there is a child who has not yet reached twenty-one and who dies before reaching that age, he does not receive his share of the interest because he has failed to satisfy the condition precedent of reaching age twenty-one. His share is divided among the remaining members of the class and distributed to those who have satisfied the condition precedent.

One important aspect of the Rule of Convenience is that if there is no one entitled to take at the time designated in the conveyance for distribution, the only class closing can be a natural closing. At least one class member (or person holding the interest of a class member) must be in existence at the time designated in the conveyance for distribution, and that person must be entitled to take without the obstacle of having failed to satisfy a condition precedent. In the conveyance "to A's children" the time for distribution is the time of conveyance, and a child must be born (or conceived, if later born alive) at that time in order to close the class under the Rule of Convenience. In the conveyance "to A's children who reach fifteen" the time for distribution is the time A's first child reaches fifteen, and actually in this case it is not possible for this time to arrive without a class member (or a person holding the interest of a class member) being entitled to take. In the conveyance "to A for life, then one year later to the children of B" the time for distribution is the time when one year has passed after A's death. A child must be born (or conceived, if later born alive) by that time in order to close the class under the Rule of Convenience. In the conveyance "to A for life, then one year later to the children of B who reach fifteen" the time for distribution is the later of the times when one year has passed after A's death or when one of the children has reached age fifteen. Once again in this case it is not possible for this time to arrive without a class member (or a person holding the interest of a class member) being entitled to take.

Note that the Rule of Convenience is a rule of construction and will yield to a contrary intent in the grantor.

2. Four Examples

Since the combination of class membership definition, conditions precedent to vesting, and class closing rules often gives rise to confusion, some of the key points discussed above are reviewed below in four examples.

(1) Where O conveys "to A's children" and there are children alive at the time of the conveyance, the class closes immediately under the Rule of Convenience and includes only those children. If A has two children, F and G, at the time of the conveyance, these children have a present interest in fee simple absolute. No other children conceived after the conveyance will become members of the class.

If there are no children alive (or in gestation and later born alive) at the time of the conveyance, the class remains open until A's death (natural closing), and the Rule of Convenience does not apply. O retains a present interest in fee simple subject to executory limitation, and A's unborn children have an executory interest in fee simple absolute. If A then bears a child, P, P takes a present interest subject to open in fee simple subject to executory limitation, fully divesting O's present interest in the process. A's unborn children continue to have an executory interest, but now the executory interest follows the condition subsequent on P's estate rather than on O's estate. P's present interest is subject to open, which means that it will not be fully divested upon the happening of the condition subsequent of another child's birth but only partially divested. If A then dies, the class closes and P and whatever other children have been born have a present interest in fee simple absolute.

(2) Where *O* conveys "to the children of *A* who reach twenty-one," the class is *A*'s children (*not A*'s children who reach twenty-one). The class closes at the time of the earlier of two events—namely, the time *A* dies (natural closing) or the time a child of *A* reaches twenty-one (Rule of Convenience). If a child of *A* has already reached twenty-one before the conveyance, then the class is closed at the time of the conveyance. When the class closes, all members who are born (or conceived, if later born alive) who have not yet reached twenty-one are entitled to a share when they do reach twenty-one. All children conceived after the class closes (or conceived before but never born alive) are not members of the class.

O's conveyance in this case where one child, *W*, has reached twenty-one and other children, *X* and *Y*, are born but not yet twenty-one, gives *W* a present interest subject to open in a fee simple subject to executory limitation and gives *X* and *Y* an executory interest. The class is closed at the time of conveyance because the time for distribution to *W* has arrived. *X* and *Y* will take a share with *W* in the present interest if and when they reach twenty-one. Reaching twenty-one is a condition precedent to transforming the interest of each into a vested present interest and is a condition subsequent to *W*'s estate to the extent that *W*'s share will be decreased to admit the share of *X* and/or *Y*. Two years later, if *X* reaches twenty-one and *Y* dies before reaching twenty-one and *Z* is born, *X* takes a share in the ownership of *W*'s estate, *Y* is excluded for not satisfying the age contingency, and *Z* is excluded for being conceived after the class closed.

(3) Where *O* conveys "to *X* for life, then one year later to *A*'s children" and *A* has two children, *G* and *H*, the ownerships are as follows: *X* has a present interest in a life estate, *O* has a reversion in fee simple subject to executory limitation, and *G* and *H* share an executory interest in fee simple absolute with *A*'s unborn children. The condition subsequent in *O*'s fee simple subject to executory limitation is the passage of one year after the termination of *X*'s life estate; this same condition is precedent to the vesting of the interest in *G* and *H*. The class closes on the earlier of two events: *A*'s death (natural closing), or the passage of one year after the termination of *X*'s life estate (Rule of Convenience). *A* has children so that they, as members of the class, or someone holding their interest, will be entitled to take one year after the termination of *X*'s life estate.

If *A* does not have children at the time of this conveyance, then *X* has a present interest in a life estate, *O* has a reversion in fee simple subject to executory limitation, and *A*'s unborn children have an executory interest in fee simple absolute. There are two conditions subsequent on *O*'s estate: the passage of one year after the termination of *X*'s life estate and the birth of a child to *A*. Both conditions must be realized before *O*'s reversion is divested. Furthermore, if *A* has not conceived children to create a member of the class by the time designated in the conveyance for distribution—that is, one year after the termination of *X*'s life estate—the Rule of Convenience does not apply, and the class remains open until *A*'s death, so that children born to *A* after the time for distribution become members.

(4) Where *O* conveys "to *L* for life, then one year later to such of *A*'s children who reach twenty-one" and *A* has no children, *O* conveys an executory interest in fee simple absolute to *A*'s children as a class. *L* has a present interest in a life estate, and *O* retains a reversion in fee simple subject to executory limitation. *O*'s estate will be cut short (another way of

saying that O's reversion will be divested) when one year has passed after the termination of L's life estate and at least one child of A has been born and reached twenty-one, or it will be cut short at the time that any child of A reaches twenty-one if that occurs for the first time more than one year after the termination of L's life estate. In either case the class will close under the Rule of Convenience (if it has not already closed naturally) by the presence of a twenty-one-year-old child of A (or someone who holds the interest of a twenty-one-year-old child of A) at or after the passage of one year from L's death. If the class closes under the Rule of Convenience, only members of the class at that time who have reached or will reach twenty-one (or those who hold the interest of these members of the class) will be permitted to take a share in the interest when the age requirement is satisfied. All children conceived after O's estate is cut short will not be entitled to take, and they will take nothing.

Thus, if A's child, X, reaches twenty-one and one year has already passed since L died, or if X reaches twenty-one and then one year passes since L died, O's estate is cut short in either case by the happening of the two events, and X's executory interest becomes a present interest. If there is only one other child, Y, who has been conceived (later to be born) by this time, Y's interest remains executory. When Y reaches twenty-one, Y joins X as a tenant in common sharing X's estate in fee simple absolute. If another child of A is conceived after O's estate is cut short, that child is not entitled to distribution.

In more precise terms for the purpose of classification of estates, if A has two children under age twenty-one, X and Y, at the time of or after the conveyance, then X and Y have an executory interest in fee simple absolute. They are said to share their executory interest in fee simple absolute with the unborn children of A, even though the unborn children of A are not yet members of the class. Their executory interest stands ready to cut short O's fee simple on the happening of both of two conditions subsequent to O's estate (one child reaching twenty-one and one year passage from the termination of L's life estate). The two conditions subsequent on O's fee simple are simultaneously conditions precedent to the executory interest held by X, Y, and the unborn children. When X reaches twenty-one and one year has passed since the termination of L's estate, if A has not conceived any other children, A's unborn children no longer have any interest because the class closes. Y continues to have an executory interest in fee simple absolute.

3. Distribution of Shares

Whenever a member of a class becomes entitled to distribution, that person may take his minimum proportionate share of the whole estate. For example, when O conveys "to the children of A who reach twenty-one," and there are three children alive at the time of the conveyance (X, Y, and Z, ages thirteen, eighteen, and twenty-two, respectively), the class is closed at the time of the conveyance, and Z is entitled to a one-third share in the property in anticipation of the other two children reaching twenty-one. If Y dies before reaching twenty-one, Z's share is increased to one-half. If X

reaches twenty-one, X is then entitled to the other half share. There is a problem in determining the minimum proportionate share in some cases. For example, when O conveys "to the children of A" and there are no children at the time of the conveyance, the class remains open until A's death. How much of the property does the first child of A take when she is born? It has been suggested that the first child takes the whole property subject to partial divestment when later children are born.

Problem Set III

The problems in this section ask for a description of an interest or an estate. The answers for interest are:

    A. present interest
    B. executory interest
    C. reversion
    D. contingent remainder
    E. right of reentry
    F. vested remainder
    G. possibility of reverter
    H. vested remainder subject to open
    I. none
    J. none of the above is correct

The answers for estate are:

    A. term of years
    B. term of years determinable
    C. life estate
    D. life estate pur autre vie
    E. life estate determinable
    F. life estate subject to condition subsequent
    G. life estate subject to executory limitation
    H. fee simple absolute
    I. fee simple determinable
    J. fee simple subject to condition subsequent
    K. fee simple subject to executory limitation
    L. none
    M. none of the above is correct

Problems

O conveys "to his children who reach twenty-one and their heirs." O has two children, who are ages five and ten.

    201. What is O's children's interest?
    202. What is O's interest?

O conveys "to *A* for life, then to *B*'s children, but if no child of *B* reaches twenty-one, then to *C*." *B* has one child, *X*, who is fifteen years old at the time of the conveyance.

203. What is *X*'s interest?
204. What is *B*'s unborn children's interest?

O conveys "to *A*, but if *A* becomes bankrupt, then to *A*'s children who shall reach twenty-one." *A* has two children, *X*, age twenty-two, and *Y*, age fifteen.

205. What is *X*'s interest?
206. What is *Y*'s interest?
207. If *A* becomes bankrupt one year later, what is *X*'s interest?
208. If *A* becomes bankrupt one year later, what is *Y*'s interest?

O has never had grandchildren born or conceived before his death. *O* devises Blackacre "to my grandchildren." Upon his death, *O* has two children, *A* and *B*.

209. What is the unborn grandchildren's interest?

O has two grandchildren, *X* and *Y*, living at her death. *O* devises Blackacre "to my grandchildren."

210. What is the unborn grandchildren's interest?

O conveys "to *A* for life, then to such of *A*'s children as survive *A*." *B* is already born to *A* at the time of the conveyance.

211. What is *B*'s interest?
212. What is *O*'s interest?

O conveys "to *A* for life, then to *B* or her children." *B* has no children at the time of the conveyance.

213. What is *B*'s interest?
214. If *B* has a child before *A*'s death, what is the child's interest?

O conveys "to *A* for life, then, if *B* goes to law school, to *B* for life, then or otherwise to *C*'s children." *C* has two children, *X* and *Y*, at the time of the conveyance.

215. What is *B*'s estate?
216. What is *X*'s estate?
217. If *B* goes to law school, what is *B*'s interest?
218. If *B* goes to law school, what is *X*'s interest?

O conveys "to *A*'s children who reach the age of twelve for the life of *S*, a stranger, and, if this happens, then to *B* and his heirs." *A* has one two-year-old child, *X*.

219.   What is *X*'s interest?
220.   What is *B*'s interest?

O conveys "to *A* for life, then to *A*'s children who reach twenty-one; and if *A* becomes bankrupt, *A*'s estate shall become void and vest in *A*'s children who reach twenty-one." *A* has one child, *X*, who is thirty years old.

221.   What is the interest in *X*?
222.   What is *A*'s estate?

O has no grandchildren living at his death. *O* devises Blackacre "to *A* for life, then to my grandchildren." *O* has two children, *M* and *N*. Thirty years later, *O*'s first grandchild, *X*, is born.

223.   What is *X*'s interest?
224.   What is the unborn grandchildren's interest?

O has no grandchildren living at his death. *O* devises Blackacre "to *A* for life, then to my grandchildren." *O* has two children, *M* and *N*. Thirty years later *O*'s first grandchild, *X*, is born. The next year *O*'s second grandchild, *Y*, is conceived. Two months later *A* dies. Seven months later *Y* is born.

225.   On *A*'s death, what is *Y*'s interest?
226.   On *A*'s death, what is the interest of the unborn grandchildren other than *Y*?

O has no grandchildren living at his death. *O* devises Blackacre "to *A* for life, then to my grandchildren." *O* has two children, *M* and *N*. Thirty years later, *O*'s first grandchild, *X*, is born. Five years later *X* dies intestate, leaving his mother, *M*, as his only heir. Two years later *A* dies.

227.   What is *M*'s interest when *X* dies?
228.   What is *M*'s interest when *A* dies?

O has no grandchildren living at his death. *O* devises Blackacre "to *A* for life, then one year later to my grandchildren." *O* has two children, *M* and *N*. Five years later *A* dies. One year after *A*'s death there are still no grandchildren who have been conceived.

229.   What is the unborn grandchildren's interest?
230.   If a grandchild, *X*, is born two years later, what is *X*'s estate?

O conveys "to *A* for life, then one year later to *B*'s children who reach fifteen and their heirs." *B* has one child, *X*, at the time of the conveyance whose age is ten. Two years later *A* dies.

231.   One year after *A*'s death what is *X*'s interest?
232.   Four years after *A*'s death what is *X*'s interest?

O conveys "to *A* for life, then to the children of *B*." At the time of the conveyance, *B* has one child, *X*. Two years later *X* dies. Three years after the death of *X*, *A* dies.

233.   What is the interest of *B*'s unborn children?
234.   What is *O*'s interest?

O conveys "to *A* and for life, then one year later to the children of *B*." At the time of the conveyance, *B* does not have children. Three years after the conveyance, *A* dies. Three years after *A*'s death, *B* has one child, *X*. Three years after *X*'s birth, *B* has another child, *Y*.

235.   What is *Y*'s estate?
236.   If *B* then dies, what is *Y*'s estate?

O conveys "to my children who reach twenty-one and their heirs." *O* has two children, *X*, who is fifteen years old, and *Y*, who is twenty-five years old.

237.   What is *Y*'s interest?
238.   What is the interest of *O*'s children other than *X* and *Y*?

O conveys "to *A* for life, then to my children who reach twenty-one and their heirs." *O* has two children, *X*, who is fifteen years old, and *Y*, who is twenty-five years old. Two years later *A* dies. One month after *A*'s death, *Z*, *O*'s third child, is born. Two years after *A*'s death, *X* dies.

239.   What is *Y*'s interest?
240.   What is the estate of *X*'s heirs?
241.   What is *Z*'s interest?

O conveys "to the nieces of *A*." At the time of the conveyance *A* has no parents and one sister, *B*, who has never had children. Three years later *B* has a son, *X*. One year later *B* has a daughter, *Y*. Five years later *B* has another daughter, *Z*.

242.   What is *Z*'s interest?

O conveys "to *A* for life, then to *B*'s grandchildren." At the time of the conveyance *B* is dead, but his two children, *R* and *S*, are alive. Two years after the conveyance, *A* dies while *R* is pregnant with *B*'s first grandchild. Two months later, *B*'s first grandchild, *X*, is born.

243.   At the time of *A*'s death, what is *X*'s estate?

O conveys "to *A* for life, then to *B* for life, then to *C* for life, then to *D*'s children." Three years after the conveyance, *A*, *B*, *C*, and *D* all die in a plane crash. *D* had a child, *X*, who died one year before the plane crash and left a will that devised all his property "to my mother, *M*." At the time of the plane crash, *D*'s wife, *M*, was pregnant, but the news of the crash caused her to miscarry two weeks later.

244.   What is *M*'s estate?

O conveys "to *A*'s children." Two years after the conveyance *A*, who is forty years old, bears her first child, *X*. Seventy years later *A* celebrates her 110th birthday.

    245.   What is the interest in *A*'s unborn children?

O devises "to *A* for life, then to my grandchildren who reach the age of ten." At the time of the devise *O*'s grandchildren are: *X* who is five years old, *Y* who is seven years old, and *Z* who is eight years old. One year after the conveyance *Z* dies. Four years after the conveyance *A* dies. At the time of *A*'s death, *O*'s fourth grandchild, *G*, is in gestation. One month later *O*'s fifth grandchild, *H*, is conceived. Two months later *G* is born a day after *Y* dies. One month later *G* and *X* die before either reaches the age of ten. Six months later *H* is born.

    246.   At the time of the conveyance, what is *Y*'s interest?
    247.   At the time of *A*'s death, what is *G*'s interest?
    248.   At the time of *H*'s birth, what is *H*'s estate?
    249.   At the time of *H*'s birth, what is the estate of *Y*'s heirs?

O devises "to *A*'s children for the life of the survivor." At the time of the conveyance, *A* has one child, *X*, who is one year old. Two years later *A* has a second child, *Y*. One year later *A* has a third child, *Z*. Five years later *X* and *Y* die in a car accident.

    250.   What is *Z*'s estate?
    251.   What is the interest of *O*'s heirs?

O devises "to my grandchildren." At the time of the conveyance one grandchild, *R*, is in gestation. Two months later another grandchild, *S*, is conceived. One month later *R* dies before birth. Eight months later *S* is born. Two years later a third grandchild, *T*, is born.

    252.   What is *T*'s estate?

O conveys "to *A* for life, then one year later to the married children of *B*." At the time of the conveyance, *B* has two children, *S*, who is married, and *T*, who is single. One year after the conveyance *A* dies and then *B* dies shortly thereafter. *T* gets married two years after *A*'s death.

    253.   When *T* marries, what is *T*'s interest?
    254.   When *T* marries, what is *S*'s estate?

O conveys "to *A*'s children, but if *L* goes to law school, then to *B*'s children." At the time of the conveyance *A* has no children, and *B* has one child, *F*.

    255.   What is the interest of *A*'s children?
    256.   What is *F*'s interest?

O conveys "to *A*'s children, but if *L* goes to law school, then to *B*'s children." At the time of the conveyance *A* has no children and *B* has one child, *F*. Two years later *A* bears triplets, *W*, *X*, and *Y*. Two years after the triplets are born *L* goes to law school. Four years after the triplets are born, *B* has another child, *G*.

    257.   What is *Y*'s estate?
    258.   What is *G*'s interest?

O conveys "to *A* for life, then to my nephews who are the children of my sister, *B*, and who reach the age of twenty-one." At the time of the conveyance, *B* has two sons, *X* (age twelve) and *Y* (age twenty-five).

    259.   What is *X*'s interest?
    260.   What is *Y*'s interest?

O conveys "to the children of *A* as long as *A* is alive, then to the children of *B*." *A* has one child, *X*, and *B* has no children.

    261.   What is *X*'s estate?
    262.   What is the interest of the children of *B*?

O conveys "to the children of *A* as long as the old oak tree remains standing on the property." *A* has no children at the time of the conveyance. Three years later his wife bears a son, *X*.

    263.   What is *X*'s estate?
    264.   What is *O*'s interest?

O conveys "to *A* for life, then to *B*'s children, but if any of *B*'s children go to law school, then to me instead of *B*'s children." At the time of the conveyance, *B* has no children. Two years later *B* has a child, *X*. When *X* is five years old, *A* dies. When *X* is ten years old, *B* has another child, *Y*.

    265.   What is *X*'s estate?
    266.   What is *O*'s interest?

O conveys "to *A* for the life of *B*, then to *C* as long as *C* does not become a doctor; otherwise to *C*'s children." *C* has one child, *X*, who is one year old at the time of the conveyance. Two years later *C* bears another child, *Y*. Five years after *X* is born, *B* dies. When *X* is seven years old, *C* becomes a doctor. When *X* is twelve years old, *C* bears another child, *Z*.

    267.   At the time of the conveyance, what is *X*'s estate?
    268.   At the time of *Y*'s birth, what is *Y*'s estate?
    269.   At the time of *Z*'s birth, what is *Z*'s estate?

O conveys "to *A*'s children for the life of *A*, then to me." At the time of the conveyance one child, *X*, is in gestation. *X* then dies before birth. Two years later *A* bears another child, *Y*. When *Y* is five years old, *A* bears another child, *Z*.

> 270. What is *Z*'s estate?
> 271. What is *O*'s interest?

O conveys Blackacre "to *A* for life, then to the children of *A* who reach twenty-one." *A* has a child, *X*, who is eighteen years old, and a child, *Y*, who is sixteen years old. One year after the conveyance, *X* sells his share to *R* for $100,000. Four years later, *Y* reaches the age of twenty-one.

> 272. What is *R*'s interest?
> 273. What is *Y*'s estate?

O conveys Blackacre "to *A* for life, then to the children of *A* who reach twenty-one." *A* has a child, *X*, who is eighteen years old, and a child, *Y*, who is sixteen years old. One year after the conveyance, *X* sells his share to *R* for $100,000. Three years after *X*'s sale *A* dies. A year after *A*'s death, *Y* reaches the age of twenty-one.

> 274. What is *R*'s interest?
> 275. What is *Y*'s estate?

O conveys Blackacre "to *A* for life, then to *A*'s children who survive *A*, and if there are no children who survive *A*, then to *B*'s children." At the time of the conveyance, *A* has only one child, *X*, and *B* has only one child, *S*. Two years later *X* dies in a car accident, and *M*, the devisee under her will, takes all her property. A year after *X*'s death, *S* dies in a plane crash, and *B*, her mother, is her only heir. Then *A* dies.

> 276. What is *M*'s estate?
> 277. What is *B*'s estate?

O conveys Blackacre "to *A* for life, then, one year later, to *A*'s children who survive *W*, and if there are no children who survive *W*, then to *B*'s children." At the time of the conveyance, *A* has only one child, *X*, and *B* has only one child, *S*.

> 278. What is *O*'s estate?
> 279. What is *B*'s estate?

O conveys Blackacre "to *A* for life, then, one year later, to *A*'s children who survive *W*, and if there are no children who survive *W*, then to *B*'s children." At the time of the conveyance, *A* has only one child, *X*, and *B* has only one child, *S*. Then *X* dies, then *A* has another child, *Y*. Then *W* dies.

> 280. What is *Y*'s interest?
> 281. What is the interest of *A*'s children who have not been conceived?

O conveys Blackacre "to A's grandchildren on condition that none of them runs for president." At the time of the conveyance, A is dead, but two of her children, X and Y, are alive without ever having had children. Two years later, X gives birth to a daughter, M, and five months after M's birth, Y gives birth to a son, N.

    282. What is N's estate?
    283. If Y dies two years after all these events, what is N's estate?

O conveys Blackacre "to A for life, then to A's nieces by her sister B for the life of B, then to C for life." B has one child, X, at the time of the conveyance.

    284. What is X's estate?
    285. What is O's interest?

O conveys Blackacre "to A for life, then to B's children as long as the old oak tree remains standing on the property." Then O conveys any interest he has left in the property "to C's children." At the time of both conveyances, B has one child, X, and C has one child, Y. Then A dies.

    286. What is X's estate?
    287. What is Y's estate?

O conveys "to A, B, and C, to take a present interest in five years." At the time of the conveyance, A, B, and C are M's only children. Two years later M bears a fourth child, D.

    288. What is O's estate?
    289. What is D's interest?

O conveys "to A for the life of B, then to C if C gets married, but if C does not get married, then to D's children." D has no children at the time of the conveyance. Then C dies without getting married.

    290. What is the interest of D's children?
    291. If D then bears a child, X, what is X's interest?
    292. When D bears a child, X, what is the interest of D's children?

O conveys "to A for life, then to B's children." B has two children, X (age five) and Y (age ten). B herself is forty-five years old and has been diagnosed with a disease that makes it impossible for her to have any more children. O then conveys any remaining interest he has in his estate to C.

    293. What is X's interest?
    294. What is C's interest?

O conveys "to A's children for the life of the survivor, then to B's children for the life of the first to die." A has two children, F and G. B has two children, X and Y. After the conveyance F and X die. Then O conveys any interest he has left in the property to C.

295. What is *G*'s estate?
296. What is *Y*'s estate?
297. What is *C*'s interest?

O devises "to my daughter, *A*, for life, then to my grandchildren who reach the age of twenty-one." *O* has one grandchild, *X*, who is nineteen at the time of the conveyance. One month after the conveyance, *X* conveys all his interest in the property to *P*. Three years later, a second grandchild, *Q*, is born. One year after *Q*'s birth, *A* dies while a third grandchild, *R*, is in gestation. *R* is later born alive.

298. What is *P*'s estate?
299. What is *Q*'s interest?
300. What is *R*'s estate?

Answers

201. *B. Executory interest* in fee simple absolute. *O*'s children are a class. The age requirement is a condition precedent on each of the children taking a vested interest. There is no life estate to support their interest as a remainder. Therefore, the children have an executory interest. When the first child reaches twenty-one, the time for distribution will arrive and the class of children will close if *O* has not died sooner. All children conceived at that time (as long as they are or will be born alive) will be a part of the class and entitled to take if and when each reaches twenty-one. Thus, if the ten-year-old reaches twenty-one and at that time there are three children of *O*, then the three children make up the class. The oldest takes a present interest subject to open in fee simple subject to executory limitation (and actually receives one-third of the property), while the other two children continue to hold an executory interest in fee simple absolute. If one of the two younger children dies before reaching twenty-one, he loses his interest and the first taker receives another one-sixth of the property. When the last child reaches twenty-one, he shares the present interest in fee simple with his brother and receives the other half of the property.

202. *A. Present interest* in fee simple subject to executory limitation. *O* retains the present interest in a freehold estate until the executory interest of the children transforms into a present interest. The condition subsequent on *O*'s estate is the age requirement for the children.

203. *H. Vested remainder subject to open* in a fee simple subject to executory limitation. *X*'s fee simple is subject to two executory interests, one that would totally cut short *X*'s estate and the other that would partially cut it short. *C*'s executory interest in fee simple absolute would totally cut short *X*'s estate if no child of *B* reaches twenty-one. The condition subsequent on *X*'s estate (which is also a condition precedent to the vesting of *C*'s interest) is the failure of any child of *B* to reach twenty-one. Note that this

condition is subsequent to *X*'s estate and not precedent to *X*'s interest because of the way it reads as a cutting off of the estate. *B*'s unborn children have the executory interest that would partially cut short *X*'s estate whenever a member of the class is born.

204. *B. Executory interest* in fee simple absolute. *B*'s unborn children are admitted to *X*'s remainder as they are born. Membership in the class increases with every new conception (if followed later by live birth) until the class closes—that is, when *B* dies (natural closing) or *A*'s life estate terminates (Rule of Convenience), whichever is sooner. Note that if *A* dies one year later and there are no other children born or in gestation, *X* takes a present interest in a fee simple subject to executory limitation because the class closes under the Rule of Convenience. The condition subsequent on *X*'s estate is still the age requirement, and if *X* then fails to reach twenty-one, *C*'s executory interest will transform into a present interest, divesting *X*'s present interest.

205. *B. Executory interest* in fee simple absolute. *A* has a present interest in a fee simple subject to executory limitation, which is subject to being cut short in favor of *X* if bankruptcy occurs.

206. *B. Executory interest* in fee simple absolute. *Y* shares the executory interest with *X*.

207. *A. Present interest* subject to open in fee simple subject to executory limitation. When the condition of bankruptcy occurs, *A*'s estate is cut short and *X*'s interest transforms into a present interest. The Rule of Convenience closes the class of *A*'s children. *Y* is still a member of the class, so *X*'s interest must remain subject to open to be shared with *Y* if *Y* reaches twenty-one.

208. *B. Executory interest* in fee simple absolute, ready to partially divest *X*'s interest when *Y* reaches twenty-one.

209. *B. Executory interest* in fee simple absolute. The time of the devise is the death of *O*. *O*'s heirs, usually *O*'s children in this case, inherit the undevised property of *O*, which is the present interest in fee simple subject to executory limitation that was retained by *O* when he made the conveyance. There are no grandchildren at the time the devise becomes effective (*O*'s death). This is the time for distribution, so the class of grandchildren will close only by a natural closing on the death of *A* and *B*, *O*'s children and the grandchildren's parents. The Rule of Convenience does not apply.

210. *I. None.* The grandchildren who are alive and entitled to distribution at the time of the devise close the class at that time under the Rule of Convenience and take a fee simple absolute without having to share it with later-born grandchildren.

211. *D. Contingent remainder* in fee simple absolute shared with the unborn children of *A*. There is a condition precedent of survival before *B*'s interest or the interest of any child of *A* can vest.

212. *C. Reversion* in fee simple absolute. If *B* or any child survives *A*, the reversion does not take; it is divested. If no children survive *A*, the reversion becomes a present interest in *O* in fee simple absolute.

213. *D. Contingent remainder* in fee simple absolute. The word "or" is usually construed as disjunctive, giving alternative contingent remainders to *B* and to her children. The implied condition

precedent to *B*'s interest is survivorship of *A*'s life estate; the implied condition precedent to the children's interest is the failure of *B* to survive *A*'s life estate. If *B* dies before the termination of *A*'s life estate, the class of *B*'s children closes naturally to include all *B*'s children who were alive between the time of the conveyance and the time of *B*'s death. The children who are alive, and the holders of the interests of those children who were members but died or conveyed their interests, take a vested remainder in fee simple absolute.

214. *D. Contingent remainder* in fee simple absolute, which is the interest of all *B*'s children, born or unborn, during the time of *A*'s life.

215. *C. Life estate. A* has a present interest in a life estate, followed by *B*'s contingent remainder in a life estate.

216. *K. Fee simple subject to executory limitation. X* and *Y* share a vested remainder (following *A*'s life estate, and, as the Backup Rule, explained in Chapter 4, shows, supporting *B*'s contingent remainder) subject to open in fee simple subject to executory limitation, and *C*'s unborn children have an executory interest in fee simple absolute. The class of *C*'s children will close when *C* dies or when *X* and *Y* are entitled to distribution, whichever is sooner. The time for distribution under the Rule of Convenience is *A*'s death or, if *B* goes to law school before *A* dies, the later of the deaths of *A* and *B*. (Note that the Destructibility of Contingent Remainders Rule discussed in Chapter 5 requires that *B* go to law school before *A* dies, or she will lose her contingent remainder.)

217. *F. Vested remainder* in a life estate. *B*'s going to law school satisfies the condition precedent on *B*'s interest and it transforms into a vested remainder.

218. *H. Vested remainder subject to open* in fee simple subject to executory limitation. *X*'s vested remainder subject to open, shared with *Y*, no longer follows *A*'s life estate after *B*'s interest vests; it now follows *B*'s life estate.

219. *B. Executory interest* in a life estate pur autre vie (for the life of *S*). *O* has a present interest in fee simple subject to executory limitation, the condition subsequent being the condition of a child of *A* reaching age twelve. *X*'s life estate pur autre vie is shared with *A*'s unborn children. When *X* reaches twelve, he will be entitled to distribution. His executory interest will transform into a present interest, and *O*'s reversion will be divested. The class will close at that time. If there are children born (or in gestation if later born alive), *X*'s present interest will be subject to open. The children under twelve will continue to hold an executory interest. As each child reaches age twelve, he or she will take a share in *X*'s present interest subject to open. When there are no more members under twelve, the present interest will no longer be subject to open. The life estate pur autre vie held by the children will end when *S* dies.

220. *B. Executory interest* in fee simple absolute following the life estate pur autre vie in *A*'s children. The age condition that is subsequent to *O*'s estate and precedent to the interest of *A*'s children is also precedent to *B*'s interest. When *X*'s executory interest transforms into a present interest, *B*'s executory interest transforms into a

vested remainder following X's life estate pur autre vie. The death of S terminates the children's estate, and B's vested remainder becomes a present interest.

221. *H. Vested remainder subject to open* in fee simple subject to executory limitation. X has a vested remainder subject to open plus an executory interest, which are considered together as a vested remainder subject to open. As for X's vested remainder subject to open, X's estate in this interest is a fee simple subject to executory limitation because it is subject to being partially cut short each time a member of the class of children reaches twenty-one and takes a share in X's estate. Before the children reach twenty-one, they have an executory interest in fee simple absolute. The class will close when X's interest becomes a present interest. As for X's executory interest, X's estate in this interest is a fee simple absolute shared with the other children. If A becomes bankrupt, the executory interest cuts short A's life estate and transforms into a present interest closing the class. Because the same class of A's children subject to the same condition precedent of reaching twenty-one takes in either case, the vested remainder subject to open and the executory interest are considered together as a vested remainder subject to open.

222. *G. Life estate subject to executory limitation* subject to being cut short by the condition subsequent of A's bankruptcy. If bankruptcy occurs and A has other children under twenty-one, then the executory interest in X will cut short A's life estate to become a present interest subject to open in a fee simple subject to executory limitation. The class will close and A's children who are born (or conceived later to be born alive) will retain an executory interest. If bankruptcy occurs and A has not conceived any other children, then the executory interest in X will cut short A's life estate to become a present interest in fee simple absolute. The class will close to exclude any other children later born to A.

223. *H. Vested remainder subject to open* in fee simple subject to executory limitation. A has a present interest in a life estate. Before X is born, O's grandchildren have a contingent remainder in fee simple absolute. After X is born, the contingent remainder transforms into a vested remainder subject to open in X. The class has not closed yet, because A has not died, nor have O's children. Therefore, O's unborn grandchildren have an executory interest that stands ready to partially cut short X's estate whenever a grandchild is born.

224. *B. Executory interest* in fee simple absolute.

225. *B. Executory interest* in fee simple absolute. On A's death X is entitled to distribution of his share, and the Rule of Convenience closes the class of grandchildren. Y is conceived and will be born alive later. Therefore, Y is a member of the class. Since Y has not yet been born, her interest is still contingent on birth. Therefore, Y has an executory interest that stands ready to partially cut short X's interest on her birth.

226. *I. None.* The class closes to exclude any future-conceived grandchildren.

227. *H. Vested remainder subject to open* in fee simple subject to executory limitation. When *X* dies, his vested remainder subject to open descends to *M* as his only heir through intestate succession.

228. *A. Present interest* in fee simple absolute. When *A* dies *M*'s interest transforms into a present interest. *M* is entitled to distribution of her share, and the Rule of Convenience closes the class of grandchildren to exclude any future-conceived grandchildren. Note that *M* is one who has received the interest of a member of the class under the Rule of Convenience.

229. *B. Executory interest* in fee simple absolute. At the time of the conveyance, *A* has a present interest in a life estate, *O* has a reversion in fee simple subject to executory limitation, and the grandchildren have an executory interest in fee simple absolute. There are no grandchildren one year after *A*'s death when the interest of the grandchildren is ready for distribution. Therefore, the class of grandchildren will close only naturally upon the death of all of *O*'s children, the grandchildren's parents. The Rule of Convenience does not apply.

230. *K. Fee simple subject to executory limitation.* When *X* is born, his executory interest divests *O*'s present interest and is transformed into a present interest subject to open. The Rule of Convenience does not apply. Therefore, the unborn grandchildren continue to have an executory interest until the natural closing.

231. *B. Executory interest* in fee simple absolute shared with the class of *B*'s children. At the time of the conveyance, *O* has a present interest in fee simple subject to executory limitation with two conditions subsequent on his estate (the passage of one year after *A*'s death and the reaching of age fifteen by a child of *B*). There are no children of *B* who have reached fifteen one year after *A*'s death. *X* is thirteen years old. Since the time designated in the conveyance for distribution is the later of two events (the passage of one year after *A*'s death and the reaching of age fifteen by a child of *B*), the class does not close.

232. *A. Present interest* in fee simple absolute. *X* is sixteen. When he reached fifteen, the time designated in the conveyance for distribution occurred and the class closed. *X*'s executory interest transformed into a present interest. *O*'s present interest in a fee simple subject to executory limitation was divested by the occurrence of the condition subsequent. The future-born children of *B* are not entitled to become members of the class.

233. *I. None.* The time for distribution, the termination of *A*'s life estate, has arrived. The heirs of *X* have inherited *X*'s interest. Therefore, the class closes and the future-born children of *B* are not entitled to become members of the class.

234. *I. None.* The heirs of *X* take *X*'s interest, which at the time of *X*'s death was a vested remainder subject to open. On the termination of *A*'s life estate, this remainder becomes a present interest in fee simple absolute.

235. *K. Fee simple subject to executory limitation* shared with *X*. The time for distribution is one year after the termination of *A*'s life estate. Since there are no members of the class of *B*'s children in existence

at that time, the Rule of Convenience does not apply. The class remains open until it closes naturally. When X and Y are born, they take a present interest subject to open in a fee simple subject to executory limitation (the condition subsequent that would partially cut short their interest is the birth of other children to B).

236. *H. Fee simple absolute.* When B dies, the class closes naturally, and the estate held by X and Y becomes a present interest in fee simple absolute.

237. *A. Present interest* subject to open in a fee simple subject to executory limitation. The time for distribution (Y's reaching twenty-one) is immediate. The class is closed at the time of the conveyance, and the only members are X and Y. X has an executory interest until she reaches twenty-one.

238. *I. None.* The class is closed.

239. *A. Present interest* subject to open in a fee simple subject to executory limitation. The time for distribution (the combination of A's death and Y's reaching twenty-one) occurs at A's death. The class closes at that time, and the only members are X, Y, and Z (who is in gestation at the time of A's death). At A's death Y has satisfied all the conditions for vesting in possession, and X and Z have an executory interest until each should reach twenty-one. Z's birth and X's death do not change Y's interest other than the expected proportionate share.

240. *L. None.* Two years after A's death when X dies, X's interest is destroyed (it does not pass to heirs) for failure of X to satisfy the condition precedent of reaching age twenty-one.

241. *B. Executory interest* in a fee simple absolute. Z continues to hold this interest two years after A's death. If Z reaches twenty-one, Z will share a present interest in fee simple absolute with Y.

242. *A. Present interest* subject to open shared with Y, the other niece, in a fee simple subject to executory limitation. The time for distribution to the class is immediately on conveyance. Since there are no class members to take at that time, the Rule of Convenience does not apply. The class will remain open until it closes naturally on B's death.

243. *H. Fee simple absolute.* Although a child in gestation ordinarily must be born before she will receive a vested interest, the law creates a fiction in this case to give X, if X is later born alive, a vested interest at the point of A's death to avoid a reversion in O. Immediately before A's death, X held a contingent remainder that stood ready to take on X's birth as a vested remainder subject to open. The vesting process was accelerated by A's death. Because X takes a present interest vested in possession at A's death, X's entitlement to distribution of this vested interest occurs at A's death even though it will be postponed actually until X is born. Therefore, the time for distribution having arrived, the class closes.

244. *H. Fee simple absolute.* At the time of the conveyance, A has a present interest in a life estate; B has a vested remainder in a life estate; C has a vested remainder in a life estate; X has a vested remainder subject to open in a fee simple subject to executory limitation; and D's unborn children have an executory interest

in a fee simple absolute. When *X* dies, *M* takes *X*'s interest by devise. The plane crash causes *A*, *B*, and *C* to lose their life estates, and *M*'s vested remainder subject to open in a fee simple subject to executory limitation transforms into a present interest. At this time the class of *D*'s children closes to include only *M* and the child in gestation if that child is later born alive. The child is not born alive, so *M*'s ownership, when it becomes a present interest, is an estate in fee simple absolute.

245. *B. Executory interest* in a fee simple absolute. The time for distribution in this conveyance is the time of the conveyance. Since there were no children in existence at that time, the Rule of Convenience does not apply. The class will close only on *A*'s death. Even though it is medically impossible for *A* to have any more children at the age of 110, the law creates the fiction that she can bear children until she dies. Therefore, *X* has a present interest subject to open in a fee simple subject to executory limitation, and the unborn children have the executory interest that stands ready to partially cut short *X*'s estate on their birth.

246. *D. Contingent remainder* in fee simple absolute shared with *X*, *Z*, and the unborn grandchildren. This contingent remainder and *O*'s reversion in fee simple absolute follow *A*'s present interest in a life estate.

247. *B. Executory interest* in a fee simple absolute. At the time of *A*'s death, *Y* is the only grandchild who has reached age ten. On *Y*'s tenth birthday, *Y*'s contingent remainder transformed into a vested remainder subject to open in a fee simple subject to executory limitation. The class closes at the time of *A*'s death when *Y*'s vested remainder subject to open becomes a present interest subject to open, and *X* and *G*, who are the only remaining members of the class, hold an executory interest that stands ready to partially cut short *Y*'s estate whenever each reaches age ten.

248. *L. None. H* never receives any interest or estate because he is conceived after the class closes.

249. *H. Fee simple absolute.* Although there are no members of the class alive at *H*'s birth, *Y*'s present interest has been inherited by *Y*'s heirs. *Y*'s heirs took a present interest subject to open in a fee simple subject to executory limitation when *Y* died. When *G* and *X* died before either had turned ten, *G* and *X* lost their interest and *Y*'s heirs then had a present interest in a fee simple absolute.

250. *L. None.* The class closes immediately upon the conveyance and the only member of the class is *X*. *Y* and *Z* take no interest. *X* takes a present interest in a life estate at the time of the conveyance. When *X* dies, the only survivor dies, and the life estate held by *X* is terminated.

251. *A. Present interest* in fee simple absolute. *O*'s reversion in fee simple absolute following *X*'s life estate, which was inherited by *O*'s heirs at the time of the conveyance, becomes a present interest in fee simple absolute at the time of *X*'s death.

252. *K. Fee simple subject to executory limitation.* The time for distribution to the class of *O*'s grandchildren is the time of conveyance. Since there are no members of the class at that time (*R* is not born alive),

the Rule of Convenience does not apply. The class can only close naturally by the death of all O's children, the parents of O's grandchildren. At the time of T's birth, both S and T share a present interest subject to open in a fee simple subject to executory limitation. The unborn grandchildren have an executory interest in fee simple absolute.

253. *A. Present interest* in a fee simple absolute. When A dies, her present interest in a life estate terminates. One year later, S's executory interest becomes a present interest subject to open in a fee simple subject to executory limitation. The class has already closed naturally by this point because B has died and no more children of B can be born; however, T is still a member of the class, although his executory interest is contingent on his getting married. When T marries, T's executory interest transforms into S's present interest, and they both share a present interest in fee simple absolute.

254. *H. Fee simple absolute.*

255. *B. Executory interest* in fee simple subject to executory limitation. The interest in A's children does not become vested until birth. At the time of the conveyance, O has a present interest in fee simple subject to executory limitation, and the interest in A's children follows the condition subsequent of birth.

256. *B. Executory interest* in fee simple absolute. F's interest follows the condition subsequent on the estate of A's children, which is L going to law school. It is shared with the other unborn children of B.

257. *L. None.* When the triplets are born, their executory interest transforms into a present interest in fee simple subject to executory limitation. The condition subsequent that wholly divests their interest if it happens is L going to law school. The condition subsequent that partially divests their interest if it happens is the birth of another child to A. When L goes to law school, their interest is divested.

258. *I. None.* When L goes to law school, F's executory interest transforms into present interest in fee simple absolute. The class closes and no other children conceived later by B can become members of the class.

259. *B. Executory interest* in fee simple absolute following the condition subsequent on Y's estate and shared with the unborn nephews of B.

260. *H. Vested remainder subject to open* in a fee simple subject to executory limitation following A's life estate.

261. *D. Life estate pur autre vie,* which ends on the death of A. The time for distribution to the class is at the time of conveyance and there is a member of the class, so the class closes.

262. *D. Contingent remainder* in fee simple absolute following X's life estate pur autre vie.

263. *M. None of the above is correct.* The time for distribution to the class of A's children is at the time of conveyance, and there were no children born at that time. Therefore, the Rule of Convenience cannot close the class. When X is born, his executory interest

transforms into a present interest subject to open in a fee simple determinable and subject to executory limitation. The durational "as long as" condition makes the fee simple determinable. The fact that other children may take a share in *X*'s estate makes the fee simple subject to executory limitation, with the unborn children holding an executory interest in fee simple absolute.

264. *G. Possibility of reverter* in fee simple absolute.

265. *J. Fee simple subject to condition subsequent* held by *X* as a present interest. The time for distribution is the death of *A*, and at that time *X* is a member of the class. Therefore, the class closes under the Rule of Convenience, and *Y* is excluded from membership.

266. *E. Right of reentry* in a fee simple absolute following the condition subsequent on *X*'s estate.

267. *H. Fee simple absolute. A* has a present interest in a life estate pur autre vie, *C* has a vested remainder in fee simple subject to executory limitation, and *C*'s children (including *X*) have an executory interest in fee simple absolute.

268. *H. Fee simple absolute. Y* shares the executory interest held by *C*'s children.

269. *L. None.* When *B* dies, *C*'s vested remainder transforms into a present interest, but her estate and the interest and estate of the children remain the same. When *C* becomes a doctor, *C*'s estate is terminated by the happening of the condition subsequent, and *X* and *Y* take a present interest. The time for distribution has arrived, and the class closes. *X* and *Y* have a fee simple absolute. *Y* is born too late to become a member of the class.

270. *M. None of the above is correct.* The time of the conveyance is the time for distribution because there are no conditions or events that must be satisfied for the children to take except birth. There is no member of the class present at that time, since *X*, the child in gestation, is not later born alive. Therefore, the Rule of Convenience does not apply, and the class remains open until the natural closing of *A*'s death. At the time of the conveyance, *O* has a present interest in fee simple subject to executory limitation, *A*'s children have an executory interest in a life estate pur autre vie, and *O* has a possibility of reverter in fee simple absolute. When *Y* is born, *Y*'s executory interest transforms into a present interest in a life estate pur autre vie subject to executory limitation, the unborn children of *A* continue to have an executory interest in a life estate pur autre vie, and *O*'s possibility of reverter transforms into a reversion in fee simple absolute. When *Z* is born, his executory interest transforms into *Y*'s present interest in a life estate pur autre vie subject to executory limitation, and they share that interest.

271. *C. Reversion.*

272. *H. Vested remainder subject to open.* At the time of the conveyance, *A* has a present interest in a life estate, and the children of *A* have a contingent remainder in fee simple absolute. When *X* reaches twenty-one, his ownership, now held by *R*, becomes a vested remainder subject to open in a fee simple subject to executory limitation. The interest of the children of *A* (other than *X*) transforms into an executory interest in fee simple absolute. When *Y*

reaches twenty-one, his interest transforms into R's vested remainder subject to open in a fee simple subject to executory limitation, partially cutting short R's interest but not changing it. Note that the time for distribution to the class has not yet arrived because A has not yet died. Therefore, the class is still open.

273. *K. Fee simple subject to executory limitation.* The unborn children of A still have an executory interest in fee simple absolute.

274. *A. Present interest.* When X reaches twenty-one, his ownership, now held by R, becomes a vested remainder subject to open in a fee simple subject to executory limitation. When A dies a year later, the class closes, and R's interest transforms into a present interest subject to open in a fee simple subject to executory limitation. When Y reaches twenty-one, his interest transforms into R's present interest, and the interest is no longer subject to open.

275. *H. Fee simple absolute.* Both X and Y have a present interest in fee simple absolute. The class is closed, and no other children of A can become members.

276. *L. None.* A's child X did not survive A, and therefore X does not own any interest in Blackacre when she dies. There is nothing of Blackacre for M to take under X's will.

277. *H. Fee simple absolute.* A's children and B's children have alternative contingent remainders under O's conveyance. The condition precedent to A's children's interest is survivorship, which did not happen. The condition precedent to B's children's interest is the nonsurvivorship of A's children, which did happen. B, who takes the interest of S as an heir when S dies, gets a contingent remainder in fee simple absolute upon S's death. This contingent remainder transforms into a present interest upon A's death. Since B, as one who has inherited the interest of a member of the class, exists at the death of A, which is the time for distribution, the class is closed. B's ownership is a present interest in fee simple absolute.

278. *K. Fee simple subject to executory limitation.* A has a present interest in a life estate, O has a reversion in fee simple subject to executory limitation, and the class of A's children and the class of B's children each have executory interests.

279. *H. Fee simple absolute.* B shares the executory interest with the whole class of B's children.

280. *B. Executory interest* in fee simple absolute. When W dies, the condition of survivorship is satisfied by X, but the satisfaction of this condition is not enough to cut short O's fee simple subject to executory limitation. There is a second condition that must also be satisfied, which is the passage of one year after A's death. So X's interest remains the same, although the interest in B's children no longer exists because they have failed to satisfy the condition of the nonsurvivorship of A's children.

281. *B. Executory interest* in fee simple absolute. The time for distribution has not yet arrived because the passage of one year after A's death has not yet occurred. Therefore, the class remains open.

282. *M. None of the above is correct.* The time for distribution to the class is the time of conveyance because there are no conditions to be

satisfied or events to occur before the grandchildren can take, except for birth. There is no one able to take at this time, so the Rule of Convenience does not apply, and the only closing will be a natural closing. At the time of the conveyance, A's grandchildren have an executory interest in fee simple subject to condition subsequent, and O has a right of reentry in fee simple absolute. When M is born, M's executory interest transforms into a present interest in fee simple subject to condition subsequent (condition broken and estate totally divested when one of the grandchildren runs for president) and subject to executory limitation (condition broken and the estate partially divested when a grandchild is born). When N is born, the same thing happens. M and N now share the present interest in a fee simple subject to condition subsequent and subject to executory limitation.

283. *M. None of the above is correct.* The estate does not change because Y's death does not bring about a natural closing. X is still alive, and more grandchildren might be born.

284. *M. None of the above is correct.* X has a life estate pur autre vie subject to executory limitation, because the time for distribution to the class of B's daughters (A's nieces by her sister B) has not yet arrived and the class remains open.

285. *C. Reversion* following the three life estates.

286. *I. Fee simple determinable.* When A dies, X's vested remainder subject to open in fee simple determinable (condition broken and estate totally divested when the old oak tree no longer remains standing) and subject to executory limitation (condition broken and estate partially divested when a child is born to B) becomes a present interest in fee simple determinable because the time for distribution has arrived and X exists as a member of the class, thus closing the class.

287. *H. Fee simple absolute.* O's possibility of reverter is conveyed to C's children, so they (including Y) have a possibility of reverter in fee simple absolute.

288. *K. Fee simple subject to executory limitation.* O's present interest remains for five years, but O cannot leave a term of years in himself. He can only leave the type of estate that he had, although it can be limited. In this case it is a fee simple limited by being subject to executory limitation, the condition being the passage of five years.

289. *I. None.* The conveyance of the executory interest in fee simple absolute to A, B, and C is not a conveyance to a class because each of the grantees is named. Therefore, class opening and closing rules do not apply.

290. *D. Contingent remainder* in fee simple absolute. At the time of the conveyance, C and D's children have alternative contingent remainders, although D's children have the additional condition precedent that they be born. When C dies without getting married, one of the conditions precedent is satisfied for D's children, but they have yet to be born.

291. *H. Vested remainder subject to open* in a fee simple subject to executory limitation. When X is born, his contingent remainder

transforms into a vested remainder subject to open because the time for distribution has not yet arrived and the class of D's children remains open.

292. *B. Executory interest* in fee simple absolute.
293. *H. Vested remainder subject to open* in a fee simple subject to executory limitation. Even though it may be physically impossible for *B* to have any more children, *B* is alive and therefore is considered capable of having children under a legal fiction.
294. *I. None.* O's first conveyance did not leave any estate in himself to convey to *C*.
295. *C. Life estate.* The time for distribution to the class of A's children is the time of conveyance, and there were two members of the class alive at that time. Therefore, the class is closed. The life estate will terminate when *G* dies.
296. *L. None.* The death of *X*, the first to die of B's children, terminates the vested remainder subject to open in a life estate pur autre vie subject to executory limitation (condition broken and the estate partially divested when a child is born to *B*).
297. *C. Reversion* in fee simple absolute. *O* had a reversion in fee simple absolute following G's life estate when he conveyed it to *C*.
298. *K. Fee simple subject to executory limitation.* *X* had a contingent remainder in fee simple absolute at the time of the conveyance, and he conveyed this ownership to *P*. When *X* turns twenty-one, P's ownership transforms into a vested remainder subject to open in a fee simple subject to executory limitation. When *A* dies, P's ownership transforms into a present interest subject to open, the class closes, and *Q* and *R* are members of the class. Since the interests of *Q* and *R* have not yet become vested, P's present interest is subject to open in a fee simple subject to executory limitation.
299. *B. Executory interest* in fee simple absolute.
300. *H. Fee simple absolute.*

4

Rules for Identification of the Conveyance

Over the years a number of rules have developed to determine the meaning of certain types of conveyances. These rules have been gathered and summarized in the ten rules below.

A. NO GAP IN SEISIN RULE

If there is a gap in a conveyance, it must be filled with a present interest in O or a reversionary interest, and the estate must be the same type (life estate or fee simple) as that which O had when she conveyed. When O conveys part of her estate, she carves out one or more estates and leaves the rest in herself.

Example: Where O, owning a present interest in fee simple absolute, conveys "to A if A gets married," and A is not married, A's interest is preceded by a gap. There is no designation of a grantee to take the interest preceding A's interest. Therefore, O retains this interest as a present interest in fee simple subject to executory limitation, with A holding an executory interest in fee simple absolute.

Example: Where O conveys "to A for life," A's life estate is followed by a gap. There is no designation of a grantee to take the interest following the life estate. Therefore, O retains this interest as a reversion in a fee simple absolute.

Example: Where O conveys "to A as long as the old oak tree stands," A's estate, a fee simple determinable, is followed by a gap if it should be cut short by the occurrence of the condition subsequent. This gap is filled with a possibility of reverter in O in a fee simple absolute.

73

Example: Where O conveys "to A but if the old oak tree falls, then not," A's estate (fee simple subject to condition subsequent) is followed by a gap if it should be cut short by the occurrence of the condition subsequent and the reentry of O. This gap is filled with a right of reentry in O in a fee simple absolute.

Example: Where O conveys "to A, but if A gets married, then to B for life," B's estate is followed by a gap if A's estate (fee simple subject to executory limitation) should be cut short by the occurrence of the condition subsequent and then B should die. This gap is filled with a possibility of reverter in O in a fee simple absolute.

Example: Where O conveys "to A, but if A becomes bankrupt, then to A's children who shall reach twenty-one," and A has one child, X, who is sixteen years old, A has the possibility of becoming bankrupt before X turns twenty-one. This leaves a gap that is filled by O's possibility of reverter in fee simple subject to executory limitation. This possibility of reverter follows the condition subsequent (bankruptcy) on A's fee simple determinable. B's executory interest follows the condition subsequent (a child of A reaching twenty-one) on O's fee simple subject to executory limitation. Note that the "but if" conditional language of the condition subsequent on A's estate does not create a fee simple subject to condition subsequent in A. This exception to the rule for such language appears to be because the grantor's intent is not to create a right of reentry but merely to fill the gap until the age condition is satisfied.

Example: Where O conveys "to A for life and then one day later to B in fee simple absolute," A's estate is followed by a reversion in O that lasts for one day. O does not have a term of years. O has retained a reversion from her original fee simple absolute estate. It is limited by the condition subsequent that one day pass after the termination of A's life estate. B has an executory interest that springs from O's estate when O's estate is cut short by the condition subsequent (passage of one day from the death of A). Therefore, O has a reversion in fee simple subject to executory limitation.

B.   PIGGYBACK RULE

A nonfreehold interest followed by a freehold interest is treated as concurrent with the freehold interest if the freehold interest is in a born, ascertained person and not otherwise subject to a condition precedent. The freehold interest is subject to the term. Some texts describe the freehold interest that "follows" a nonfreehold interest as a remainder or a reversion. This may be a modern usage, but it is both confusing and misleading. Not only is it confusing when applying the rules of estates and future interests, but the concept of a freehold interest subject to a term is not so unusual that it need be avoided. The landlord-tenant relationship evokes the idea of an owner holding his interest concurrently with a tenant in possession.

Example: Where O conveys "to A for ten years, and then to B in fee simple absolute," B has a present interest in fee simple absolute subject to a term of years in A—that is, B is the landlord, and A is the tenant.

Example: Where O conveys "to A for ten years, and then to B if B gets married," O has a present interest in the freehold estate of a fee simple subject to executory limitation subject to the nonfreehold estate of a term of years in A, and B has an executory interest in fee simple absolute. (Note that "subject to" is used in two different senses here.) When the condition subsequent ("if B gets married"), which is precedent to B's executory interest, is satisfied, the executory interest becomes a present interest in fee simple absolute either subject to the term in A or not, depending on whether A's term has expired.

Example: Where O conveys "to A for life, then to B for ten years, then to C if C gets married," A has a present interest in a life estate, O has a reversion in fee simple absolute following A's life estate and subject to a term of years in B, and C has a contingent remainder in fee simple absolute following A's life estate and supported by O's reversion. B's nonfreehold estate of a term of years is supported by O's freehold estate of a fee simple absolute in the sense that it runs concurrently with it; C's contingent remainder is supported by O's reversion in the sense that O's reversion will remain to become a present interest if the condition precedent on C's remainder is not realized. If C gets married, the condition precedent is realized, and C's contingent remainder vests in interest while O's reversion is divested. B's term of years will then run concurrently with C's estate; in other words, A will have a present interest in a life estate, following which C will have a vested remainder in fee simple absolute subject to a term of years in B.

C.   BACKUP RULE

A contingent remainder is always supported by a vested interest, either a vested remainder or a reversion.

Example: Where O conveys "to A for life, then to B if B gets married," B has a contingent remainder in a fee simple absolute, and O has a reversion in a fee simple absolute. Both these future interests follow A's life estate, and the contingent remainder is supported by the reversion.

Example: Where O conveys "to A for life, then to B for life if B gets married, then to C," C has a vested remainder supporting B's contingent remainder. Both follow A's life estate. There is no reversion in O because A's present interest in a life estate and C's vested remainder in a fee simple absolute fully exhaust O's original fee simple absolute estate that O conveyed. If B gets married, B's life estate will push C's vested remainder back until the death of B, and the interests will then be a present interest in a life estate in A, a vested remainder in a life estate in B, and a vested remainder in a fee simple absolute in C.

D. CONTINGENT REMAINDER CANNOT DIVEST A VESTED REMAINDER RULE

In the Backup Rule an example is given where a contingent remainder is supported by a vested remainder. This is permitted because the contingent remainder is in a life estate, and when the contingent remainder vests, the vested remainder that supports it is pushed back in time to follow the life estate. If the contingent remainder is in a fee simple, it cannot be supported by a vested remainder because it would violate the rule that a contingent remainder is not allowed to divest a vested remainder. What might look like a vested remainder must be treated as a contingent remainder in order to satisfy this rule.

> *Example:* Where O conveys "to A for life, then if B gets married, to B, then to C," B and C have alternative contingent remainders, each in a fee simple absolute, and both of which are supported by a reversion in O. C cannot have a vested remainder in fee simple absolute because the vesting of B's contingent remainder would divest C's vested remainder (not merely postpone it) and such divestment is not permitted. O's reversion is the only type of vested interest that can be divested in such a case.

> *Example:* Where O conveys "to A for life, then to such of B's children who reach twenty-one, then to C," the condition precedent to the interest of B's children is "who reach twenty-one." C cannot have a vested remainder. Therefore, the implied condition precedent to C's interest is "if no child reaches twenty-one by the time A dies." B's children and C have alternative contingent remainders. The reason for including the words "by the time A dies" is explained by the Destructibility of Contingent Remainders Rule, discussed in Chapter 5.

E. SUBSUMPTION RULE

A condition that merely states the essence of an estate in a conveyance is not a condition in that conveyance. It may be superfluous or it may actually constitute words of limitation that create the estate.

> *Example:* Where O conveys "to A for life, but if A dies, then to B in fee simple absolute," B has a vested remainder because A's death terminates A's life estate by definition of that estate. Mention of A's death in the condition is considered superfluous and therefore the condition is ignored. Technically, A's life estate might terminate unnaturally by forfeiture before A's death, but this possibility is not considered when rendering the condition ineffective.

> *Example:* Where O conveys "to A and his heirs, but if A dies, then to B in fee simple absolute," A has a life estate and B a vested remainder,

because the condition becomes part of the words of limitation to define *A*'s life estate.

Example: Where *O* conveys "to *A* for life, then if *A* dies before *B*, to *B* for life," *A* has a present interest in a life estate and *B* a vested remainder in a life estate, leaving a reversion in a fee simple absolute in *O*. The condition is superfluous because the conveyance means the same thing with or without the condition: *B*'s vested remainder will become a present interest if *A* dies before *B*, and it will be destroyed if *B* dies before *A*.

Example: Where *O* conveys "to *A* for life, then if *A* dies before *B*, to *B* in fee simple absolute," *A* has a life estate, *B* has a contingent remainder in fee simple absolute, and *O* has a reversion in fee simple absolute. The condition is *not* superfluous; it is a real condition. If *B* dies before *A*, *B*'s interest is destroyed because of the condition; without the condition *B*'s interest would be vested from the time of the conveyance and would pass to *B*'s heirs on *B*'s death before *A* (if *B* has not conveyed or devised it).

F.   MODIFIED RULE IN WILD'S CASE

The rule in Wild's Case in 1599 was stated in two resolutions: The first resolution was to interpret the devise "to *A* and his children" (children not living) as a fee tail in *A* (an estate not considered in this book because of its statutory conversion to other estates in most jurisdictions when it makes a rare appearance). The second resolution was to interpret the devise "to *A* and his children" (children then living) as a life estate held concurrently by *A* and his children as joint tenants. Each of these resolutions has been modified by jurisdictions applying the rule today to give the following interpretations:

If the children are living at the time of the conveyance, a conveyance "to *A* and *A*'s children" is interpreted in the same way as if there were no rule—that is, to give a present interest in fee simple absolute to *A* and *A*'s children as a tenancy in common. There is some difference of opinion on how *A* and her children take their interest. If they take as a class, they share equally. If they take an individual gift and a class gift, it may be an undivided one-half gift to *A* and an undivided one-half gift to the children.

If the children are *not* living at the time of the conveyance, a conveyance "to *A* and *A*'s children" is interpreted to give a present interest in a life estate to *A* followed by a contingent remainder in fee simple absolute in the unborn children.

If the conveyance "to *A* and *A*'s children" is postponed to some future date, such as in a conveyance "to *X* for life, then to *A* and *A*'s children," the Modified Rule in Wild's Case still applies, but it should not be applied until the preceding estates have terminated. When *X* dies, if no children were alive at the time of the conveyance or born since that time, *A* will have a life estate and *A*'s children will have a contingent remainder. When *X* dies, if any children were alive at the time of the conveyance or born since that time, they (or the person who holds their estate) should share a tenancy in common with *A*.

Note also that this rule is a rule of construction that will give way to a contrary intent expressed by the grantor.

G. PREFERENCE FOR VESTING EXCEPTION

Conditions are determined to be precedent or subsequent in large part by the way they read. Professor George Haskins advocated the use of a general rule of thumb that if a condition describes the terms on which one *takes* an interest it is precedent; if it describes the terms on which one *loses* it, it is subsequent.

> *Example:* Where O conveys "to A for life, then to B and her heirs, but if B gets married, then to C and his heirs," the but-if condition describes the terms on which B loses her interest and C takes his. B has a vested remainder in fee simple subject to executory limitation (note the condition subsequent) and C has an executory interest in fee simple absolute (note the condition precedent aspect of the condition subsequent).
>
> *Example:* Where O conveys "to A for life, then if B gets married, to B and her heirs; otherwise to C and his heirs," the condition describes the terms on which B takes her interest and even C takes his interest. B and C both have contingent remainders (note the conditions precedent: "if B gets married" and "otherwise").

One exception to this rule of construction is worth noting. Because of a preference for vesting, two future interests, each with an apparent condition precedent referring to an age contingency and appearing seriatim, may not be classified as two contingent remainders but rather as a vested remainder subject to divestment followed by an executory interest. This preference for vesting exception exists to avoid the destruction of contingent remainders through the Merger Rule (discussed next) and the Destructibility of Contingent Remainders Rule (discussed in Chapter 5).

> *Example:* Where O conveys "to A for life, then to B if B reaches twenty-one, but if B does not reach twenty-one, then to C," the two conditions are read together under this exception as one condition that is subsequent to B's estate and precedent to C's interest. B has a vested remainder subject to divestment (more specifically, a vested remainder in fee simple subject to executory limitation), and C has an executory interest in fee simple absolute. If the conditions were separated in this conveyance, B and C would have alternative contingent remainders. Examples of conveyances with alternative contingent remainders are where O conveys "to A for life, then if B reaches twenty-one to B, but if B does not reach twenty-one, then to C"; where O conveys "to A for life, then to B if B reaches twenty-one, then to C if B does not reach twenty-one"; and where O conveys "to A for life, then if B reaches twenty-one, to B, then to C if B does not reach twenty-one."

H. MERGER RULE

Merger occurs when one person holds two immediately successive vested interests (or contingent interests that are contingent on the satisfaction of the same condition precedent) or two vested interests that are successive except for an intervening contingent remainder(s). With one exception, the two interests then become one, and any intervening contingent remainders are destroyed.

Example: Where O conveys "to A for life, then to A," A has a present interest in a life estate and also a vested remainder in a fee simple absolute. These two immediately successive vested interests merge to give A a present interest in a fee simple absolute at the time of the conveyance.

Example: Where O conveys "to A for life, then if B gets married, both to B for life and then to C; otherwise to O," A has a present interest in a life estate, B has a contingent remainder in a life estate following A's life estate, C has a contingent remainder (subject to the same condition precedent as B's contingent remainder) in a fee simple absolute following B's life estate, and O has a reversion in a fee simple absolute following A's life estate and supporting the contingent remainders in B and C. Both B and C are prepared to take vested interests if B gets married before the death of A, and, if this happens, O's reversion is divested. If B conveys her interest to C, C takes a contingent remainder in a life estate pur autre vie that merges with her contingent remainder in a fee simple absolute to form a contingent remainder in a fee simple absolute. At this point A would have a present interest in a life estate, C would have a contingent remainder in a fee simple absolute (subject to the condition precedent of B's marriage), and O would have a reversion in a fee simple absolute.

Example: Where O conveys "to A for life, then to B if B gets married," A has a present interest in a life estate, B has a contingent remainder in a fee simple absolute, and O has a reversion in a fee simple absolute. If A conveys his interest back to O (or O conveys her reversion to A), the two vested interests in one person merge, and the intervening contingent remainder in B is destroyed. The present interest in a life estate pur autre vie in O and the reversion in a fee simple absolute in O (or the present interest in a life estate in A and the reversion in a fee simple absolute in A) merge to form one present interest in fee simple absolute.

The *one exception* to the Merger Rule is that two vested interests simultaneously created in the same person do not merge in that person if there is an intervening contingent remainder created in another person at the same time.

Example: Where O conveys "to A for life, then to B for life if B gets married, then to A in fee simple absolute," B has a contingent remainder and A has a present interest in a life estate plus a vested remainder in fee simple absolute. B's contingent remainder is not destroyed because of the exception to the Merger Rule. This exception does not apply if *A* conveys away both his interests and they come into the hands of one person. Thus, if *A* conveys both his interests to *X*, *X* receives a present interest in a life estate pur autre vie and a vested remainder in fee simple absolute, each of which merges with the other to form one present interest in fee simple absolute in *X* as *B*'s contingent remainder is merged out.

Note that the Merger Rule is not only a rule for identification but also a rule to govern events subsequent to the conveyance.

I.   RULE IN SHELLEY'S CASE

If a conveyance or will gives a freehold estate in real property to a person and a remainder in fee simple to that same person's heirs, and the estates are both legal or both equitable, the remainder is considered a remainder in fee simple in the ancestor. This rule applies even where the freehold estate is held by the ancestor as a cotenant, and where the freehold estate is held as a vested remainder preceding the remainder in the heirs or as a contingent remainder subject to the same condition precedent as the following remainder in the heirs. The Rule in Shelley's Case (1581) operates on a delayed basis when the requirements of the rule are satisfied at a later point in time, such as when the interest in the ancestor is subject to a condition precedent not made applicable to the remainder interest in the heirs and the condition precedent is satisfied, or when the interest in the heirs is an executory interest that later becomes a remainder.

> *Example:* Where *O* conveys "to *A* for life, then to *B* for life, then to *A*'s heirs," *A* has a present interest in a life estate plus a vested remainder in fee simple absolute that follows a vested remainder in a life estate in *B*. (There is no merger because *B* has an intervening vested remainder.)
>
> *Example:* Where *O* conveys "to *A* for life, then to the heirs of *A*," *A* has a present interest in a life estate and, under the Rule in Shelley's Case, a vested remainder in fee simple absolute. Under the Merger Rule, these two interests immediately merge to form a present interest in fee simple absolute.
>
> *Example:* Where *O* conveys "to *A* for life, then to *A*'s heirs if *B* gets married," *A* has a present interest in a life estate plus a contingent remainder in fee simple absolute (subject to the condition precedent that *B* get married). *O* has a reversion in fee simple absolute. When *B* gets married, *A* has a present interest in a life estate plus a vested remainder in fee simple absolute, each of which merges with the other under the Merger Rule to form a present interest in fee simple absolute in *A*.
>
> *Example:* Where *O* conveys "to *A* and *B* for the life of *A*, then to *A*'s heirs," *A* takes a shared present interest in a life estate plus a vested remainder in a fee simple absolute.

Example: Where O conveys "to A for life, then to B for life, and then to B's heirs," A has a present interest in a life estate and B has a vested remainder in a fee simple absolute. B takes a vested remainder in a life estate plus, under the Rule in Shelley's Case, a vested remainder in a fee simple absolute, each of which merges with the other under the Merger Rule.

Example: Where O conveys "to A for life, then, if B gets married, both to B for life and then to B's heirs," A has a present interest in a life estate and B has a contingent remainder in a fee simple absolute. B takes a contingent remainder in a life estate plus, under the Rule in Shelley's Case, a contingent remainder in a fee simple absolute, each of which merges with the other under the Merger Rule because they are both subject to the same condition precedent.

Example: Where O conveys "to A for life, then, if B gets married, to B for life, then, if B and C each get married, to B's heirs," A has a present interest in a life estate, B has a contingent remainder in a life estate and a contingent remainder in a fee simple absolute. The contingent remainder in B's heirs is subject to the same condition precedent as the contingent remainder in B (B getting married). Therefore, the Rule in Shelley's Case changes the remainder in B's heirs into a remainder in B. The Merger Rule does not operate at this point, because the contingent remainder in fee simple absolute is still subject to an additional condition (C getting married). If C gets married, B (still unmarried) has two immediately successive contingent interests that are contingent on the satisfaction of the same condition precedent (B getting married), and each merges with the other under the Merger Rule.

Example: Where O conveys "to A and her heirs, but if A gets married, then to B for life, and then to B's heirs," A has a present interest in a fee simple subject to executory limitation, B has an executory interest in a life estate, and B's heirs have an executory interest in a fee simple absolute. The Rule in Shelley's Case does not apply at this point because the heirs have an executory interest and not a remainder. If A gets married, B takes a present interest in a fee simple absolute. The satisfaction of the condition subsequent on A's estate destroys that estate, leaving a present interest in a life estate in B plus, under the Rule in Shelley's Case operating on a delayed basis, a vested remainder in a fee simple absolute in B, each of which merges with the other under the Merger Rule.

Note that the Rule in Shelley's Case is usually a rule of law, not a rule of construction. Furthermore, most states have abrogated the rule and left the remainder in the designated heirs. The problems in this book assume the operation of the Rule in Shelley's Case.

J. DOCTRINE OF WORTHIER TITLE

The attempt by a grantor in an inter vivos conveyance to create a future interest (a remainder or an executory interest) in real or personal property in his or her heirs creates instead a reversion or a possibility of reverter in the grantor.

>   *Example:* Where *O* conveys "to *A* for life, then to the heirs of *O*," *A* has a present interest in a life estate and *O* has a reversion.
>
>   *Example:* Where *O* conveys "to *A* and her heirs until (or but if) *A* gets married, then to the heirs of *O*," *A* has a present interest in a fee simple determinable, and *O* has a possibility of reverter. Note that the "but if" language of the condition subsequent will not change the implied intent of the grantor to create a condition whose occurrence will automatically terminate the preceding estate.

This is a rule of construction, which means that the presumption created by the rule can be rebutted by the manifestation of a contrary intent. Note that some states have abrogated the Doctrine of Worthier Title.

Problem Set IV

The problems in this section ask for a description of an interest or an estate. The answers for interest are:

>   A. present interest
>   B. executory interest
>   C. reversion
>   D. contingent remainder
>   E. right of reentry
>   F. vested remainder
>   G. possibility of reverter
>   H. vested remainder subject to open
>   I. none
>   J. none of the above is correct

The answers for estate are:

>   A. term of years
>   B. term of years determinable
>   C. life estate
>   D. life estate pur autre vie
>   E. life estate determinable
>   F. life estate subject to condition subsequent
>   G. life estate subject to executory limitation
>   H. fee simple absolute
>   I. fee simple determinable
>   J. fee simple subject to condition subsequent
>   K. fee simple subject to executory limitation
>   L. none
>   M. none of the above is correct

Problems

O conveys "to Max for two years, then to Carl for life, then to the heirs of his boss Fred and their heirs."

- 301. What is Max's estate?
- 302. What is Carl's interest?
- 303. What is Fred's heirs' interest?
- 304. What is *O*'s interest?

O conveys "to Pam for life, then to Bill and his heirs, but if Bill dies without issue, then to Cathy and her heirs."

- 305. What is Bill's interest?
- 306. What is *O*'s interest?

O conveys "to Andy and his children. Andy has a son, Casper, and a grandson, Jim."

- 307. What is Andy's estate?

O conveys "to *A* for ten years and then to *A*'s heirs."

- 308. What is the interest of *A*'s heirs?

O conveys "to *A* and his heirs, but if *A* dies, to *B* and his heirs."

- 309. What is *A*'s estate?

O conveys "to *A* and his heirs to take effect after *A* gets married."

- 310. What is *A*'s interest?

O conveys "to Andy and his children." Andy has no children at the time.

- 311. What is Andy's estate?

O conveys "to *A* for life, then if *B* has a son, to *B* and his heirs, but if *B* does not have a son, to *C* and his heirs."

- 312. What is *C*'s interest?

O conveys "to *A* and his heirs until twenty years after *A*'s death, then to *B* and his heirs."

- 313. What is *B*'s interest?

O conveys "to *A* and his heirs until *A* gets married, then to the heirs of *O*."

- 314. What is the interest of *O*'s heirs?

O conveys "to *A* for thirty years, then to *B* for life, then to the heirs of *B* if *B* gets married."

    315.   What is the interest of *B*'s heirs?

O conveys "to *A* for life, then to *B* for one day, then to the heirs of *A*."

    316.   What is the interest of *A*'s heirs?

O conveys "to *A* for life, then one day after *A*'s death to *O*'s heirs."

    317.   What is the interest of *O*'s heirs?

O conveys "to *A* for life, then to *B* and her heirs if *B* reaches fifteen, but if she dies before reaching fifteen, to the heirs of *B*."

    318.   What is the interest of the heirs of *B*?

O conveys "to *A* for life, then to *B* for life if *B* has a son, then or otherwise to the heirs of *A* and their heirs."

    319.   What is *A*'s interest?

O conveys "to *A* for life, then to *B* for life if *B* gets married."

    320.   What is *O*'s interest?

O conveys "to *A* for life, then to such of *A*'s children as shall attain the age of twenty-one and their heirs, then to *C* and his heirs." At the time of the conveyance, *B* is *A*'s only child and is nineteen years old.

    321.   What is *B*'s interest?
    322.   What is *C*'s interest?

O devises "to *A* for life, then to *B* if *B* has children." At *O*'s death, *B* has no children and *A* is *O*'s only heir.

    323.   What is *B*'s interest?

O conveys "to *A* for life, then to *O*'s son *B* and his heirs." If *O* were dead at the time of the conveyance, she would have no other heirs in the world but *B*.

    324.   What is *B*'s interest?

O conveys "to *A* for life, then to *O*'s children who reach twenty-one and their heirs." *O* has two children, *X* (age five) and *Y* (age ten).

    325.   What is *O*'s children's interest?
    326.   If *A* dies twelve years later, what is *Y*'s interest?

O conveys "to *A* for life or until she gets married, then, in either case, to *B*." *B* then conveys all his interest "to *A*."

    327.   What is *A*'s estate?

O devises "to *A*, but if *A* dies without issue, then to *B* for life, then to *C* for life, then to *B*'s heirs."

    328.   What is *A*'s estate?
    329.   What is the interest of *B*'s heirs?
    330.   What is *O*'s heirs' interest?
    331.   If *A* then dies without issue, what is the interest of *B*'s heirs?

O conveys "to *A*, but if *B* gets married, then to the heirs of *A*."

    332.   What is *A*'s heirs' interest?
    333.   What is *A*'s estate?

O conveys "to *A* for life, then to *B* for life if *B* has a son, then to *C* for life."

    334.   What is *C*'s interest?

O conveys "to *A* for life, then to *B*, if *B* turns twenty-one; otherwise to *C* if *B* does not turn twenty-one."

    335.   What is *C*'s interest?

O conveys "to *A* for life as long as *A* has no son; otherwise to the heirs of *O*."

    336.   What is *O*'s heirs' interest?

O conveys "to *A* for life, but if *B* has a son, then to the heirs of *B*." After the conveyance, *A* dies, and at his death *B* still does not have a son.

    337.   What is *B*'s heirs' interest?

O conveys "to *A* for life, then to the heirs of *A*." After the conveyance, *A* conveys all his interest "to *B*." After *A*'s conveyance, *A* dies, leaving *C* as his only heir.

    338.   What is *C*'s interest?

O conveys "to *A* for life, then to *B* if *A* dies before *B*."

    339.   What is *B*'s interest?

O conveys "to *A* for life, then to *B* for life, then to the heirs of *A* if *A* gets married."

    340.   What is *A*'s interest?

O conveys "to *A* for life, then, if *A* reaches the age of twenty-one, to *B*, and, if *A* dies before the age of twenty-one, to the heirs of *A*."

    341.   What is the interest in the heirs of *A*?

O conveys "to *A* for life, then to *A*'s heirs for the life of the survivor."

    342.   What is *A*'s heirs' estate?

O conveys "to *A* for life, and if she gets married, then, on the termination of her life estate, to the heirs of *O*."

    343.   What is *O*'s heirs' estate?

O conveys "to *A* for life, but if *B* gets married, then to the heirs of *A*." After the conveyance, *B* gets married.

    344.   What is *A*'s estate?
    345.   If *A* then dies without any heirs, what is *O*'s estate?

O conveys "to *A* for life, then, if *B* gets married, to *B* for life unless *B* divorces; otherwise to *C* and her heirs."

    346.   What is *B*'s estate?
    347.   What is *C*'s interest?

O conveys "to *A* and *B* for their joint lives, then to the heirs of *A*."

    348.   What is *A*'s interest?

O conveys "to *A* for life, then to *B* and his heirs, if *A* dies without a son, but if *A* dies with a son, to the heirs of *B*."

    349.   What is the interest of *B*'s heirs?

O conveys "to *A* for life, then to *B* and his heirs as long as *B* does not get married, then to *O*'s heirs."

    350.   What is *B*'s estate?

O conveys "to *A* for life, then to *B* for life if *A* dies before *B*."

    351.   What is *B*'s interest?

O conveys "to *A* during widowhood, then to *B*." At the time of the conveyance, *A* is a widow.

    352.   What is *A*'s estate?
    353.   What is *B*'s interest?

O conveys "to *A* for life, then to *B* and her children." Then *A* dies without *B* ever having conceived children. Two years later, *B* has her first child, *X*.

    354.   What is *X*'s interest?

O conveys "to *A* for life, then to her surviving children, then to *B*."

    355.   What is *B*'s interest?

O conveys "to *A* and his heirs, but if *A* dies without issue, then to *B* and his heirs as long as *B* is alive."

    356.   What is *B*'s estate?
    357.   What is *O*'s interest?

O conveys "to *A* for life, then, if *B* gets married, both to *B* for life and then to the heirs of *B*."

    358.   What is *B*'s estate?

O conveys "to *A* for life, then to *B* for life, but if *B* dies without issue, then to *C* for life, then to *D* and her heirs."

    359.   What is *C*'s interest?

O conveys "to *A* for life, then to *B* for life, then, if *A* dies before *C*, to *C* for life."

    360.   What is *C*'s interest?

O conveys "to *A* for life, then to the heirs of *O*, with my express desire to leave nothing in the property in myself despite the Doctrine of Worthier Title."

    361.   What is the interest of *O*'s heirs?

O conveys "to *B* for life, then to *C* and his heirs when *C* reaches the age of ten, but if *C* dies under the age of ten, to *D* and her heirs." *C* is two years old at the time of the conveyance.

    362.   What is *C*'s interest?

O conveys "to *A* for the life of *B*, then to the heirs of *A*."

    363.   What is *A*'s estate?

O devises "to *A* for life, then to *B* for life, then to *C* if *C* gets married, then to *D* as long as *D* never drinks alcohol."

    364.   What is *C*'s estate?

365. What is *D*'s interest?
366. What is *D*'s estate?

O conveys "to *A* for life, then to *B* if *B* gets married, but if *B* does not get married, then to *C* for life and following *C*'s life estate to *D*."

367. What is *D*'s interest?
368. What is *O*'s interest?

O conveys "to *A* for life, then to *B*, but if *B* gets married, then to *C* for life and following *C*'s life estate to *D*."

369. What is *D*'s interest?

O conveys "to *A* for life, then to *B* if *B* gets married; otherwise to *C* for life and following *C*'s life estate to *D*."

370. What is *D*'s interest?

O conveys "to *A* for life, then to *B* and her children." *B* has no children at the time of the conveyance, but after the conveyance, *B* has her first child, *X*. After *X*'s birth, *A* dies.

371. What is *B*'s estate?

O conveys "to *A* for life, then to *B* and her children." *B* has one child, *X*, at the time of the conveyance. After the conveyance, *X* dies, after which *A* dies.

372. What is the estate of *X*'s heirs?

O conveys "to *A* for the life of *B*, then to *A* for life, then to *C* and his heirs."

373. What is *A*'s estate?

O conveys "to *A* for life, then to such of *B*'s children who reach twenty-one, then to *A*'s heirs." Two years later, *B*'s only child, *X*, reaches twenty-one.

374. What is *X*'s estate?
375. What is *A*'s estate?

O conveys "to *A* for life or for as long as it takes his sister, *B*, to finish law school in *A*'s lifetime, then to *B* for eight years."

376. What is *A*'s estate?
377. What is *B*'s estate?

O conveys "to *A* for life, then to *B* for life, but if *B* gets married, then *B* loses his estate."

378. What is *B*'s estate?

379. What is *O*'s interest?

O conveys "to *A* for life, then, one day later, to *B*, but if *B* gets married, then to *C*."

380. What is *O*'s interest?

381. What is *C*'s interest?

O conveys "to *A* for life, then to *B* for ten years, then to *C* if *C* gets married, but if *C* does not get married, then to *D*."

382. What is *B*'s estate?

383. What is *O*'s interest?

O conveys "to *A* for life, then, if *B* reaches the age of fifteen, to *B*, and to *C* for life, if *B* does not reach the age of fifteen."

384. What is *C*'s interest?

385. What is *O*'s interest?

O conveys "to my heirs."

386. What is *O*'s estate?

O conveys "to *A* for life, then, if *A* goes to business school, to *B* for life, then to *B*'s heirs, and if *A* does not go to business school, then to *C* for life, then to *O*'s heirs." *O* then conveys all his interest left in the property to *C*.

387. What is *B*'s estate?

388. What is *C*'s interest?

O conveys "to *A* for life, then to *B* for life if *B* gets married, then to *A*'s heirs." Then *B* gets married, after which *A* conveys all his ownership in the property to *C*.

389. What is *B*'s interest?

390. What is *C*'s interest?

O conveys "to *A* for the life of *X*, then to *B* for the life of *Y*, then to *C*." Then *A* dies. Then *Y* dies.

391. What is *O*'s interest?

392. What is *C*'s interest?

O conveys "to *A* for life, then to *A*'s heirs, but if *A* does not have a gravestone on her grave two years after her death, then to *B* for life."

393. What is *A*'s estate?

394. What is *O*'s interest?

O conveys "to *A* for life, but if *A* gets married, then *O* shall have the right to reenter and retake the property as of his former estate." *O* then conveys any interest he has in the property to *B*.

    395.   What is *B*'s interest?

O conveys "to *A* for life, then if *B* divorces, to *B* and her children, but if *B* does not divorce, to *B*'s heirs." At the time of the conveyance, *B* has conceived no children. Then *B* divorces.

    396.   What is *B*'s interest?
    397.   If *B* then has a child, *X*, two years later, what is *X*'s interest?

O conveys "to *A* for ten years, then to *O*'s heirs for ten years."

    398.   What is *O*'s estate?
    399.   What is *O*'s heirs' estate?
    400.   If *O* then conveys any interest he has left in the property "to *A*'s heirs," what is *A*'s heirs' interest?

Answers

    301.   *A. Term of years.* It is a fixed calendar time period.
    302.   *A. Present interest* in a life estate under the Piggyback Rule.
    303.   *D. Contingent remainder* in fee simple absolute. Fred is still alive and his heirs remain unascertained until he dies.
    304.   *C. Reversion* in fee simple absolute that follows Carl's life estate and supports the heirs' contingent remainder under the Backup Rule.
    305.   *F. Vested remainder* in fee simple subject to executory limitation, followed by an executory interest in fee simple absolute in Cathy. The executory interest in Cathy transforms into a vested remainder (or a present interest if Pam's life estate has terminated) if Bill has no issue at his death. Note that "issue" are the direct descendants of a person, to be distinguished from "heirs" who are the takers upon a person's death, whether they be descendants or other persons.
    306.   *I. None. O* has no interest left after his conveyance.
    307.   *H. Fee simple absolute* shared with his son Casper as a tenancy in common under the Modified Rule in Wild's Case.
    308.   *B. Executory interest* in fee simple absolute. The Rule in Shelley's Case does not apply because *A*'s estate is a nonfreehold. *A*'s heirs are not ascertained, so they cannot take a present interest. *O* retains a present interest in fee simple subject to executory limitation and subject to a term of years in *A* under the Piggyback Rule.
    309.   *C. Life estate.* The words of limitation are "and his heirs, but if *A* dies." The apparent condition is really part of the words of limitation under the Subsumption Rule. *B* has a vested remainder in fee simple absolute.

310. *B. Executory interest* in a fee simple absolute springing from a present interest in fee simple subject to executory limitation retained by *O*. *O* has an interest under the No Gap in Seisin Rule.

311. *C. Life estate.* The children have a contingent remainder in fee simple absolute under the Modified Rule in Wild's Case.

312. *D. Contingent remainder* in fee simple absolute. *B* and *C* have alternative contingent remainders because each interest is accompanied by a condition that reads like, and therefore is treated as, a condition precedent.

313. *B. Executory interest* in fee simple absolute. Although a time is specified, it depends on *A*'s death. Therefore, *A* does not have a term of years but rather a present interest in fee simple subject to executory limitation.

314. *I. None.* Under the Doctrine of Worthier Title, *A* has a present interest in a fee simple determinable, and *O* has a possibility of reverter in fee simple absolute.

315. *I. None. A* has a term of years. *B* has a present interest in a life estate subject to the term of years in *A*. *B*'s heirs would have had a contingent remainder in a fee simple absolute, but the Rule in Shelley's Case converts this contingent remainder into one in *B*. *O* has a reversion following *B*'s life estate and supporting *B*'s contingent remainder.

316. *I. None.* The Piggyback Rule makes the freehold interest "following" the term of years a remainder that actually follows *A*'s life estate. The Rule in Shelley's Case gives this remainder to *A* as a vested remainder in fee simple absolute in addition to her present interest in a life estate. The Merger Rule combines the two interests. *A* has a present interest in fee simple absolute subject to a term of one day in *B*, which will start in possession after *A*'s death.

317. *I. None. O*'s heirs do not take an executory interest. Under the Doctrine of Worthier Title, *O* takes a possibility of reverter that merges with his reversion. *O*'s conveyance thus gives *A* a present interest in a life estate, and *O* retains a reversion in fee simple absolute.

318. *B. Executory interest. B* has a vested remainder in fee simple subject to executory limitation under the Preference for Vesting Exception. *B*'s heirs have an executory interest in fee simple absolute. The condition on the vesting of their executory interest is *B*'s death before age fifteen, at which point the condition is satisfied and the heirs are ascertained. The Rule in Shelley's Case does not apply where the heirs have an executory interest.

319. *J. None of the above is correct. A*'s interests are a present interest in a life estate plus a vested remainder in fee simple absolute. The interest designated for *A*'s heirs, before application of the Rule in Shelley's Case, is a contingent remainder following *A*'s present interest in a life estate and alternative to, as well as following, the contingent remainder in a life estate in *B*. The Rule in Shelley's Case operates to give the remainder designated for *A*'s heirs to *A* as a vested remainder following *A*'s life estate, leaving the heirs with nothing. The two vested interests in *A* do not merge out the now intervening contingent remainder in *B* because of the

exception to the Merger Rule. (However, *A* could convey her interests to *X*, giving *X* a present interest in fee simple absolute under the Merger Rule and thus destroying *B*'s intervening contingent remainder.)

320. *C. Reversion* in fee simple absolute to support the contingent remainder in *B*, and, if *B*'s remainder vests, to follow it. *O* retains this interest under the No Gap in Seisin Rule.

321. *D. Contingent remainder* in fee simple absolute following *A*'s life estate. The condition is incorporated in the words of purchase. *B*'s interest will transform into a vested remainder subject to open in two years if *A*'s life estate has not terminated.

322. *D. Contingent remainder* in fee simple absolute following *A*'s life estate. Although *C* appears to have a vested remainder since there is no explicit condition on *C*'s taking, the Contingent Remainder Cannot Divest a Vested Remainder Rule requires that *C*'s interest be an alternative contingent remainder with the implicit condition precedent that *A*'s children not reach the age of twenty-one on or before *A*'s death. *O* has a reversion in fee simple absolute that supports the two contingent remainders.

323. *D. Contingent remainder* in fee simple absolute. *O*'s reversion created by *O*'s devise immediately descends to *A* at the same time that *A* receives the present interest in a life estate by *O*'s devise. Since these two vested interests are created simultaneously, under the exception to the Merger Rule they do not merge out the intervening contingent remainder in fee simple absolute in *B*. Therefore, *A* is left with a present interest in a life estate plus a reversion in fee simple absolute.

324. *F. Vested remainder* in fee simple absolute. *B* cannot be an heir until *O* dies. The Doctrine of Worthier Title applies to heirs; it does not apply when an heir apparent is designated by name in a conveyance.

325. *D. Contingent remainder* in fee simple absolute. *O*'s children are not "heirs," therefore the Doctrine of Worthier Title does not apply. *O*'s children are a class. The age requirement is a condition precedent to each of the children taking a vested interest. *O* has a reversion to support the contingent remainder in *O*'s children under the Backup Rule.

326. *J. None of the above is correct.* *Y* has a present interest subject to open in a fee simple subject to executory limitation. When *Y* reached twenty-one, her contingent remainder transformed into a vested remainder subject to open (divesting *O*'s reversion), and the other children's contingent remainder transformed into an executory interest in fee simple absolute. Upon *A*'s death, *Y*'s vested remainder subject to open transforms into a present interest subject to open, and the class closes. Under the class closing rules, all children alive at that time, such as *X*, are considered part of the class and take a share in the estate if they reach twenty-one.

327. *H. Fee simple absolute.* After *O*'s conveyance, *A* has a present interest in a life estate subject to executory limitation, followed by a vested remainder in fee simple absolute in *B* (which includes *B*'s executory interest prepared to cut short *A*'s estate on the

happening of the condition subsequent of marriage). *B*'s convey-ance gives *A* a vested remainder in fee simple absolute (which includes the possibility of cutting short *A*'s estate on the happen-ing of the condition subsequent of marriage). Under the Merger Rule, *A*'s present and future interests combine to form a present interest in fee simple absolute. Note that the future interest that follows the life estate is a remainder even though the life estate may be cut short by a condition subsequent. It takes as a remain-der whether the life estate terminates naturally, unnaturally, or by operation of the condition subsequent.

328. *K. Fee simple subject to executory limitation.* The condition subse-quent whose occurrence will cut short *A*'s estate in favor of the next interest is *A* dying without direct descendants surviving her.

329. *B. Executory interest* in fee simple absolute following *C*'s executory interest in a life estate. The Rule in Shelley's Case does not operate on an executory interest.

330. *G. Possibility of reverter* in fee simple absolute following *C*'s execu-tory interest in a life estate. It is possible that after the conveyance *B*'s life estate could be forfeited for waste, then *A* could die with-out issue, and then *C* could die before the death of *B*. In this case there would be no one to take a present interest since *B*'s heirs would not be ascertained. This gap is filled by *O* (replaced by *O*'s heirs upon his devise) retaining an interest in himself under the No Gap in Seisin Rule.

331. *I. None.* When *A* dies without issue, *B*'s executory interest trans-forms into a present interest in a life estate, *C*'s executory interest transforms into a vested remainder in a life estate, and *B*'s heirs' executory interest transforms into a vested remainder in fee simple absolute in *B* under the Rule in Shelley's Case. *O*'s possi-bility of reverter is divested.

332. *B. Executory interest* in fee simple absolute. The Rule in Shelley's Case does not apply when the future interest in the heirs is an executory interest.

333. *I. Fee simple determinable.* The condition subsequent that cuts short *A*'s estate is *B*'s marriage, but this can happen before *A*'s heirs are ascertained by *A*'s death. Therefore, *O* must retain an interest that fills this gap. The conveyance gives *A* a present interest in fee simple determinable (the condition subsequent on this estate being *B*'s marriage), *O* a possibility of reverter in fee simple subject to executory limitation (the condition subsequent on this estate being the ascertainment of *A*'s heirs), and *A*'s heirs an executory interest in fee simple absolute. The Rule in Shelley's Case does not operate here where the interest in *A*'s heirs is an executory interest.

334. *F. Vested remainder* in a life estate following *A*'s life estate and supporting *B*'s contingent remainder under the Backup Rule. *A* has a present interest in a life estate, *B* has a contingent remain-der in a life estate, and *O* has a reversion in fee simple absolute.

335. *D. Contingent remainder* in fee simple absolute. There is no Prefer-ence for Vesting Exception because the conditions are separated in this conveyance. One does not follow immediately after the other

because the words of purchase for *C*'s ownership intervene. *A* has a present interest in a life estate, *B* has a contingent remainder in fee simple absolute, *C* has an alternative contingent remainder in fee simple absolute, and *O* has a reversion in fee simple absolute supporting the two contingent remainders under the Backup Rule.

336. *I. None.* Before application of the Doctrine of Worthier Title, the two interests in *O*'s heirs are an executory interest following the condition of *A* having a son and a contingent remainder following *A*'s life estate and contingent on the ascertainment of the heirs. These are converted by the Doctrine of Worthier Title to give *O* a possibility of reverter and a reversion. The possibility of reverter and the reversion are considered together as a reversion in *O*.

337. *B. Executory interest.* The conveyance gives *A* a life estate subject to executory limitation, *B*'s heirs an executory interest in fee simple absolute, and *O* a reversion in fee simple subject to executory limitation. Neither the Rule in Shelley's Case nor the Doctrine of Worthier Title applies. When *A* dies, *O* has a present interest in fee simple subject to executory limitation, and *B*'s heirs have an executory interest in fee simple absolute.

338. *I. None.* The Rule in Shelley's Case gives the contingent remainder in *A*'s heirs to *A* as a vested remainder, and the Merger Rule combines *A*'s two interests into a present interest in fee simple absolute. *A*'s conveyance to *B* gives the whole interest to *B*, leaving nothing to be inherited by *C*.

339. *D. Contingent remainder* in fee simple absolute. The condition makes a difference whether the remainder in fee simple in *B* will continue after the death of *A*. It is not superfluous under the Subsumption Rule.

340. *J. None of the above is correct.* *A* has a present interest in a life estate plus a contingent remainder in fee simple absolute following *B*'s life estate. The Rule in Shelley's Case operates to give *A* the remainder designated for the heirs of *A*. This remainder is still subject to the condition precedent of marriage. *B*'s vested remainder for life and *O*'s reversion (supporting *A*'s contingent remainder) remain unaffected.

341. *I. None.* *A* has a present interest in a life estate followed by a contingent remainder in *B* in fee simple absolute and a contingent remainder in *A* in fee simple absolute, both of which are supported by a reversion in *O* in fee simple absolute following *A*'s life estate. The Preference for Vesting Exception does not operate here because the conditions precedent, even though they concern age, do not appear seriatim. The Rule in Shelley's Case changes the contingent remainder that would otherwise have been in the heirs into a contingent remainder in *A*.

342. *D. Life estate pur autre vie.* The Rule in Shelley's Case does not operate here since the remainder in *A*'s heirs is not in fee simple. *A*'s heirs have a contingent remainder following *A*'s life estate, and *O* has a reversion following *A*'s life estate and supporting the contingent remainder.

343. *L. None. A* has a present interest in a life estate. Before application of the Doctrine of Worthier Title, *O*'s heirs have a contingent remainder in fee simple absolute, and *O* has a reversion. Under the Doctrine of Worthier Title, *O* takes the contingent remainder in addition to her reversion. Since the reversion includes the contingent remainder by being ready to take any time *A*'s life estate terminates, *O* is considered to have merely the reversion.

344. *L. None.* The conveyance gives *A* a life estate determinable (condition subsequent is *B*'s marriage), *O* a possibility of reverter in fee simple subject to executory limitation (condition subsequent is the ascertainment of *A*'s heirs), *A*'s heirs an executory interest in fee simple absolute, and *O* a reversion in fee simple subject to executory limitation (conditions subsequent are *B*'s marriage and the ascertainment of *A*'s heirs). The Rule in Shelley's Case does not apply when the heirs have an executory interest. When *B* gets married, *A*'s life estate is cut short and *O* has a present interest in fee simple subject to executory limitation (condition subsequent is the ascertainment of *A*'s heirs), and *A*'s heirs have an executory interest in fee simple absolute.

345. *H. Fee simple absolute.* No heirs of *A* are ascertained because there are none. Therefore, the condition subsequent is not satisfied, and *O*'s fee simple subject to executory limitation is transformed into a fee simple absolute. Note that in the absence of heirs in intestate succession, property escheats to the state, but the state is not an heir as required by the terms of this conveyance.

346. *G. Life estate subject to executory limitation. B*'s interest is a contingent remainder subject to the condition precedent of marriage. The condition subsequent that stands ready to cut short *B*'s life estate is divorce.

347. *F. Vested remainder* in fee simple absolute following *A*'s present interest in a life estate and supporting *B*'s contingent remainder under the Backup Rule. This vested remainder stands ready to take at any time the preceding estates terminate or are sooner cut short. If *A*'s life estate terminates before *B* gets married, *C*'s interest becomes a present interest in fee simple absolute. If *B* gets married before *A*'s estate terminates, *B*'s interest becomes a vested remainder in a life estate subject to executory limitation. *B*'s vested remainder follows *A*'s life estate and is followed by *C*'s vested remainder, which stands ready to take as soon as *A*'s estate and *B*'s estate terminate (or, in the case of *B*'s estate, if it is sooner cut short by the condition subsequent of divorce).

348. *J. None of the above is correct. A* has a present undivided half interest in a fee simple absolute plus a vested remainder in fee simple absolute. Before applying the Rule in Shelley's Case, *A* and *B* share as tenants in common in a life estate pur autre vie (life estate measured by the life of the first to die) and the heirs of *A* have a contingent remainder in fee simple absolute. The rule applies in the case where there is a cotenancy in the freehold estate. After applying the rule, *A* has a vested remainder in place of the interest in her heirs.

349.   *D. Contingent remainder* in fee simple absolute. There is no Preference for Vesting Exception here because there is no age contingency. *A* has a present interest in a life estate. *B* and *B*'s heirs have alternative contingent remainders in fee simple absolute. *O* has a reversion in fee simple absolute following *A*'s life estate and supporting the contingent remainders. The Rule in Shelley's Case does not apply because the interest in the ancestor, *B*, is subject to a condition precedent different from the condition precedent to the remainder in the heirs.

350.   *I. Fee simple determinable. A* has a present interest in a life estate. *B* has a vested remainder in fee simple determinable. The Doctrine of Worthier Title operates in this case to give a possibility of reverter to *O* rather than an executory interest to *O*'s heirs.

351.   *F. Vested remainder* in a life estate following *A*'s present interest in a life estate and followed by a reversion in *O*. The condition ("if *A* dies before *B*") is considered superfluous under the Subsumption Rule. *B* gets his estate only if *A*'s life estate terminates before he dies, whether the condition exists or not. Now it is technically possible to argue that *A*'s life estate may terminate by forfeiture before *A*'s death and later on for *B* to die before *A* and that this makes the condition not superfluous, but this possibility is not considered by the Preference for Vesting Exception. The exception argues for the construction that the condition is superfluous—that is, subsumed in the definition of the preceding life estate—thus giving *B* a vested remainder that transforms into a present interest whenever *A*'s life estate terminates.

352.   *G. Life estate subject to executory limitation.* This seems the logical label to apply. Widowhood is interpreted as a situation that can exist only while a woman remains alive and unmarried. Termination by death makes *A*'s estate a life estate. Since the estate may also be cut short by the condition subsequent of marriage in favor of an interest in the grantee *B*, it is subject to executory limitation.

353.   *F. Vested remainder* in fee simple absolute. *B* stands ready to take on the natural termination of *A*'s life estate if not sooner (on *A*'s marriage). Note that *B* would have an executory interest if he took only on *A*'s marriage; however, his vested remainder includes this interest.

354.   *H. Vested remainder subject to open* in fee simple subject to executory limitation. The Modified Rule in Wild's Case is applied on a delayed basis when the interests in the parent and the children are future interests. The time to apply the rule here is when *A* dies. At that time there are no children, so the rule gives *A* a present interest in a life estate and the children a contingent remainder in fee simple absolute. When *X* is born, *X*'s contingent remainder transforms into a vested remainder subject to open in a fee simple subject to executory limitation, and the other unborn children's contingent remainder transforms into an executory interest in fee simple absolute.

355.   *D. Contingent remainder* in fee simple absolute. The children have a contingent remainder in fee simple absolute dependent on survival. *B* cannot have a vested remainder because the vesting of

the children's contingent remainder would divest B's vested remainder (not merely postpone it) and such divestment is not permitted under the Contingent Remainder Cannot Divest a Vested Remainder Rule. The nonoccurrence of survival is the condition precedent to B's contingent remainder. O has a reversion following A's life estate and supporting the two alternative contingent remainders.

356. *C. Life estate.* A has a present interest in fee simple subject to executory limitation (condition subsequent is A's dying without issue at the time of his death). B has an executory interest. B's estate is defined by the words "as long as B is alive," which are therefore words of limitation.

357. *G. Possibility of reverter* in fee simple absolute following B's life estate to fill the gap under the No Gap in Seisin Rule where no one is designated to take. The reason that O has a possibility of reverter is not because of the words "as long as B is alive" because these words are not a condition. Rather, it is because of the fact that O has an interest that follows an executory interest in a life estate after the condition subsequent "but if A dies without issue."

358. *H. Fee simple absolute.* Before application of the Rule in Shelley's Case, A has a life estate followed by a reversion in O, B has a contingent remainder (subject to the condition precedent of marriage) in a life estate following A's life estate, and B's heirs have a contingent remainder (subject to the two conditions precedent of marriage and ascertainment of the heirs) in fee simple absolute following B's life estate. The Rule in Shelley's Case applies when the freehold is subject to a condition precedent to which the remainder in the heirs also is subject. Here B's contingent remainder and the contingent remainder in the heirs are both subject to the condition precedent of marriage. The Rule in Shelley's Case gives the remainder in B's heirs to B. The two contingent remainders in B are now each subject to only the one condition precedent of marriage. The Merger Rule combines B's two interests.

359. *D. Contingent remainder* in a life estate. A has a present interest in a life estate. B has a vested remainder in a life estate. The die-without-issue condition can take place only at the end of B's life estate and therefore cannot cut it short, despite the "but if" language of the condition. It must be treated as a condition precedent to C's and D's interests. O has a reversion in fee simple absolute following B's life estate and supporting the two consecutive contingent remainders in C and D.

360. *F. Vested remainder* in a life estate. The condition "if A dies before C" is superfluous. A has a present interest in a life estate, followed by a vested remainder in a life estate in B, followed by a vested remainder in a life estate in C, followed by a reversion in fee simple absolute in O.

361. *D. Contingent remainder* in fee simple absolute. The contingency lies in the fact that the heirs are unascertained. A has a life estate. O retains a reversion despite his express desire. However, the express desire should be sufficient to show a contrary intent to

that presumed in the Doctrine of Worthier Title. Therefore, the Doctrine is not applied to give the interest in O's heirs to O.

362. *F. Vested remainder* in fee simple subject to executory limitation. The two conditions "when C reaches the age of ten, but if C dies under the age of ten" appear together and are treated as one condition (which one could read as "but if C dies under the age of ten") that is subsequent to C's estate and precedent to D's executory interest. This construction is imposed because of the Preference for Vesting Exception.

363. *H. Fee simple absolute.* Without applying the Rule in Shelley's Case, A has a life estate pur autre vie, the heirs of A have a contingent remainder in fee simple absolute, and O has a reversion in fee simple absolute. The Rule in Shelley's Case applies when there is a freehold in the ancestor even if it is a life estate pur autre vie. The rule gives the contingent remainder in A's heirs to A as a vested remainder, and the Merger Rule combines A's two interests into one present interest in a fee simple absolute.

364. *H. Fee simple absolute.* There are no words of limitation. C's interest is a contingent remainder following a present interest in A in a life estate and a vested remainder in B in a life estate.

365. *D. Contingent remainder.* D's interest looks like a vested remainder, but if it were, C's contingent remainder could divest it. This is not permitted under the Contingent Remainder Cannot Divest a Vested Remainder Rule. Therefore, D's interest is a contingent remainder (condition precedent is C's not getting married by the time A and B die).

366. *I. Fee simple determinable.* The "as long as" durational language of the condition subsequent, coupled with the fact that D's fee simple will be cut short in favor of the grantor by the occurrence of the condition, makes this estate determinable. There is a gap in the conveyance, and under the No Gap in Seisin Rule O takes the interest. O has a possibility of reverter in fee simple absolute following this condition. O also has a reversion in fee simple absolute following B's life estate and supporting the two alternative contingent remainders in C and D. O's two interests do not merge.

367. *D. Contingent remainder* in fee simple absolute. The first condition ("if B gets married") is a condition precedent to B's remainder. The second condition ("but if B does not get married") is a condition precedent to C's and D's contingent remainders. C's and D's remainders together are alternative to B's remainder. The contingencies do not concern age; therefore, the Preference for Vesting Exception does not apply.

368. *C. Reversion* in fee simple absolute. Since there is no vested interest following A's life estate, there is a gap in the conveyance that must be filled with a reversionary interest under the No Gap in Seisin Rule.

369. *B. Executory interest* in fee simple absolute. The condition ("but if B gets married") is a condition subsequent to B's estate and a condition precedent to the interests of C and D. B has a vested remainder in fee simple subject to executory limitation, and C and D have consecutive executory interests.

370.   *D. Contingent remainder* in fee simple absolute (condition prece-
        dent is *B* not getting married by the time *A* dies). Although *C* and
        D appear to have consecutive vested remainders, they have con-
        secutive contingent remainders under the Contingent Remainder
        Cannot Divest a Vested Remainder Rule. *O* has a reversion in fee
        simple absolute following *A*'s life estate and supporting the con-
        tingent remainders in *B*, *C*, and *D*. *C*'s and *D*'s remainders are
        alternative to *B*'s.

371.   *H. Fee simple absolute.* Upon the conveyance, *A* has a life estate
        followed by a vested remainder in a life estate in *B*, followed by
        a contingent remainder in fee simple absolute in *B*'s unborn chil-
        dren and a reversion in *O*. The Modified Rule in Wild's Case
        operates to divide the interests of *B* and *B*'s children in this way
        unless *B* has a child before the termination of *A*'s life estate. *B* has a
        child before *A*'s life estate ends, thus transforming *A*'s vested
        remainder in a life estate and the children's contingent remainder
        in fee simple absolute into a vested remainder subject to open in *B*
        and *X* in a fee simple subject to executory limitation (condition
        subsequent is the birth of each new child) and an executory inter-
        est in fee simple absolute in the unborn children. When *A* dies, the
        class closes and the vested remainder subject to open transforms
        into a present interest in fee simple absolute in *B* and *X*.

372.   *H. Fee simple absolute.* Upon the conveyance, *A* has a life estate, *B*
        and *X* have a vested remainder subject to open in a fee simple
        subject to executory limitation (condition subsequent is the birth
        of each new child), and the unborn children have an executory
        interest in fee simple absolute. When *X* dies, *X*'s heirs inherit his
        share. When *A* dies, the class closes and the vested remainder
        subject to open transforms into a present interest in fee simple
        absolute in *B* and the heirs of *X*. The fact that there are no children
        at the time that *A*'s life estate terminates does not matter in this
        instance since a child has already been born.

373.   *D. Life estate pur autre vie.* *A* has a present interest in a life estate pur
        autre vie and a vested remainder in a life estate, followed by *C*'s
        vested remainder in fee simple absolute. The Merger Rule merges
        the two interests in *A*, but the life estate pur autre vie that results
        from the merger now extends in time to the death of the survivor
        of *A* and *B*.

374.   *K. Fee simple subject to executory limitation.* Before application of the
        Rule in Shelley's Case, the conveyance gives *A* a present interest in
        a life estate, *B*'s children a contingent remainder in fee simple
        absolute (contingent on a child of *B* reaching twenty-one by the
        time of *A*'s death), and *A*'s heirs a contingent remainder in fee
        simple absolute (contingent on *A*'s heirs being ascertained and on
        no child of *B* reaching twenty-one by the time of *A*'s death), and *O*
        a reversion in fee simple absolute following *A*'s life estate and
        supporting the two contingent remainders. The Rule in Shelley's
        Case gives the contingent remainder in *A*'s heirs to *A*. Therefore, at
        the time of the conveyance, *A* and the children of *B* have alter-
        native contingent remainders. When *X* reaches the age of twenty-
        one, the children's contingent remainder transforms into a vested

remainder subject to open in X in fee simple subject to executory limitation with an executory interest in the unborn children in fee simple absolute.

375. *C. Life estate.* When X reached twenty-one, A could no longer satisfy one of the conditions on her contingent remainder and it is destroyed. She is left with a present interest in a life estate.

376. *E. Life estate determinable.* A's present interest is not followed by any future interest in a grantee in freehold. The durational condition ("for as long as") makes A's estate determinable. O has a reversion in fee simple absolute (which includes O's possibility of reverter).

377. *A. Term of years.* B's ownership is a nonfreehold since it is defined by a set period of time. If B finishes law school in A's lifetime, B will take possession of her nonfreehold estate, and it will ride piggyback on O's freehold estate, which O takes as a present interest by the happening of the same condition. If B does not finish law school before A dies, then B will take possession of her estate and O will take a present interest in his estate upon the death of A.

378. *F. Life estate subject to condition subsequent.* The conditional condition ("but if") followed by an interest in O is what gives B an estate subject to condition subsequent. No one is designated to take when B loses his estate, so this gap is filled by O under the No Gap in Seisin Rule.

379. *J. None of the above is correct.* O has a right of reentry, which always follows an estate subject to condition subsequent. O also has a reversion, which follows A's life estate. The two do not combine into one interest.

380. *C. Reversion* in fee simple subject to executory limitation. There is no one designated to take for one day following A's life estate. Under the No Gap in Seisin Rule, O takes this interest. O does not take a term of years but rather retains his fee simple interest, albeit limited as a fee simple subject to executory limitation.

381. *B. Executory interest* in fee simple absolute. B's executory interest (following the condition subsequent on O's estate, which is the passage of one year) in fee simple subject to executory limitation (the condition subsequent on B's estate being B's getting married) is followed by this interest in C.

382. *A. Term of years.* B's term starts in the future upon the termination of A's life estate.

383. *C. Reversion* in fee simple absolute. B and C have alternative contingent remainders because the Preference for Vesting Exception is not applicable in the absence of an age contingency. O's reversion follows A's life estate and supports both these contingent remainders under the Backup Rule. O's estate also supports B's term of years under the Piggyback Rule. The support is different in each case. O's freehold estate is that of a landlord in relation to the nonfreehold estate of the tenant B under the Piggyback Rule (although by the time B's nonfreehold becomes a present interest, B's landlord may be C or D or someone who took or inherited from one of them). On the other hand, O's reversion, which supports

the contingent remainders, is designed to fill the gap in the conveyance that is left if the contingent remainders are destroyed.

384. *D. Contingent remainder* in a life estate. The alternative contingencies for *B*'s and *C*'s ownerships involve an age contingency, but the Preference for Vesting Exception does not apply because the conditions are separated from each other by the words of purchase for *B*'s and *C*'s ownerships. Therefore, *B* and *C* have alternative contingent remainders.

385. *C. Reversion* in fee simple absolute following *A*'s life estate. There is no additional interest held by *O* after *C*'s life estate because, if *C*'s life estate becomes a present interest, *O*'s reversion is not divested but merely pushed back until the termination of *C*'s estate.

386. *H. Fee simple absolute.* Before application of the Doctrine of Worthier Title, *O* has a present interest in fee simple subject to executory limitation, and *O*'s heirs have an executory interest in fee simple absolute. When the Doctrine is applied, *O* takes *O*'s heirs interest, and it becomes one with *O*'s estate to make it a fee simple absolute.

387. *H. Fee simple absolute. B* has a contingent remainder in a life estate and, under the Rule in Shelley's Case, the contingent remainder in fee simple absolute that follows the life estate and is designated for *B*'s heirs. These two ownerships merge under the Merger Rule so that *B* has one contingent remainder in fee simple absolute.

388. *C. Reversion* in fee simple absolute. The conveyance gives *A* a present interest in a life estate, *B* a contingent remainder in fee simple absolute, *C* an alternative contingent remainder in a life estate, and *O* a reversion in fee simple absolute (*O* getting *O*'s heirs' interest under the Doctrine of Worthier Title, which interest blends with *O*'s reversion in fee simple absolute). *O* then conveys his interest to *C*, and *C*'s contingent remainder in a life estate blends with the reversion.

389. *F. Vested remainder* in a life estate. The conveyance gives *A* a present interest in a life estate, *B* a contingent remainder in a life estate, and, under the Rule in Shelley's Case, *A* a vested remainder in fee simple absolute following *A*'s life estate and supporting *B*'s contingent remainder. Although usually the Merger Rule would merge *A*'s two successive vested interests, the exception to the Merger Rule spares the destruction of *B*'s contingent remainder at this time because it was created simultaneously with *A*'s two interests. When *B* gets married, *B*'s contingent remainder becomes a vested remainder. *A*'s conveyance does not change this.

390. *J. None of the above is correct.* If *B* had not married before the conveyance to *C*, *C* would have had a present interest in fee simple absolute under the Merger Rule. However, *B*'s marriage causes *B*'s interest to transform into a vested remainder, and *C* takes *A*'s two separate interests, a present interest in a life estate and a vested remainder in fee simple absolute following *B*'s life estate.

391. *I. None.* The conveyance gives *A* a present interest in a life estate pur autre vie, *B* a vested remainder in a life estate pur autre vie,

and *C* a vested remainder in fee simple absolute. There is nothing left that remains in *O*.

392. *F. Vested remainder* in fee simple absolute. When *A* dies, *A*'s heirs, who are ascertained upon *A*'s death, inherit *A*'s present interest in a life estate pur autre vie. When *Y* dies, *B*'s estate is terminated. *C*'s interest now follows *A*'s heirs' life estate pur autre vie.

393. *K. Fee simple subject to executory limitation.* The contingent remainder in fee simple subject to executory limitation in *A*'s heirs satisfies the Rule in Shelley's case so that at the time of the conveyance it is created in *A* as a remainder in fee simple subject to executory limitation. Since the contingency of ascertaining the heirs no longer exists, this remainder in *A* is vested. Since it follows *A*'s life estate, which is also vested as a present interest, the two interests merge under the Merger Rule. *A* now has a present interest in fee simple subject to executory limitation.

394. *G. Possibility of reverter* in fee simple absolute following *B*'s executory interest in a life estate. The "but if" language of the condition subsequent on *A*'s estate does not determine the nature of the reversionary interest in *O* because *O*'s interest is not the first interest to follow the condition subsequent. *B*'s interest is the first to follow the condition subsequent.

395. *J. None of the above is correct.* The conveyance gives *A* a life estate subject to condition sulbsequent, and *O* a right of reentry in fee simple absolute plus a reversion in fee simple absolute. These two interests do not combine into one. *O*'s second conveyance gives *B* the same interests, a right of reentry in fee simple absolute plus a reversion in fee simple absolute.

396. *F. Vested remainder.* The conveyance gives *A* a present interest in a life estate, *B* a contingent remainder in a life estate following *A*'s life estate, *B*'s children a contingent remainder in a life estate following *B*'s life estate, *B*'s heirs a contingent remainder in a life estate (the two conditions precedent being *B*'s not divorcing and the heirs being ascertained), and *O* a reversion in fee simple absolute supporting the two lines of contingent remainders. Of course, *B*'s estate will be revised in accordance with the Modified Rule in Wild's Case if *B* has children, since this rule can operate on a delayed basis. The Rule in Shelley's Case does not apply because the interest in *B* is not subject to the same condition subsequent as the interest in *B*'s heirs. When *B* divorces, the interests become a present interest in a life estate in *A*, a vested remainder in a life estate in *B*, a contingent remainder in fee simple absolute in *B*'s children, and a reversion in fee simple absolute in *O*.

397. *H. Vested remainder subject to open.* When *X* is born, *X*'s contingent remainder transforms into a vested remainder subject to open in a fee simple subject to executory limitation. Under the Modified Rule in Wild's Case, this interest is held with *B*. The children of *B* have an executory interest in fee simple absolute. The interest of *O* disappears. Note how the Modified Rule in Wild's Case also revised *B*'s estate from a life estate to a fee simple estate when *X* was born.

398. *H. Fee simple absolute*. Estates for terms of years do not affect freehold estates. *O* has a present interest in fee simple absolute.

399. *A. Term of years*. The Doctrine of Worthier Title does not operate here because the interest in *O*'s heirs is not a remainder or an executory interest.

400. *B. Executory interest* in fee simple absolute. *O* is not able to convey all the interest he has in the property to *A*'s heirs since they are not ascertained and therefore cannot take a present interest. *O* retains a present interest in fee simple subject to executory limitation.

5

Rules to Govern Events Subsequent to the Conveyance

In addition to rules for identification at the time of conveyance, there are rules to determine what happens to the interests in a conveyance on the happening of certain events. These are described in the five rules below.

A. DESTRUCTIBILITY OF CONTINGENT REMAINDERS RULE

Contingent remainders are destroyed if they do not take immediately on the termination of all the preceding estates.

Example: Where O conveys "to A for life and then to B if B gets married," B has a contingent remainder in fee simple absolute, preceded by a present interest in a life estate in A and supported by a reversion in fee simple absolute in O. If B gets married on or before the termination of A's life estate, B's remainder becomes vested and will become a present interest in fee simple absolute on the termination of A's life estate. If B has not married by the time A's life estate terminates, B's remainder is destroyed at that time. O's reversion then becomes a present interest in fee simple absolute.

If the condition that must be satisfied to vest a remainder on time is birth, it should be remembered that a child who is in gestation at the time the preceding life estate terminates is considered as if he or she were born at that time if that child is later born alive.

Example: Where O conveys "to A for life, then to the children of A," and A dies while his wife is pregnant with their first child, the child is entitled to her interest on birth. The Destructibility Rule does not apply as long as the child is born alive.

Note that the Destructibility Rule applies only to legal contingent remainders in freehold estates. It does not apply to equitable contingent remainders, or to remainders in personal property, or to future interests in a term of years. Note also that many states have abrogated the Destructibility Rule.

B. INDESTRUCTIBILITY OF EXECUTORY INTERESTS RULE

Executory interests are not destroyed if they do not take immediately on the termination of all the preceding estates. In other words, executory interests do not need preceding estates in grantees to support them.

Example: Where *O* conveys "to *A* for life, but if *B* gets married then to *B*," *A* has a present interest in a life estate subject to executory limitation, *B* has an executory interest in fee simple absolute, and *O* has a reversion in fee simple subject to executory limitation. If *B* gets married before the termination of *A*'s life estate, *A*'s life estate along with *O*'s reversion is cut short and *B*'s executory interest becomes a present interest in fee simple absolute. If *B* has not married by the time *A*'s life estate terminates, *B*'s executory interest is preserved, and *O*'s reversion becomes a present interest in fee simple subject to executory limitation. Then, if *B* gets married, *O*'s estate is cut short, and *B*'s executory interest becomes a present interest in fee simple absolute.

Likewise, executory interests are not destroyed if they do not take immediately on the cutting short of a preceding estate.

Example: Where *O* conveys "to *A* and his heirs until *A* gets married, then to *B* if *B* reaches twenty-one," *A* has a present interest in fee simple determinable that is cut short if he gets married; *O* has a possibility of reverter in fee simple subject to executory limitation; and *B* has an executory interest that cuts short *O*'s estate if she becomes twenty-one. If *B* reaches age twenty-one before *A* gets married, *A*'s estate becomes a fee simple subject to executory limitation, and *B*'s interest remains an executory interest that will cut short *A*'s estate if *A* gets married. If *B* does not reach twenty-one by the time *A* gets married, *O*'s possibility of reverter becomes a present interest in fee simple subject to executory limitation and *B*'s interest remains an executory interest that will cut short *O*'s estate if *B* reaches twenty-one. If *B* dies without reaching twenty-one, the condition precedent to *B*'s interest (*B*'s reaching twenty-one) is impossible to fulfill and her executory interest is destroyed by that fact. The condition subsequent to *O*'s estate (*B*'s reaching twenty-one) is eliminated and O is left with a present interest in fee simple absolute. If A never gets married, the possibility of reverter in O and the executory interest in B are destroyed by that fact, and A's estate becomes one in fee simple absolute (inherited by A's heirs on A's death if A has not conveyed or devised).

C. RULE IN PUREFOY v. ROGERS

A remainder may not transform into an executory interest in order to escape the Destructibility of Contingent Remainders Rule. This is the Rule in Purefoy v. Rogers (1670), which is really a corollary of the Destructibility Rule.

> *Example:* Where O conveys "to A for life, then to B if B gets married," B has a contingent remainder that cannot transform into an executory interest if B has not married by or at the termination of A's life estate. B's interest is destroyed by the Destructibility of Contingent Remainders Rule, and B loses her interest at that time.

Note that there is nothing to prevent an executory interest from transforming into a remainder by reason of subsequent events, or even a remainder from transforming into an executory interest, as long as it is not to escape the Destructibility Rule.

> *Example:* The transformation of an executory interest into a remainder is illustrated by O's conveyance "to A and his heirs, but if A gets married, then to B for life, then to C." A has a present interest in fee simple subject to executory limitation, and B and C each have executory interests at the time of the conveyance. If A were to get married, B then would have a present interest in a life estate, and C would have a vested remainder in fee simple absolute.
>
> *Example:* The transformation of a remainder into an executory interest is described in 3 Restatement of Property §278e (Illustration 5), at 1442 (1940):

>> 5. A, owning Blackacre in fee simple absolute, transfers Blackacre "to B for life, remainder to B's children and their heirs, but if B has no children alive at the time of his (B's) death, then to C and his heirs." B has no child when A makes this transfer. C has a remainder subject to the stated condition precedent. B has a son D. . . . D thereupon acquires a remainder vested subject to complete defeasance and thenceforth C has an executory interest.

To explain this last example more fully, at the time of the conveyance, B has a present interest in a life estate; A has a reversion in fee simple absolute; B's unborn children have a contingent remainder (condition precedent is birth by the time of B's death) in fee simple subject to executory limitation (condition subsequent is failure to survive B's death); and C has an alternative contingent remainder (condition precedent is B's children remaining unborn by the time of *B*'s death) in fee simple absolute plus an executory interest (condition precedent is failure of *B*'s children to survive *B*'s death) in fee simple absolute, which together are considered a contingent remainder in fee simple absolute. When *D* is born, *A*'s reversion is divested, and *D* takes a vested remainder subject to open (the contingent remainder in the unborn children transforming into an executory interest in the unborn children) in fee simple subject to executory limitation (the contingent remainder in *C* transforming into an executory interest).

D. MERGER RULE

See section H in Chapter 4.

E. TRANSFERABILITY

All interests are alienable except, in some jurisdictions, the possibility of reverter, the right of reentry, and the contingent remainder. All interests are devisable unless they are in a life estate (except that a life estate pur autre vie is devisable) and, in some jurisdictions, if they are a possibility of reverter or a right of reentry. All interests are inheritable unless they are in a life estate (except that a life estate pur autre vie is inheritable).

Problem Set V

The problems in this section ask for a description of an interest or an estate. The answers for interest are:

   A.   present interest
   B.   executory interest
   C.   reversion
   D.   contingent remainder
   E.   right of reentry
   F.   vested remainder
   G.   possibility of reverter
   H.   vested remainder subject to open
   I.   none
   J.   none of the above is correct

The answers for estate are:

   A.   term of years
   B.   term of years determinable

C. life estate
D. life estate pur autre vie
E. life estate determinable
F. life estate subject to condition subsequent
G. life estate subject to executory limitation
H. fee simple absolute
I. fee simple determinable
J. fee simple subject to condition subsequent
K. fee simple subject to executory limitation
L. none
M. none of the above is correct

Problems

O conveys "to *A* for life, then to *A*'s children who shall attain the age of eighteen and their heirs, but if *A* dies and no child of *A* has attained the age of eighteen, then to *A*'s children when they reach eighteen and their heirs." *B* is an only child of *A* and is two years old at the time of the conveyance. *A* then dies a year later.

401. When *A* dies, what is *B*'s interest?
402. If *B* attains the age of eighteen and at that time one other child, *C*, has been born, what is *B*'s estate?

O conveys "to *A* for life, then to *B* for life, then to the children of *D* who survive *D* and their heirs." *C* is *D*'s only child at the time of the conveyance. *A* and *B* die shortly after the conveyance, leaving *C* and *D* surviving them.

403. What is *C*'s interest?
404. What is *O*'s estate?

O conveys "to *A* for life, then to *B* if *B* has a son." *O* then conveys all interest he has left in the property to *A* and her heirs.

405. After *O*'s first conveyance, what is *A*'s estate?
406. After *O*'s second conveyance, what is *A*'s estate?

O conveys "to *A* for life, then, if *B* reaches eighteen, to *B* and his heirs, but if he has not reached eighteen by the time *A* dies, to *B* and his heirs when he does reach eighteen." *B* is fifteen at the time of the conveyance. Five years after the conveyance *A* has not yet died.

407. Five years after the conveyance, what is *B*'s interest?

O conveys "to *A* for the life of *B*." *A* then conveys all interest she has in the property to *B* and his heirs.

408. What is *B*'s estate?

O conveys Blackacre "to *A* for life." *O* then conveys his remaining interest in Blackacre "to *B* for life."

409.   What is *B*'s interest?

O conveys "to *A* for life, then if *B* gets married, to *B*, but if *B* does not get married, to *C*." *A* then conveys her life estate back "to *O*."

410.   What is *O*'s estate?

O conveys "to *A* for life, then to *B* for life, then to the children of *D* who survive *D* and their heirs." *C* is presently *D*'s only child. *A* then conveys any interest he has in the property back "to *O*." After *A*'s conveyance, *D* dies, leaving *C* as her only heir.

411.   After *A*'s conveyance but before *D* dies, what is *O*'s interest?
412.   After *D* dies, what is *C*'s estate?

O conveys "to *A* for life, then to *B* for life, then to the children of *D* who survive *D* and their heirs." *C* is *D*'s only child at the time of the conveyance. One year later *A* dies. One year after *A*'s death, *O* conveys any interest he has remaining in the property "to *B*." One year after this second conveyance by *O*, *D* dies, leaving *C* as his only heir.

413.   On *D*'s death, what is *C*'s interest?

O conveys "to *A* for life." *A* then conveys "to *B* for ten years, and then to *C*." One year later *A* dies.

414.   What is *O*'s estate?

O conveys "to *A* and her heirs, but if *A* dies without issue, then to *B* and his heirs." *A* loses her only child in a car accident. One month later, *A* has a heart attack and dies.

415.   What is *B*'s interest?

O conveys "to *A* for life, then to *B* and her heirs if *X* gets married." *B* dies, and then *X* gets married. *A* is still alive.

416.   What is the interest in *B*'s heirs?

O conveys Blackacre "to *A* for life, then to *B* if *B* gets married, but if *B* does not get married, to my heirs." One day later *O* conveys all his remaining interest in Blackacre "to *A*."

417.   What is *A*'s estate?

O conveys Blackacre "to *A* for life, then to *B* for life if *B* has a son, then to *C* for life." When it becomes apparent that *B* will not get married, *O* makes a second conveyance "to *C*" of all his remaining interest in Blackacre.

418.   What is *B*'s estate?

O conveys "to *A* for life, then to my son, *B*, and his heirs." *O* then dies, devising all his property "to *X*."

   419.   What is *B*'s interest?

O conveys "to *A* for life, then to the children of *A*." *A* has one child, *X*, at the time of the conveyance. *A* conveys all her interest "to *O*."

   420.   What is *O*'s estate?

O conveys "to *A* for life, then to the children of *A* for the life of the survivor, then to *B*." *A* has one child, *X*, at the time of the conveyance. *A* conveys all her interest "to *B*."

   421.   What is *B*'s interest?

O conveys Blackacre "to *A* and her heirs, but if *A* quits high school, then to me, who shall have the right to reenter and take Blackacre as of my former estate." *A* quits high school.

   422.   What is *O*'s interest?

O conveys "to *A* and her heirs, but if *A* gets married, then to *B* for life, then if *C* gets married, to *C* for life." *B* conveys all his interest back "to *O*." Then *A* gets married. Then *C* gets married.

   423.   What is *C*'s interest?

O conveys Blackacre "to *A* for life." *A* then conveys Blackacre "to *B* for *B*'s life."

   424.   What is *B*'s estate?

O conveys "to *A* for the life of *X*, then to *B* for life." *A* then conveys "to *Y* for life." *A* then dies, leaving a son, *Z*, surviving her as her only heir.

   425.   What is *Z*'s estate?

O conveys "to *A* for life as long as *B* does not get married, then or otherwise to *C* for life." *B* then gets married. *C* then dies.

   426.   What is *O*'s estate?

O conveys "to *A* for the life of *B*. *A* then conveys all her interest to *C* and her children." *C* has one child, *X*, at the time of *A*'s conveyance.

   427.   What is *X*'s estate?

O conveys "to *B* for life, then to *B*'s children if they get married." *B* has one child, *C*, who has not married at the time of the conveyance. Then *B* dies. Then *C* gets married.

428.   When *C* gets married, what is *C*'s interest?

O conveys "to the children of *A*." *A* has lost all her children by the time of the conveyance, but she has one grandchild, *X*. *A* then bears a child, *M*.

429.   What is *M*'s interest?

O conveys "to *A* for life, then to the children of *A*." *A* then forfeits her life estate. Three years later *A* bears her first child, *X*.

430.   What is *X*'s interest?

O conveys "to *A* and his heirs until *A* gets married, then to *B* if *B* reaches twenty-one." *A* gets married when *B* is eighteen years old.

431.   What is *B*'s interest?

O conveys "to *A* and his heirs, but if *A* dies without issue, then to *B*." Two years later *A*'s wife bears *A*'s first child, *X*. *X* then dies. *A* then dies.

432.   What is *B*'s interest?

O conveys "to *A* for life, then, if *B* gets married, to *B* for life; otherwise to *C*." *A* then conveys all her interest in the property "to *C*."

433.   What is *C*'s interest?

O conveys "to *A* for life, then, if *B* gets married, to *B* and his heirs; otherwise to *C*." *A* then conveys all her interest in the property "to *C*."

434.   What is *B*'s interest?

O conveys "to *A* for life, then, if *B* gets married, to *B* for life; otherwise to *A*'s heirs." *B* then gets married. *A* then conveys all her interest in the property "to *C*."

435.   What is *C*'s interest?

O conveys "to *A* for life, then, if *B* gets married, to *B* for life; otherwise to *A*'s heirs." *A* then conveys all interest in the property "to *C*." *B* then gets married.

436.   What is *C*'s interest?

O conveys "to *A* for life, then, if *B* gets married, to *B*, and if *B* does not get married, to *C*." *O* then dies without a will, leaving *A* as his only heir. *B* is unmarried.

437.   What is *C*'s interest?

O conveys "to *A* and her children." At the time of the conveyance, *A* has no children. Two years later *A* has her first child, *B*. *A* then conveys all her interest "to *O*."

438.   What is *O*'s estate?

O conveys "to *A* for one hundred years if she should live so long, then to *B* for life, then in fee simple to the children of *A* and *B* who should survive *A* and *B*." At the time of the conveyance, *A* has one child, *X*, and *B* has one child, *Y*. *B* then dies.

439.   What is *A*'s estate?
440.   What is the interest of *X* and *Y*?

O conveys "to *A* for life, then, if *B* reaches eighteen, to *B* and his heirs, but if he has not reached eighteen by the time *A* dies, to *B* and his heirs when he does reach eighteen." *B* is fifteen at the time of the conveyance. Two years after the conveyance, *A* dies.

441.   What is *B*'s interest?

O conveys "to *A* for life, then to *B*'s first son and his heirs." Then *A* dies. *B*'s first son, *X*, is born to *B*'s wife one month after *A*'s death.

442.   What is *X*'s interest?

O conveys "to *A* and his heirs, but if *A* gets married, then to *B* for life, then to *C* for life, then to the heirs of *C*." *A* gets married.

443.   What is *C*'s interest?

O conveys "to *A* for ten years." One year later, *A* conveys her interest "to *B* for life." Then *O* dies, leaving *H* as his only heir. Then *A* dies, leaving *X* as his only heir.

444.   What is *B*'s estate?

O conveys "to *A* for life, then to *B* and his heirs." *B* then conveys "to *O* as long as *B* does not get married." *O* dies, leaving *X* as his only heir. Then *A* dies. *B* is still unmarried.

445.   What is *B*'s interest?

O conveys Blackacre "to *A* for life, and if *A* dies without issue, to *B* and his heirs." *A* then conveys her interest in Blackacre "to *C* and his heirs." *A* then marries *D* and has a son, *E*. *A* then dies, devising all her interest in Blackacre "to *F*."

446.   What is *F*'s interest?

O conveys Blackacre "to *A* for life, then one year after the termination of *A*'s estate, to such of *A*'s children as attain the age of fifteen." At the time of the conveyance, *A* has two twin children, *B* and *C*, who are each thirteen years old. Two years later, *B* and *C* reach fifteen. Then *A* has another child, *D*. Then *B* dies, devising all his interest "to *X*." Then *A* dies, devising all her interest "to *X*." Then, several years later, *D* reaches fifteen with *C* still alive.

447.   What is *D*'s interest?

O conveys Blackacre "to *A* for life, then one day later to the children of *B*." *A* dies. Two years later, *B* has her first child, *X*. One year later, *B* has a second child, *Y*, and *B* dies in childbirth.

448.   What is *Y*'s interest?

O conveys Blackacre "to *A* for life, then to the children of *B*." *A* dies. Two years later *B* has her first child, *X*. One year after that, *B* has a second child, *Y*, and *B* dies in childbirth.

449.   What is *X*'s interest?

O conveys Blackacre "to *A* for life, then to *B* for the life of *Y*, then to *C* and his heirs." *A*, *B*, and *C* are killed in a car crash, each leaving a son (*D*, *E*, and *F*, respectively) as his only heir. The three sons are killed in a plane crash, each leaving a spouse (*X*, *Y*, and *Z*, respectively) as his only heir.

450.   What is *Y*'s interest?

O conveys Blackacre "to *A* for life, then to *A*'s widow for life, then to the heirs of *A*." Two years later, *O* sells any remaining interest he has in the property "to *A*." One year later, *A* dies, leaving his wife surviving him but giving all his interest in Blackacre "to *X*" in his will.

451.   Upon *O*'s second conveyance, what is the interest of *A*'s widow?
452.   Upon *A*'s death, what is *X*'s interest?

O conveys "to *A* for life, then, if *B* gets married, to *B* for life." Two months later, *A* dies devising her interest, if any, "to *X*." *B* is still unmarried.

453.   What is *O*'s interest?

O conveys "to *A* and her heirs until *A* gets married, then to my heirs." *O* dies, leaving a will in which he devises all his property "to *X*." *O* has one living relative at the time of his death, his son, *S*.

454.   What is *X*'s interest?

O conveys "to *A* for ten years, then to *B* for life." *B* dies one year later, leaving *H* as his only heir. Then *A* dies, leaving *S* as his only heir.

455.   What is *S*'s estate?

O devises "to *A* for life, then to *B* for thirty years, then to *C* for life as long as the property is used as a farm." The next year *A* and *B* die, leaving *H* and *S* as their respective heirs.

456.   What is *C*'s estate?

O conveys "to *A* and her children." At the time of this conveyance, *A* has no children. One day later, *O* conveys all interest he has remaining in Blackacre "to *A*." Two years later, *A* dies while giving birth to her only child, *B*. In her will, *A* leaves all her property "to *X*."

457.   What is *B*'s interest?

O conveys "to *A* for life, then to *B* if *B* places a red rose on *A*'s grave each year at Christmas for the first five Christmases after her death." Then *A* dies, and *B* places a red rose on her grave the next Christmas.

458.   What is *B*'s interest?

O conveys "to *A* and *A*'s children, but if *A* dies without issue, then to *B*." *A* has children, *X* and *Y*, at the time of the conveyance. Then *X* has a son, *S*, and *Y* has a daughter, *D*. Then *X* and *Y* die, leaving *S* and *D* respectively as their only heirs. Then *A* dies, devising all her interest "to *T*."

459.   What is *S*'s estate?

O conveys "to *A* for life, then to *B* for life if *B* gets married, but if *B* does not get married, to *C* for life." *O* then conveys any remaining interest in the property "to *A*." Then *B* gets married.

460.   What is *A*'s interest?

O conveys "to *A* so long as she lives and maintains the property, but if she fails to maintain the property, then I, *O*, shall have the right to reenter and retake the property as of my former estate." *O* dies leaving *H* as his only heir. *A* fails to maintain the property. Then *A* dies leaving *M* as her only heir.

461.   What is *M*'s interest?

O conveys "to *A* for life, then to *B* if *B* has a son." Then *O* conveys any remaining interest he has in the property "to *A* and *A*'s children." Two years later, *B*'s first son, *Y*, is born. Then *B* dies, leaving *Y* as his only heir. *A*'s first son, *Z*, is born shortly thereafter, and *A*'s wife dies in childbirth. Then *A* dies.

462.   What is *Y*'s interest?
463.   What is *Z*'s interest?
464.   What is *O*'s interest?

O conveys "to *A* for life." Then *A* conveys "to *B* for life." Then *B* conveys "to *C* for ten years."

465.   What is *B*'s estate?
466.   What is *A*'s interest?

O devises "to *A* and her heirs, but if *A* ever goes to jail, then I, *O*, may reenter and possess the premises as of my former estate." *O*'s heirs are *X* and *Y*. After *O*'s death, *A* goes to jail.

467.   What is *A*'s estate?

O conveys "to *A* for life, then to the children of *B*." At the time of the conveyance, *B* has no children. Thereafter, *B* has a child, *X*. *X* dies when she is one month old, leaving *B* as her only heir.

468.   What is *B*'s interest?

O conveys "to *A* for life, then to *B* and his heirs, but if *X* dies without issue, then to *C* and his heirs instead of to *B*." *X* dies without issue living at his death.

469.   What is *C*'s interest?

O conveys Blackacre "to *A* for life, then to *B* and his heirs if *B* gets married, but to *C* and his heirs if *B* does not get married." *O* then conveys Whiteacre "to *A* for life, then to *B* and his heirs, but, if *B* does not get married, then to *C* and his heirs." *A* dies. Then *B* gets married.

470.   What is *B*'s interest in Blackacre?
471.   What is *B*'s interest in Whiteacre?

O conveys "to *A* and his heirs, but if *A* dies without issue, then to the heirs of *B*." *B* bears her first two children, *X* and *Y*. Then *A* dies without issue. Then *B* dies, leaving *X* and *Y* as her only heirs.

472.   After *A*'s death and before *B*'s death, what is the interest of *B*'s heirs?

O devises "to *A* for life, then to *B* if *B* gets married." Then *A* conveys all her interest in the property "to *X*." Then *B* gets married. Then *A* dies. At the time of *O*'s death, *A* is *O*'s only heir. At the time of *A*'s death, *B* is *A*'s only heir.

473.   What is *X*'s estate?
474.   What is *B*'s interest?

O conveys "to *A* for life, then to the heirs of *B*, but if *M* ever goes to law school, then the property, no matter who owns it, shall automatically revert to me, *O*, and my heirs." *A* dies, leaving *X* as her only heir. Then *O* dies leaving *Y* as his only heir. Then *B* dies, leaving *Z* as his only heir.

475.   What is *Y*'s estate?

O conveys "to *A* for life, then to the heirs of *B*, but if *M* ever goes to law school, then the property, no matter who owns it, shall automatically revert to me, *O*, and my heirs." *B* dies, leaving *Z* as his only heir. Then *A* dies, leaving *X* as her only heir. Then *O* dies, leaving *Y* as his only heir.

476.   What is *Y*'s interest?

O conveys Blackacre "to *A* for life, then to the children of *A* for the life of the survivor, then to the heirs of *A*." *A* dies two years later. *A*'s will gives all of *A*'s interest in Blackacre "to *M*." Six months later, *A*'s only child, *X*, is born.

477.   What is *M*'s interest?

O conveys Blackacre "to *A* for life, then to my heirs." *O* sells Blackacre to *X* and then dies, leaving *H* as his only heir.

478.   What is *H*'s interest?

O conveys "to *A* for life, then to *B* for the life of *X* if he gets married on or before the termination of *A*'s life estate; otherwise to *B* for the life of *X* if he gets married afterward." *A* dies and one month later *B* gets married. One year later *B* dies, leaving his spouse, *S*, and his son, *T*, as his only heirs. *X* is still alive.

479.   What is *T*'s interest?

O conveys "to *A* for life, then to the children of *B* and their heirs, but if any of *B*'s children dies before the time of *B*'s death, then to *C* and his heirs." Two years after the conveyance, *B* has his first child, *X*.

480.   What is *X*'s interest?
481.   What is *X*'s estate?

O conveys Blackacre "to *A* and his heirs, but if *A* dies childless, then I, *O*, shall have the right to reenter and take the property as of my former estate." Two years later, *A* dies childless and leaves his grandson, *S*, as his only heir.

482.   What is *S*'s estate?

O conveys "to *A* for life, then to the children of *B*." *B* has one child, *X*, who is twenty years old. Two years later, *X* dies, leaving all his property "to *H*." One year later, *A* dies. Three years later, *B* has another child, *Y*.

483.   What is *Y*'s estate?

O conveys "to *A* for life, then to *B*, but if *B* gets married, then, instead of *B*, both to *C* for life, then to *D* for the life of *X*." *O* dies and wills all his property to *B*. Then *B* gets married.

484.   What is *B*'s interest?

O conveys "to *A* for life, then to *B* for life, then to *C* for life if *C* gets married, then to the heirs of *B*." *B* dies, leaving *X* as her only heir. Then *C* gets married.

485.   What is *C*'s interest?

O conveys Blackacre "to *A* for the life of *Z*, then, if *B* gets married, to *B*, and if *B* does not get married, to my heirs." *O* then dies and wills any remaining interest in Blackacre "to *A*'s children." *O*'s heir is *X*. *A*'s children at the time of *O*'s conveyance and at the time of *O*'s will are *J* and *K*. Then *A* dies, leaving *J* and *K* as his only heirs. Then *B* gets married.

486.   What is *X*'s interest?
487.   What is *B*'s interest?
488.   What is *J*'s estate?

O conveys Blackacre "to *A* as long as Blackacre is used as a farm." *A* conveys Blackacre "to *B*, but, if *B* gets married, I, *A*, shall have the right to reenter and retake Blackacre as of my former estate."

489.   What is *A*'s interest?
490.   What is *A*'s estate?

O conveys Blackacre "to *A* and her heirs, but, if *A* dies without issue, then to *B* for life, then one day after the death of *B*, to *C* for the life of *Z*, then to *D*." *O* then conveys any remaining interest in Blackacre "to *B*."

491.   What is *D*'s interest?

O conveys Blackacre "to *A* for life, then to *B*." Then *O* sells Blackacre to *X* and then dies, leaving *B* as his only heir.

492.   What is *B*'s interest?

O conveys "to *A* for life, and, if *B* gets married, then to *B*, but if *B* flunks the first-year property course in law school, then to *C* instead of *B*, and, if *B* does not get married, the property shall revert to me, *O*." *B* flunks the first-year property course in law school and then gets married.

493.   What is *C*'s interest?

O conveys "to *A* for life, then to *B* for life if *B* gets married, then, if *B* gets married, either to *A*'s heirs if *C* gets married or to *D* if *C* does not get married." *C* gets married.

494.   What is *A*'s interest?

O conveys Blackacre "to *A* for life, then to *B* for ten years, then to *C* for the life of *Z*, but, if *C* uses Blackacre as a tavern, then, instead of *C*, to *D* and his heirs." *C* dies, leaving her son, *X*, as her only heir.

495.   What is X's interest?
496.   What is X's estate?

O conveys "to A for life, then one day later to B for life, then to C for ten years, then to D if D gets married." A dies, and a week passes.

497.   After the week passes, what is D's interest?

O conveys "to A for her life or until all her children have died, whichever is longer, then to B for the life of Z, if B gets married." Then A's only child living at the time of O's conveyance dies.

498.   What is A's estate?
499.   What is B's interest?

O conveys Blackacre "to A and her heirs as long as Blackacre is used as a farm." Then O conveys any interest he has remaining in Blackacre "to B for life." B then conveys "to C for C's life."

500.   What is C's interest?

Answers

401.   *B. Executory interest* in fee simple absolute. O conveys two interests to A's children, a contingent remainder following A's life estate (and supported by O's reversion) and an executory interest to cut short O's fee simple subject to executory limitation that is held by O in his reversion. Both interests are contingent on the children of A reaching the age of eighteen. When A dies, the contingent remainder is destroyed by the Destructibility of Contingent Remainders Rule. The executory interest, now in B and the unborn children, is not destroyed (Indestructibility of Executory Interests Rule) but must await the occurrence of the condition subsequent ("if they reach eighteen") before O's present interest in a fee simple subject to executory limitation can be cut short and each child within the class reaching eighteen can take a present interest.

402.   *K. Fee simple subject to executory limitation.* B has satisfied the condition subsequent and O's estate has been cut short. The class closes as B takes a present interest. Since there is another member of the class who still holds an executory interest, B's interest is a present interest subject to open in a fee simple subject to executory limitation. No other children who are later conceived can become members of the class since the class is closed.

403.   *I. None.* By the conveyance, A receives a present interest in a life estate, B receives a vested remainder in a life estate, the children of D receive a contingent remainder in fee simple absolute, and O retains a reversion in fee simple absolute. The condition of survivorship is not satisfied at the time the preceding estates terminate, and, therefore, the children's contingent remainder is destroyed

by the Destructibility of Contingent Remainders Rule. If *A* alone had died or *B* alone had died, the contingent remainder would still be supported by a preceding estate.

404.   *H. Fee simple absolute. O*'s reversion at the time of the conveyance has now become a present interest.

405.   *C. Life estate.* The first conveyance gives *A* a present interest in a life estate, *B* a contingent remainder in fee simple absolute, and *O* a reversion in fee simple absolute.

406.   *H. Fee simple absolute. O*'s second conveyance gives *A* a reversion in fee simple absolute to follow *A*'s life estate and support *B*'s contingent remainder. Note that this interest was created as a reversion in *O* in the first conveyance and remains a reversion when it is transferred to *A*. Since *A* now owns two successive vested interests that were not created in *A* at the same time, they merge out the intervening contingent remainder under the Merger Rule and leave *A* with a present interest in a fee simple absolute.

407.   *F. Vested remainder* in fee simple absolute. At the time of the conveyance, *B* has a contingent remainder in fee simple absolute plus an executory interest in fee simple absolute. When the condition of reaching eighteen is satisfied, the contingent remainder becomes vested, thus divesting *O*'s reversion. The condition on which the executory interest depends (*B*'s not reaching eighteen by the time *A* dies) will never happen. The executory interest is thus destroyed. (Note that executory interests may be destroyed by the failure of their conditions ever to happen—not by the failure of their conditions to happen on the termination of preceding estates.)

408.   *C. Life estate. O*'s conveyance gives *A* a present interest in a life estate pur autre vie, and *O* retains a reversion in fee simple absolute. *A*'s conveyance gives *B* a life estate for the life of *B* or, in other words, a life estate.

409.   *C. Reversion* in a life estate. *O* retains a reversion in himself with the first conveyance, and he conveys a life estate to *B* in this reversion in the second conveyance. At that point, *A* has a life estate, *B* has a reversion in a life estate, and *O* has a reversion in fee simple absolute to follow *B*'s estate.

410.   *H. Fee simple absolute.* On the conveyance, *A* has a present interest in a life estate, followed by a reversion in fee simple absolute in *O*. *B* and *C* have alternative contingent remainders. When *A* conveys to *O*, *O* takes a life estate pur autre vie. The merger of this life estate pur autre vie with *O*'s reversion in fee simple absolute under the Merger Rule causes the destruction of the contingent remainders in *B* and *C*.

411.   *J. None of the above is correct.* On the conveyance, *A* has a life estate, *B* has a vested remainder for life, the children of *D* (including *C*) have a contingent remainder in fee simple absolute, and *O* has a reversion. *A*'s conveyance to *O* does not cause a merger because *B*'s vested interest cannot be merged out. *O* has a present interest in a life estate pur autre vie plus a reversion in fee simple absolute.

412.   *H. Fee simple absolute.* On *D*'s death, the condition precedent to *C*'s contingent remainder occurs and *C*'s interest transforms into a

vested remainder. Since the class closes naturally and there are no other members of the class, C's estate is a fee simple absolute.

413.   *I. None.* At the time of the conveyance, A has a life estate, B has a vested remainder in a life estate, D's children have a contingent remainder in fee simple absolute, and O has a reversion in fee simple absolute. When A dies, B's interest is transformed into a present interest in a life estate. When O conveys his reversion in fee simple absolute to B, B's two interests merge to become a present interest in fee simple absolute, thus merging out the intervening contingent remainder in C and the unborn children of D. C no longer has an interest after this point in time.

414.   *H. Fee simple absolute.* O conveyed a present interest in a life estate to A and retained a reversion in fee simple absolute. A then conveyed to C a life estate pur autre vie subject to a term of years determinable in B. When A dies, the term of years as well as the life estate pur autre vie terminates. (A could not convey more than she had.) O's reversion becomes a present interest.

415.   *A. Present interest* in fee simple absolute. On the conveyance, A has a present interest in fee simple subject to executory limitation. B has an executory interest in fee simple absolute. The words "dies without issue" mean "dies without issue alive at the time of A's death." A died without issue even though she had had issue. Therefore, the condition precedent to B's taking a present interest is satisfied and A's estate is cut off.

416.   *F. Vested remainder* in fee simple absolute. On the conveyance, B has a contingent remainder, following A's present interest in a life estate and supported by O's reversion in fee simple absolute. B does not have to be alive when X gets married to satisfy the condition precedent. B's heirs inherit B's contingent remainder when B dies. The contingent remainder transforms into a vested remainder when X marries.

417.   *H. Fee simple absolute.* On O's first conveyance, A has a present interest in a life estate, B has a contingent remainder in fee simple absolute, and O has a reversion in fee simple absolute. The Preference for Vesting Exception does not apply because the condition (B getting married) is not an age contingency. O appears to have conveyed an alternative contingent remainder to the heirs of O, but the Doctrine of Worthier Title construes this conveyance as a reversion in O himself. O then conveys this reversion in fee simple absolute to A. It merges with A's present interest in a life estate under the Merger Rule and destroys the intervening contingent remainder in B.

418.   *C. Life estate.* On the first conveyance, A has a life estate, B has a contingent remainder in a life estate supported by C's vested remainder in a life estate, and O has a reversion in fee simple absolute. B's contingent remainder is not an intervening contingent remainder between C's life estate and O's reversion. It is intervening between A's life estate and C's vested remainder. On the second conveyance, C receives O's reversion, which merges with C's vested remainder. B's contingent remainder still follows A's life estate and is supported by C's vested remainder.

419. *F. Vested remainder* in fee simple absolute. The Doctrine of Worthier Title does not apply because the interest in remainder is not to "heirs" but rather to a specific person, *B*. *O*'s death and devise has no effect on the ownerships.

420. *D. Life estate pur autre vie*. On the conveyance, *A* has a life estate, *X* has a vested remainder subject to open in a fee simple subject to executory limitation, and the unborn children of *A* have an executory interest in fee simple absolute. *A*'s conveyance gives *O* a life estate for the life of *A*. Note that the Rule in Shelley's Case does not apply when the remainder is to "children."

421. *J. None of the above is correct*. On the conveyance, *A* has a life estate, *X* has a vested remainder subject to open in a life estate pur autre vie subject to executory limitation, the unborn children of *A* have an executory interest in a life estate pur autre vie, and *B* has a vested remainder in fee simple absolute. *A*'s conveyance gives *B* a present interest in a life estate pur autre vie. This vested interest does not merge with *B*'s vested remainder because of the intervening vested interest in *X*. Therefore, *B* has two separately identifiable interests.

422. *E. Right of reentry* in fee simple absolute. On the conveyance, *A* has a present interest in a fee simple subject to condition subsequent and *O* has a right of reentry in fee simple absolute. When the condition subsequent occurs, *O* has the power to terminate *A*'s estate, but that power must be exercised before *A*'s estate is terminated. It has not yet been exercised here.

423. *I. None*. At the time of the conveyance, *A* has a present interest in a fee simple subject to executory limitation, *B* has an executory interest in a life estate, *C* has an executory interest in a life estate following *B*'s life estate, and *O* retains a possibility of reverter in fee simple absolute following *B*'s life estate. *B*'s conveyance gives *O* an executory interest in a life estate pur autre vie followed immediately by *O*'s possibility of reverter. Both interests are subject to the same condition (*A*'s marriage). It would seem that merger would occur in this situation to merge out *C*'s interest, but the fact that *C*'s interest is an executory interest gives pause. In any case, when the condition subsequent (*A*'s marriage) occurs, *A*'s estate is cut short, and *O*'s interests, if they have not yet merged (and they probably have not), transform into a present interest in a life estate pur autre vie plus a reversion in fee simple absolute. They do merge and *C*'s interest, which would have transformed into a contingent remainder for life, is merged out by the Merger Rule, leaving *O* with a present interest in fee simple absolute. *C* gets married too late to save his interest.

424. *D. Life estate pur autre vie*. Since *A* specified "for *B*'s life," the estate in *B* is a life estate for the life of *A* or *B*, whoever dies first (life estate pur autre vie). If *B* dies before *A*, the interest will revert to *A*. If *A* dies before *B*, the interests of both *A* and *B* are terminated and *O*'s reversion becomes a present interest. On the other hand, if *A* had merely specified "to *B*" in her conveyance, *B* would have had a life estate for the life of *A*.

425. *D. Life estate pur autre vie.* On the conveyance, *A* has a present interest in a life estate pur autre vie, *B* has a vested remainder in a life estate, and *O* has a reversion in fee simple absolute. *A*'s conveyance gives *Y* a present interest in a life estate for the life of *X* or *Y*, whoever dies first. *A* retains a reversion in a life estate pur autre vie from this second conveyance. Upon *A*'s death, her heir, *Z*, inherits her interest.

426. *H. Fee simple absolute.* On the conveyance, *A* has a present interest in a life estate subject to executory limitation, *C* has a vested remainder in a life estate (ready to follow the natural termination of *A*'s life estate, if not sooner through *B*'s marriage), and *O* has a reversion in fee simple absolute. *B*'s marriage transforms *C*'s vested remainder into a present interest in a life estate. This life estate ends with the death of *C*, and *O*'s reversion transforms into a present interest in fee simple absolute.

427. *D. Life estate pur autre vie* shared as a one-half undivided share with *C*. Under the Modified Rule in Wild's Case, *C* and *X* share a tenancy in common in the life estate pur autre vie conveyed by *A*. The class is closed to other children who might be born because of the Rule of Convenience. *O* has a reversion in fee simple absolute.

428. *I. None.* *C*'s contingent remainder is destroyed by the Destructibility of Contingent Remainders Rule before the condition precedent (*C*'s marriage) occurs.

429. *J. None of the above is correct.* *M* has a present interest subject to open in a fee simple subject to executory limitation. On *O*'s conveyance, *O* retains a present interest in a fee simple subject to executory limitation, and *A*'s children have an executory interest in fee simple absolute. The class of children does not include the children who are dead at the time of the conveyance. When *M* is born, *O*'s estate is cut short, and *M*'s interest vests in possession as a present interest, but it does not close the class. Since the time for distribution to the class of children is immediate upon *O*'s conveyance and there are no takers at the time of *O*'s conveyance, the Rule of Convenience does not operate to close the class. The class will close only naturally on the death of *A*. *A*'s unborn children continue to have an executory interest in fee simple absolute.

430. *I. None.* *A*'s children have a contingent remainder (following *A*'s life estate and supported by *O*'s reversion) that fails to vest before the termination of *A*'s life estate. It is destroyed by the Destructibility of Contingent Remainders Rule. *O* now has a present interest in fee simple absolute.

431. *B. Executory interest* in fee simple absolute. On *O*'s conveyance, *A* has a present interest in fee simple determinable (condition subsequent being *A*'s marriage), *O* has a possibility of reverter in fee simple subject to executory limitation (condition subsequent being *B* reaching twenty-one), and *B* has an executory interest in fee simple absolute. *A*'s marriage cuts short *A*'s estate, but the age contingency that is a condition to the vesting of *B*'s interest has not yet occurred. Since executory interests are indestructible,

B's interest is not destroyed. *O* has a present interest in fee simple subject to executory limitation.

432. *A. Present interest* in fee simple absolute. On *O*'s conveyance, *A* has a present interest in fee simple subject to executory limitation, and *B* has an executory interest in fee simple absolute. Although *A* had issue, he did not have issue at his death. Therefore, the condition is satisfied, and *A*'s estate is cut short at his death in favor of *B*.

433. *A. Present interest* in fee simple absolute. *C* receives a vested remainder in fee simple absolute by *O*'s conveyance and a vested present interest in a life estate pur autre vie by *A*'s conveyance. These successive interests, created in *C* at different times, merge, thus merging out the intervening contingent remainder in a life estate in *B*.

434. *D. Contingent remainder* in a fee simple absolute. On *O*'s conveyance, *A* has a present interest in a life estate, *B* and *C* each have alternative contingent remainders in fee simple absolute, and *O* has a reversion in fee simple absolute. *C* cannot have a vested remainder because it would be subject to divestment by *B*'s contingent remainder, and this would violate the Contingent Remainder Cannot Divest a Vested Remainder Rule. *C* receives a present interest in a life estate pur autre vie by *A*'s conveyance. There is no merger between *C*'s present interest and *C*'s contingent remainder.

435. *J. None of the above is correct.* On *O*'s conveyance, *A* has a present interest in a life estate and, with the application of the Rule in Shelley's Case, a vested remainder in fee simple absolute. *B* has a contingent remainder in a life estate. Although *A*'s successive interests are vested in the same person, there is no merger because of the exception to the Merger Rule that occurs when the vested interests are created in one person at the same time the contingent remainder is created. When *B* gets married, *B*'s contingent remainder transforms into a vested remainder. At this point, *A*'s vested interests are no longer successive because *B*'s interest follows *A*'s life estate and *B*'s estate precedes *A*'s vested remainder. When *A* conveys to *C*, *C* receives a present interest in a life estate pur autre vie and a vested remainder in fee simple absolute.

436. *A. Present interest* in fee simple absolute. On *O*'s conveyance, *A* and *B* have the same interests as mentioned in problem 435. The exception to the merger rule no longer exists when *A* conveys her two back-to-back vested interests to *C*. The two interests are merged, merging out *B*'s contingent remainder. *B*'s later marriage is to no avail.

437. *I. None.* On *O*'s conveyance, *A* has a present interest in a life estate, *B* and *C* each have an alternative contingent remainder in fee simple absolute, and *O* has a reversion in fee simple absolute. *A* receives *O*'s reversion by inheritance and the reversion merges with *A*'s vested present interest, merging out the contingent remainders of *B* and *C*. On *A*'s inheritance, *A* has a present interest in fee simple absolute. Note that the condition precedent to *C*'s contingent remainder is not yet satisfied even though *B* is unmar-

ried. The condition is the failure to marry by the termination of A's life estate (otherwise the condition would not make sense), which has not occurred at the time of O's death.

438. *D. Life estate pur autre vie.* On O's conveyance, the Modified Rule in Wild's Case gives A a life estate and A's unborn children a contingent remainder. Upon birth, B takes a vested remainder subject to open, and A's unborn children have an executory interest in fee simple absolute. A's conveyance gives O what A had, a life estate for the life of A.

439. *B. Term of years determinable.* A's life is the determining condition.

440. *I. None.* On O's conveyance, B has a present interest in a life estate subject to a term of years determinable in A, the children of A and B have a contingent remainder in fee simple absolute, and O has a reversion in fee simple absolute. On B's death, B's life estate terminates. The remainder in the children is contingent on survivorship of both parents and thus does not become vested on the death of B. This contingent remainder is destroyed by the Destructibility of Contingent Remainders Rule since there is no preceding life estate and the condition precedent has not been satisfied. The future interest in the children could have been preserved from destruction if both A and B had been given terms of years determinable—that is, "O conveys to A for one hundred years if she should so long live, then to B for one hundred years if he should so long live, then in fee simple to the children of A and B who should survive A and B." O would have had a present interest in fee simple subject to executory limitation, and the children would have had an executory interest in fee simple absolute. Whether A or B had died or both forfeited their estates before death, the executory interest would not have been destroyed. It would have transformed into a present interest in fee simple absolute on the deaths of both A and B if there had been surviving children.

441. *B. Executory interest* in fee simple absolute. B has two future interests at the time of the conveyance: (1) a contingent remainder following A's present interest in a life estate and supported by O's reversion, and (2) an executory interest prepared to cut short O's reversion on the happening of the condition subsequent ("but if he has not reached eighteen by the time A dies"). The death of A destroys B's contingent remainder. O's interest becomes a present interest in fee simple subject to executory limitation (condition subsequent is B reaching eighteen). The alternative limitations in this conveyance are one means of sidestepping the Rule in Purefoy v. Rogers.

442. *A. Present interest* in fee simple absolute. On O's conveyance, A has a present interest in a life estate, B's unborn son has a contingent remainder in fee simple absolute, and O has a reversion in fee simple absolute. A child born after the termination of the life estate is considered to be in existence during his gestation period so that the Destructibility of Contingent Remainders Rule does not operate here. If the son had not been born alive, the Destructibility Rule would have operated to destroy the contingent remainder.

443.   *F. Vested remainder* in fee simple absolute. At the time of the conveyance, *A* has a fee simple subject to executory limitation, *B* has an executory interest in a life estate, *C* has an executory interest in a life estate, the heirs of *C* have an executory interest in fee simple absolute, and *O* has a possibility of reverter in fee simple absolute following *C*'s executory interest in a life estate. When *A* gets married, the condition subsequent divests *A*'s estate. *B* then has a present interest in a life estate, and before application of the Rule in Shelley's Case, *C* has a vested remainder in a life estate and *C*'s heirs have a contingent remainder in fee simple absolute. The rule operates when *A*'s marriage occurs to give *C* a vested remainder in fee simple absolute in place of the remainder in *C*'s heirs. The Merger Rule combines the two interests in *C* to give *C* a vested remainder in fee simple absolute to follow *B*'s present interest. Note that the freehold of the ancestor in the Rule in Shelley's Case need not be in a present interest, and the rule may operate on a delayed basis.

444.   *B. Term of years determinable. A* has a term of years that she conveys to *B* to terminate on *B*'s death. The deaths of *O* and *A* do not affect the interest in *B*. On *O*'s death, *O*'s present interest in fee simple absolute descends to his heir, *H*. On *A*'s death, *A*'s remaining interest in the term of years descends to *X*.

445.   *G. Possibility of reverter* in fee simple absolute. *O* conveys a present interest in a life estate to *A* and a vested remainder in fee simple absolute to *B*. *B* conveys a vested remainder in fee simple determinable to *O* and keeps the rest of the vested remainder in fee simple absolute as a possibility of reverter in fee simple absolute in himself. One might call this interest a possibility of reverter within a vested remainder. *O*'s vested remainder in fee simple determinable is inherited by *X* on *O*'s death. When *A* dies, the vested remainder becomes a present interest in *X* in fee simple determinable. Whenever *B* gets married, *B* will take a present interest in fee simple absolute. Note that if *O* had conveyed "to *A* for life, then to *B* and his heirs if *B* gets married," *B* would have had a contingent remainder that would have been destroyed under the Destructibility of Contingent Remainders Rule when *A* died before *B* got married. The conveyance in this problem is a method for avoiding the effect of the Destructibility Rule.

446.   *I. None. O*'s conveyance gives *A* a present interest in a life estate and *B* a contingent remainder in fee simple absolute, leaving a reversion in *O* in fee simple absolute. *A* conveys her interest to *C* as a present interest in a life estate pur autre vie (for the life of *A*). When *A* dies, her estate, which is then in *C*, ends. The condition precedent to *B*'s interest (*A* having issue) is satisfied, and *B*'s contingent remainder transforms into a present interest in fee simple absolute. *O*'s reversion is divested.

447.   *A. Present interest* in fee simple absolute shared as an undivided one-third interest in a tenancy in common. On *O*'s conveyance, *A* has a present interest in a life estate, *O* has a reversion in fee simple subject to executory limitation (condition subsequent being the passage of one year after the termination of *A*'s life estate and a

child reaching fifteen), and *A*'s children have a springing executory interest in fee simple absolute. The class of children is open to include all children alive (or conceived later to be born alive) between the time of the conveyance and the time of *A*'s death plus one year. At that time the class will close if there is someone in the class (or a representative) to take distribution. In fact there is: *X*, *C*, and *D* are the only members (or representatives of members) included in the class one year after *A*'s death because the class does close, since *C* and *X* are capable of taking distribution. Since all these children satisfy or eventually satisfy the condition of reaching fifteen, they are entitled to shares in the estate. When *B* and *C* reach fifteen, they need to satisfy only one more condition (one year passage of time after *A*'s life estate) while the other children still need to satisfy two. When *B* dies, *X* takes *B*'s share in the executory interest. When *A* dies, *O* takes a present interest in fee simple subject to executory limitation. One year after *A* dies, *B*'s heir, *X*, and *C* take in possession undivided shares in a present interest subject to open in fee simple subject to executory limitation. *D* receives her share on reaching fifteen.

448. *A. Present interest* in fee simple absolute shared as an undivided one-half interest with *X* in a tenancy in common. On *O*'s conveyance, *A* has a present interest in a life estate, *O* has a reversion in fee simple subject to executory limitation, and *B*'s children have an executory interest in fee simple absolute. There are two conditions subsequent on *O*'s estate: the passage of one day from the termination of *A*'s life estate and the birth of a child. On *A*'s death *O* takes a present interest in fee simple subject to executory limitation. Since there are no members of the class alive at the time designated in the conveyance for distribution (one day after *A*'s death), the class may close only naturally on *B*'s death. When *X* is born, she takes a present interest subject to open in fee simple subject to executory limitation—that is, subject to partial divestment of the estate in favor of other children when they are born. When *Y* is born, her executory interest transforms into *X*'s present interest subject to open in fee simple subject to executory limitation. When *B* dies, the interest held by *X* and *Y* is no longer subject to open, since there is a natural closing.

449. *I. None.* On *O*'s conveyance, *A* has a present interest in a life estate, *B*'s children have a contingent remainder in fee simple absolute, and *O* has a reversion in fee simple absolute. When *A* dies, the children of *B* are as yet unborn. Therefore, the Destructibility of Contingent Remainders Rule operates to destroy the contingent remainder in the children on *A*'s death. *O* now has a present interest in fee simple absolute.

450. *A. Present interest.* When *A* dies, *A*'s present interest in a life estate terminates. *B*'s vested remainder becomes a present interest in a life estate pur autre vie (for the life of *Y*) and, with *B*'s death, is inherited by *E*. *C*'s vested remainder in fee simple absolute, with *C*'s death, is inherited by *F*. When *E* and *F* are killed, their spouses inherit their interests. *Y* inherits a present interest in a life estate because the life estate extends the length of her life.

451. *D. Contingent remainder* in a life estate. At the time of the conveyance, *A* has a present interest in a life estate, *A*'s widow has a contingent remainder in a life estate (she is unascertained), *A* has a vested remainder in fee simple absolute (on application of the Rule in Shelley's Case). There is no merger between *A*'s two vested interests because of the exception to the Merger Rule dealing with an intervening contingent remainder. *O*'s second conveyance is ineffective because *O* does not own any part of Blackacre at this point.

452. *F. Vested remainder* in fee simple absolute. When *A* dies, his life estate terminates. *A*'s widow's contingent remainder transforms into a present interest in a life estate. *A*'s vested remainder in fee simple absolute is devised to *X*.

453. *A. Present interest* in fee simple absolute. At the time of the conveyance, *A* has a present interest in a life estate, *B* has a contingent remainder in a life estate, and *O* has a reversion in fee simple absolute. On *A*'s death, *X* receives nothing because *A* has nothing to convey. *B*'s interest is destroyed by the Destructibility of Contingent Remainders Rule because the condition precedent is not satisfied on time.

454. *G. Possibility of reverter* in fee simple absolute. At the time of the conveyance, *A* has a present interest in a fee simple determinable. Under the Doctrine of Worthier Title, the interest in the heirs of *O* becomes an interest in *O*. *O*'s will leaves this possibility of reverter to *X*. *S* receives nothing.

455. *A. Term of years.* *B*'s present interest in a life estate terminates on his death and *O*'s reversion in fee simple absolute becomes a present interest. *A*'s term is inherited by *S* on *A*'s death.

456. *E. Life estate determinable.* *O*'s devise gives *A* a present interest in a life estate, *B* a term of years, and *C* a vested remainder in a life estate determinable. *O* retains a reversion, which includes *O*'s possibility of reverter. *A*'s death terminates *A*'s life estate. *C*'s vested remainder becomes a present interest. *S* inherits *B*'s term when *B* dies.

457. *I. None.* Under the Modified Rule in Wild's Case, *A* receives a present interest in a life estate and the children receive a contingent remainder in fee simple absolute on *O*'s conveyance. *O* retains a reversion in fee simple absolute. *O*'s second conveyance to *A* gives *A* a reversion in fee simple absolute immediately following *A*'s present interest in a life estate. Merger leaves *A* with a present interest in fee simple absolute, merging out the contingent remainder in the children. On *A*'s death, *X* receives *A*'s interest by will.

458. *B. Executory interest* in fee simple absolute. *B*'s interest cannot vest until after *A*'s death. Therefore, on *O*'s conveyance, *A* takes a present interest in a life estate, *O* takes a reversion in fee simple subject to executory limitation, and *B* takes an executory interest in fee simple absolute. The executory interest remains such after *A*'s death until the condition (placing a red rose for the first five Christmases) is satisfied. After *A*'s death, *O* has a present interest in fee simple subject to executory limitation.

459. *H. Fee simple absolute.* At the time of the conveyance, *A*, *X*, and *Y* share a present interest in fee simple subject to executory limitation as tenants in common. *B* has an executory interest in fee simple absolute. When *X* dies, *S* inherits her one-third undivided share. When *Y* dies, *D* likewise inherits her one-third undivided share. When *A* dies, *T* takes *A*'s interest by will. *A*'s death with issue causes the failure of the condition subsequent, and the executory interest is eliminated. *S*'s share in a fee simple subject to executory limitation becomes a share in a fee simple absolute.

460. *A. Present interest* in fee simple absolute. At the time of the conveyance, *A* has a present interest in a life estate, *B* has a contingent remainder in a life estate, *C* has a contingent remainder in a life estate, and *O* has a reversion in fee simple absolute. The two conditions do not involve an age contingency; therefore, there is no preference for vesting. *B* and *C* have alternative contingent remainders that are merged out when *O* conveys his reversion to *A*. *B*'s subsequent marriage is too late.

461. *I. None.* At the time of the conveyance, *A* has a present interest in a life estate subject to condition subsequent, and *O* has a reversion in fee simple subject to condition subsequent plus a right of reentry in fee simple absolute. The "so long as" language of the condition suggests that *A*'s life estate is determinable, but the "but if" language and the "right to reenter" language weigh heavier in the balance, thus allowing a classification of *A*'s life estate as one subject to condition subsequent. When *O* dies, *H* inherits the reversion and the right of reentry. When *A* fails to maintain the property, *H* does not exercise the right of reentry and therefore does not divest *A*'s estate. When *A* dies, *A*'s life estate terminates naturally, and *H*'s reversion becomes a present interest in fee simple absolute. The right of reentry disappears because it is no longer necessary to transfer ownership to *H*. When *A* dies, she has nothing for *M* to inherit.

462. *I. None.* On *O*'s first conveyance, *A* has a present interest in a life estate, *B* has a contingent remainder in fee simple absolute, and *O* has a reversion in fee simple absolute. On *O*'s second conveyance, *A* takes a reversion (*O*'s interest) in a life estate (Modified Rule in Wild's Case) immediately following his own life estate, and *A*'s unborn children take a contingent remainder in fee simple absolute, leaving *O* with a reversion in fee simple absolute following *A*'s second life estate. *A*'s present interest in a life estate and reversion in a life estate merge under the Merger Rule, merging out the intervening contingent remainder in *B* and leaving nothing for *Y* to inherit when *B* dies. When *A*'s first son, *Z*, is born, *O*'s reversion is divested and *Z*'s contingent remainder becomes a vested remainder subject to open in fee simple subject to executory limitation (*A* can still have children at this point even though his wife died in childbirth). When *A* dies, *Z*'s interest transforms into a present interest in fee simple absolute because *A*'s life estate terminates, and the class of *A*'s children closes naturally.

463. *A. Present interest* in a fee simple absolute.

464. *I. None.*

465.   *D. Life estate pur autre vie* (for the life of *A* or *B*, whoever is the first to die) subject to a term of years in *C*.

466.   *J. None of the above is correct. A* has a reversion within a present interest in a life estate. *A*'s interest will transform into a present interest in a life estate if *B* dies first. If *A* dies first, *O*'s reversion in fee simple absolute will become a present interest.

467.   *J. Fee simple subject to condition subsequent.* On *O*'s death, *A* takes a present interest in a fee simple subject to condition subsequent. *O*'s heirs, *X* and *Y*, inherit the right of reentry from *O*. Although the condition subsequent (*A*'s going to jail) occurs thereafter, *A* still has her present interest because *O*'s heirs have not yet exercised their right of reentry.

468.   *H. Vested remainder subject to open* in fee simple absolute. On the conveyance, *A* has a present interest in a life estate, *B*'s children have a contingent remainder in fee simple absolute, and *O* has a reversion in fee simple absolute. When *X* is born, *X* takes a vested remainder subject to open in fee simple absolute, which divests *O*'s reversion. The unborn children then have an executory interest in fee simple absolute. *B* inherits *X*'s interest. If *B* were to have more children, they would share in the vested remainder with *B*.

469.   *F. Vested remainder* in fee simple absolute. At the time of the conveyance, *A* has a present interest in a life estate, *B* has a vested remainder in fee simple subject to executory limitation, and *C* has an executory interest in fee simple absolute. The condition subsequent (*X*'s death without surviving descendants) occurs and cuts short *B*'s fee simple subject to executory limitation. *C*'s executory interest is transformed into a vested remainder.

470.   *I. None.* At the time of the conveyance, *A* has a present interest in a life estate, *B* and *C* each have an alternative contingent remainder in fee simple absolute (no Preference for Vesting Exception), and *O* has a reversion in fee simple absolute. On *A*'s death, *B* has not yet married. *B*'s condition precedent is not satisfied, causing *B*'s contingent remainder to be destroyed under the Destructibility of Contingent Remainders Rule. *C*'s condition precedent is satisfied. *B* has not married by the time of *A*'s death. *C* takes a present interest in fee simple absolute.

471.   *A. Present interest* in fee simple absolute. At the time of the conveyance, *A* has a present interest in a life estate, *B* has a vested remainder in fee simple subject to executory limitation, and *C* has an executory interest in fee simple absolute. On *A*'s death, *B*'s vested remainder becomes a present interest. *B*'s marriage ensures that the condition subsequent that would have cut short *B*'s estate will never occur. *C*'s executory interest is destroyed.

472.   *B. Executory interest* in fee simple absolute. At the time of the conveyance, *A* has a present interest in a fee simple determinable (condition subsequent being *A* dying without issue), *O* has a possibility of reverter in fee simple subject to executory limitation (condition subsequent being the ascertainment of *B*'s heirs upon *B*'s death), *B*'s heirs have an executory interest in fee simple absolute. The birth of the children to *B* do not change any of these interests or estates. *A*'s death causes *O*'s possibility of reverter

to transform into a present interest. It is only on B's death that the heirs of B are ascertained.

473. *H. Fee simple absolute.* At the time of the devise, A has a present interest in a life estate by devise from O and a reversion in fee simple absolute by inheritance from O. B has a contingent remainder in fee simple absolute. Merger does not occur because of the exception to the Merger Rule. A's conveyance allows merger of A's two successive interests in X, merging out B's contingent remainder. X has a present interest in fee simple absolute. The subsequent events do not affect this conveyance.

474. *I. None.*

475. *H. Fee simple absolute.* At the time of O's conveyance, A has a present interest in a life estate determinable ("automatically revert" is stronger than the "but if" language), B's heirs (unascertained) have a contingent remainder in fee simple determinable, and O has a reversion in fee simple absolute plus a possibility of reverter in fee simple absolute. M's going to law school is the condition subsequent on A's estate and B's heirs' estate. A's death occurs while the remainder in B's heirs is still contingent (because B is not yet dead). A's estate terminates. The remainder in B's heirs is destroyed under the Destructibility of Contingent Remainders Rule. O's reversion transforms into a present interest in fee simple absolute. Y inherits this interest on O's death.

476. *G. Possibility of reverter* in fee simple absolute. At the time of O's conveyance, A, B's heirs, and O have the interests and estates designated in problem 475. At B's death the contingent remainder in B's heirs becomes a vested remainder in Z in fee simple determinable. O's reversion is divested and O is left with a possibility of reverter in fee simple absolute. At A's death, Z's vested remainder becomes a present interest. At O's death, Y inherits O's possibility of reverter.

477. *F. Vested remainder* in fee simple absolute. O's conveyance gives A a life estate. The unborn children have a contingent remainder in a life estate pur autre vie (for the life of the survivor). The remainder in A's heirs is a remainder in A by operation of the Rule in Shelley's Case. Therefore, A has both a present interest in a life estate and a vested remainder in fee simple absolute. There is no merger between these two vested interests in A despite the fact that the intervening remainder is contingent because of the exception to the Merger Rule for simultaneous creation. When A dies, the contingent remainder in A's children is not destroyed because a child in gestation and later born alive, such as X, is considered in existence at that time. Therefore, at the time of A's death, the contingent remainder in A's children is actually considered to transform into a present interest in X in a life estate pur autre vie. The class is closed and X is considered capable of taking distribution, even though he is still unborn. M takes A's vested remainder by devise.

478. *I. None.* On O's conveyance, A has a present interest in a life estate, and O (by operation of the Doctrine of Worthier Title) has a reversion in fee simple absolute. X buys the reversion, and there is nothing for H to inherit on O's death.

479. *A. Present interest* in a life estate pur autre vie. *O*'s conveyance gives *A* a present interest in a life estate, *B* a contingent remainder in a life estate pur autre vie, *O* a reversion following *A*'s life estate in a fee simple subject to executory limitation (condition subsequent being *B*'s marriage after *A*'s death), *B* an executory interest in a life estate pur autre vie, and *O* a possibility of reverter in a fee simple absolute following *B*'s executory interest in a life estate. On *A*'s death, *A*'s life estate terminates, *B*'s contingent remainder is destroyed under the Destructibility Rule, *O*'s reversion becomes a present interest in fee simple subject to executory limitation, and all the other interests and estates remain the same. *B*'s marriage causes *O*'s estate to be cut short and transforms *B*'s interest into a present interest and *O*'s interest into a reversion. *B*'s death causes *B*'s interest to be inherited by *S* and *T*.

480. *H. Vested remainder subject to open* in fee simple subject to executory limitation. At the time of the conveyance, *A* has a present interest in a life estate, the unborn children have a contingent remainder in fee simple subject to executory limitation, *C* has an executory interest in fee simple absolute, and *O* has a reversion in fee simple absolute. *X*'s interest becomes vested on birth but remains open to include other children if and when they are born. *X*'s interest is also subject to complete divestment if any of *B*'s children dies before *B* dies.

481. *K. Fee simple subject to executory limitation.* There are two conditions subsequent, one whose occurrence will completely cut short *X*'s estate (death of any of *B*'s children before *B*), and one whose occurrence will partially cut short *X*'s estate (birth of a child).

482. *J. Fee simple subject to condition subsequent.* On *O*'s conveyance, *A* has a present interest in fee simple subject to condition subsequent, and *O* has a right of reentry in fee simple absolute. *O* has not yet exercised his right of reentry, and *S* inherits *A*'s estate.

483. *L. None.* At the time of the conveyance, *A* has a present interest in a life estate, *X* has a vested remainder subject to open in fee simple subject to executory limitation, and *B*'s unborn children have an executory interest in fee simple absolute. When *X* dies, *H* takes *X*'s interest. When *A* dies, *H* (holding the interest of a member of the class of *B*'s children) becomes entitled to distribution at the time designated in the conveyance for distribution. The Rule of Convenience closes the class, and *Y* is excluded. *H* has a present interest in fee simple absolute.

484. *C. Reversion* in fee simple absolute. On *O*'s conveyance, *A* has a present interest in a life estate, *B* has a vested remainder in fee simple subject to executory limitation, *C* has an executory interest in a life estate, *D* has an executory interest in a life estate pur autre vie, and *O* retains a possibility of reverter in fee simple absolute following *D*'s executory interest in a life estate. On *O*'s death, *B* takes *O*'s interest. When *B* gets married, *B*'s fee simple is cut short and *C* has a vested remainder in a life estate, *D* has a vested remainder in a life estate pur autre vie, and *B*'s possibility of reverter becomes a reversion.

485. *F. Vested remainder* in a life estate. *O*'s conveyance gives *A* a present interest in a life estate, *B* a vested remainder in a life estate, *C* a contingent remainder in a life estate, and *B* (by operation of the Rule in Shelley's Case) a vested remainder in fee simple absolute. There is no merger of *B*'s two successive vested interests despite the intervening contingent remainder because of the exception to the Merger Rule for simultaneous creation. *B*'s death allows *X* to inherit *B*'s remainder in fee simple absolute. There is no merger with *B*'s life estate because *B*'s life estate has terminated with *B*'s death. When *C* gets married, *C*'s contingent remainder becomes vested.

486. *I. None.* On *O*'s conveyance, *A* has a present interest in a life estate pur autre vie, *B* has a contingent remainder in fee simple absolute, and *O* has a reversion. The conveyance to *O*'s heirs is the retention of a reversion in *O* under the Doctrine of Worthier Title. *O*'s reversion passes to *A*'s children under *O*'s will. *J* and *K* take a reversion subject to open in fee simple subject to executory limitation, and the unborn children take an executory interest in the reversion in fee simple absolute. At no time does *X* take an interest in Blackacre.

487. *I. None.* On *A*'s death, *A*'s life estate pur autre vie is inherited by *A*'s children, *J* and *K*. The two successive vested interests—present interest in a life estate pur autre vie and reversion subject to open in fee simple subject to executory limitation—in *J* and *K* merge, thus merging out the intervening contingent remainder in *B*. The time for distribution has arrived, and the class closes. *J* and *K* no longer have an interest subject to open.

488. *H. Fee simple absolute.* *J* shares a present interest in fee simple absolute with *K* as a tenant in common.

489. *E. Right of reentry* in a fee simple determinable. On *O*'s conveyance, *A* has a present interest in fee simple determinable, and *O* has a possibility of reverter in fee simple absolute. On *A*'s conveyance, *B* has a present interest in fee simple subject to condition subsequent (*A* has a right of reentry) and determinable (*O* has a possibility of reverter).

490. *I. Fee simple determinable.*

491. *B. Executory interest* in fee simple absolute. On *O*'s conveyance, *A* has a fee simple subject to executory limitation (condition subsequent being *A* dying without issue). *B* has an executory interest in a life estate, *O* has a possibility of reverter in fee simple subject to executory limitation (condition subsequent being the passage of one day after the death of *B*), *C* has an executory interest in a life estate pur autre vie, and *D* has an executory interest in fee simple absolute. When *O* makes a second conveyance to *B*, *B*'s executory interest in a life estate merges with the possibility of reverter in fee simple subject to executory limitation to produce an executory interest in fee simple subject to executory limitation. The merger does not affect *D*'s interest.

492. *F. Vested remainder* in fee simple absolute. On *O*'s conveyance, *A* has a life estate and *B* has a vested remainder in fee simple

absolute. *O* has nothing to sell to *X*. The fact that *B* is *O*'s only heir does not bring the Doctrine of Worthier Title into operation.

493. *F. Vested remainder* in fee simple absolute. On *O*'s conveyance, *A* has a present interest in a life estate, *O* has a reversion in fee simple absolute, *B* has a contingent remainder in fee simple subject to executory limitation (condition subsequent being *B*'s flunking first-year property), *C* has an executory interest in fee simple absolute. The condition subsequent on *B*'s estate (flunking first-year property) occurs to cut short *B*'s estate. *C* is left with a contingent remainder in fee simple absolute. *B*'s later marriage satisfies the condition precedent on *C*'s interest. *C*'s interest vests, and *O*'s reversion is divested. Note that the condition "if *B* does not get married" is treated as superfluous.

494. *J. None of the above is correct.* On *O*'s conveyance, *A* has a present interest in a life estate, *B* has a contingent remainder in a life estate, *A* (by the operation of the Rule in Shelley's Case) has a contingent remainder in fee simple absolute, *D* has an alternative contingent remainder in fee simple absolute, and *O* has a reversion in fee simple absolute. When *C* gets married, *D*'s contingent remainder is destroyed by the failure of one of the conditions precedent to *D*'s interest. *B* now has a contingent remainder in a life estate followed by a contingent remainder in *A* in fee simple absolute. The remainders of *B* and *A* are contingent on the same condition precedent. *A* also continues to have her present interest in a life estate. There is no merger.

495. *F. Vested remainder* in a life estate pur autre vie. On *O*'s conveyance, *A* has a present interest in a life estate and *B* has a term of years to begin on the termination of *A*'s life estate. *C*'s interest follows *A*'s interest under the Piggyback Rule, and *C* has a vested remainder in a life estate pur autre vie subject to executory limitation (condition subsequent being *C* using Blackacre as a tavern). *D* has an executory interest in fee simple absolute. *O* has a reversion in fee simple absolute. On *C*'s death, *X* inherits *C*'s interest in a life estate pur autre vie but without the condition subsequent because the condition has failed to happen.

496. *D. Life estate pur autre vie.*

497. *D. Contingent remainder* in fee simple absolute. On *O*'s conveyance, *A* has a present interest in a life estate, *O* has a reversion in fee simple subject to executory limitation (condition subsequent being the passage of one day after *A*'s life estate is over), *B* has an executory interest in a life estate. *C* has a term of years, *O* has a possibility of reverter in fee simple absolute (following *B*'s executory interest in a life estate), and *D* has an executory interest in a fee simple absolute (following *B*'s executory interest in a life estate). On the passage of one day from *A*'s death, *B* has a present interest in a life estate, *O* has a reversion in fee simple absolute, *C* has a term of years, and *D* has a contingent remainder to follow *B*'s estate. The condition precedent on *D*'s interest is *D*'s marriage.

498. *D. Life estate pur autre vie.* On *O*'s conveyance, *A* has a present interest in a life estate pur autre vie, *B* has a contingent remainder in a life estate pur autre vie, and *O* has a reversion in fee simple

absolute. The death of *A*'s only child does not change *A*'s estate into a life estate because *A* may have more children.

499. *D. Contingent remainder* in a life estate pur autre vie.

500. *G. Possibility of reverter* in a life estate pur autre vie. On *O*'s first conveyance, *A* has a present interest in a fee simple determinable, and *O* retains a possibility of reverter in fee simple absolute. On *O*'s second conveyance, *B* has a possibility of reverter in a life estate, and *O* has a possibility of reverter in fee simple absolute following *B*'s life estate. On *B*'s conveyance, *C* has a possibility of reverter in a life estate pur autre vie. The life that determines the length of *C*'s estate is that of *B* or *C*, whichever is shorter. *B* has a reversion in a life estate in a possibility of reverter in a life estate.

6

The Rule Against Perpetuities

> No interest is good unless it must vest, if at all, not later than twenty-one years after some life in being at the creation of the interest.
>
> —*John Chipman Gray*

The Rule Against Perpetuities (RAP) is applied at the time of the conveyance after the interests and estates have been identified and all other rules have been applied. It is not a rule to limit the duration of interests; it is focused only on preventing future interests from vesting too remotely. It takes into consideration facts that *actually* exist at the time of the conveyance and any facts that *hypothetically* could occur after the conveyance, not facts that actually occur after the conveyance. It invalidates interests that have a chance to vest too remotely when considering all the facts at the time of conveyance and all the various hypothetical facts that could occur afterward, even if subsequent actual events show that these interests do not vest too remotely. For many years, the common law RAP was applied "remorselessly" and mechanically by courts, sometimes leading to bizarre results not intended by the drafter or justified by policy. As a result, in most jurisdictions today it has been modified by variations of "wait-and-see" statutes, cy pres, and the Uniform Statutory Rule Against Perpetuities. Still, to understand this most difficult area of the law, it is important to start with the common law rule. This book focuses only on that rule as summarized in the quotation from John Chipman Gray above.

A. ELEMENTS

1. *Must Vest*

In particular, the rule is used to invalidate contingent remainders, executory interests, and interests subject to open that vest too remotely. These interests must vest within a certain time period, if they vest at all, or else they will be invalid. On the other hand, all reversionary interests (because they are interests that remain in the grantor), present interests *not* subject to open, and vested remainders *not* subject to open are considered vested for purposes of the rule.

How does an interest vest? Contingent remainders become vested when the grantee is born and ascertained and the remainder is not otherwise subject to a condition precedent. Executory interests only vest in possession (that is, when they become present interests) or when they are transformed into vested remainders. Present interests subject to open and vested remainders subject to open vest for purposes of the rule when the last member of the class takes a vested interest.

It is the quality of being vested, not merely possessed, that makes the interest valid.

> *Example:* Where O conveys Blackacre "to A for as long as Blackacre is used as a farm," A has a present interest in fee simple determinable. O has a reversionary interest called a possibility of reverter. Both interests are valid. Even though it may be five hundred years before Blackacre ceases to be used as a farm and O's possibility of reverter is transformed into a present interest, O's interest is vested from the time of its creation. If O then conveys her possibility of reverter to B, B will have a possibility of reverter that continues to be vested as a reversionary interest even though it may not vest in possession for another five hundred years.
>
> *Example:* Where O conveys "to A for as long as Blackacre is used as a farm, then to B and his heirs," the attempted conveyance to B is an executory interest. Since executory interests do not vest until they vest in possession, B's executory interest is invalid because it may vest too late. (Note that this invalidity could have been avoided by creating a possibility of reverter in O and then transferring the possibility of reverter to B as in the first example above.)

Pay particular attention to the fact that the interests of the members of a class are dependent on each other. None of these interests at the time of the conveyance can have the possibility of vesting too remotely or else all the interests of the members of the class are invalid. Thus, vested remainders subject to open may be invalid if even one executory interest in one member of the class might vest too remotely.

> *Example:* Where O conveys "to A for life, then to A's grandchildren who graduate from college," and A has two grandchildren at the time of the conveyance, both of whom have graduated from college, the

attempted interest in A's grandchildren is invalid because the interest of another grandchild might vest too late.

How does one know that the interest in the grandchildren is invalid? One imagines a case where, if the RAP were not applied, one of the grandchildren could take a vested interest too late. If the RAP is not applied, A's two grandchildren share a vested remainder subject to open in a fee simple subject to executory limitation and A's unborn grandchildren have an executory interest in fee simple absolute. If two grandchildren, X and Y, are born after O's conveyance and X graduates from college, and then all lives in being at the time of the conveyance die (including A), X will have a present interest subject to open in a fee simple subject to executory limitation (shared with the heirs of the other grandchildren who have died), and Y will have an executory interest in fee simple absolute. It is possible for Y to graduate from college more than twenty-one years later. If so, then Y's interest will vest too late. Therefore, because of this possibility of remote vesting of one member of the class, the other members of the class who would have had a vested interest from the beginning of the conveyance have no interest at all under the RAP. Their interest is void ab initio. What O has conveyed is a present interest in a life estate to A, and O has left a reversion in a fee simple absolute in himself.

2. *If at All*

It is not necessary that a future interest vest for it to be valid. It merely must not be able to vest too remotely, even if the chance of this happening is very unlikely and, in some cases, even medically impossible.

> *Example:* Where O conveys "to A for life, then to the children of A for the life of the survivor, then, on the death of the last surviving child of A, to the first grandchild of A," and A is eighty years old and has two children but no grandchildren at the time of the conveyance, the contingent remainder in the grandchild of A is invalid.

It is obvious that as a practical matter A will have no more children, and if there is a grandchild, it will be born to one of A's two children. If the RAP is not applied, on birth this grandchild would receive a vested interest well within the perpetuities period (by being born to a life in being). So why is the remainder interest in the first grandchild of A invalid under the RAP? The medically impossible is considered legally possible here. It is hypothesized that, after O's conveyance, A could have another child, then all the lives in being at the time of the conveyance could die, then more than twenty-one years later this after-born child of A could have A's first grandchild. The vesting of this grandchild's interest would be too late under the RAP; therefore, the remainder in the first grandchild of A is invalid because of this legal possibility. This example of an invalid interest under the RAP has been called the *fertile octogenarian rule.*

3. *Not Later than Twenty-One Years*

The perpetuities period is twenty-one years after a certain point in time. This twenty-one-year period may be increased by one or more actual periods of gestation but only if the child in each period is born alive.

> *Example:* Where *O* devises "to my great-grandchildren when my first grandchild reaches twenty-one and no later," the executory interest in *O*'s great-grandchildren is valid.

This is true even though at *O*'s death his wife could be pregnant with their first child, *A*, who could die thirty years later leaving his twenty-five-year-old wife pregnant with their first child, *B*, who could become pregnant with her first child, *C*, when she reaches twenty-one. In this hypothetical *O*'s child, *A*, is considered a life in being at the time of the devise, despite the fact that his birth occurs after *O*'s death. Therefore, *A*'s death is the earliest point in time when all lives in being at the creation of the interest can die. At this point, if all lives in being at the creation of the interest have died, the twenty-one-year period starts to run. The grandchild, *B*, when she reaches twenty-one, does so more than twenty-one years after *A*'s death, but the extra time is permitted for the actual period of her gestation. The great-grandchild, *C*, is born after the end of the twenty-one-year period, but again the extra time is permitted for the actual period of his gestation. Thus *C*'s interest vests in this hypothetical within the twenty-one-year period envisaged by the RAP.

Note that the class closing rule, which keeps a class open until it closes naturally only if there is no member (or representative of a member) of the class at the time designated for distribution, is a rule of construction. In the preceding example, there may be no great-grandchildren at the time that the first grandchild reaches twenty-one, and ordinarily under the class closing rule, the class of great-grandchildren would close only naturally. However, this class closing rule is not applicable here because the grantor has manifested an intent to close the class no later than the time the first grandchild reaches twenty-one. Therefore, since no great-grandchild may take an interest more than twenty-one years after the death of a life in being at the creation of the interest (except for periods of actual gestation, which are permitted as shown above), the interest in the great-grandchildren is valid under the RAP.

Note also that such techniques as artificial insemination, in vitro fertilization, and frozen embryos are not considered under the common law RAP although they may be considered by statutory modifications.

4. *After Some Life in Being at the Creation of the Interest*

This phrase is perhaps the hardest to understand in the RAP. The twenty-one-year period is measured from the hypothesized deaths of all persons alive at the time of the conveyance. Yes, you read it right: *all* persons alive at the time of the conveyance. Remember that the time of conveyance is delivery of the deed if it is inter vivos and the death of a testator if it is testamentary. Any person alive at this time is included in the designation "lives in being." Once one has understood the significance of this phrase, one must then hypothesize different situations in which all lives in being at the time of the conveyance could die, and if there is any possibility that an interest might vest beyond twenty-one years after one of these situations, the interest is void under the RAP.

Since it is possible that a life in being may die at any time, it is important to find a way of ensuring that a contingent remainder or executory interest or interest subject to open becomes vested, if at all, within the proper period. This is done by finding a measuring life (or lives). The rule does not void a future interest if there is a measuring life (or lives) that ensures that the interest will not vest beyond the appropriate period designated by the rule.

Example: In the example in section 3, where *O* devises "to my great-grandchildren when my first grandchild reaches twenty-one and no later," the children alive at the time of the testator's death (including those in gestation and later born alive) are the measuring lives. These children are lives in being because the testator's death is the time of the conveyance. On the death of these children we know that all grandchildren will have had to be born or to be in gestation, thus ensuring that the time for vesting of the great-grandchildren's interest must take place on or before twenty-one years (plus actual periods of gestation) from the date of the children's deaths, if it takes place at all.

Example: Where *O* conveys "to *A* for life, then to *B* if *C* gets married," *B* has a valid contingent remainder because *B* or her grantees or heirs stand ready to take whenever the condition is satisfied and the life estate terminates. *B*'s interest cannot vest beyond the death of *A* because of the Destructibility of Contingent Remainders Rule, and therefore *A* is a measuring life which ensures that the perpetuities period is not exceeded before *B*'s interest vests. Note that even if the Destructibility Rule does not operate, *B*'s interest is still valid because it cannot vest beyond the death of *C* (who is therefore a measuring life) since *C* will marry or not within his own lifetime.

Example: Where *O* conveys "to *A* and her heirs, but if *A*'s first son (as yet unborn) gets married, to *B*," *B* has no interest. What may be identified as an executory interest in *B* is void under the RAP because it may conceivably vest beyond the perpetuities period, whether it in fact does so or not. The following hypothetical, conceived as a situation that could occur if the RAP were not applied, demonstrates this possibility: *A*'s first son, *B*'s daughter, and *W* may be born after the conveyance. *O*, *A*, *B*, and all lives in being may die. *A*'s first son (as *A*'s heir) would continue to hold *A*'s present interest in fee simple subject to executory limitation, and *B*'s daughter (as *B*'s heir) would continue to hold *B*'s executory interest in fee simple absolute. Then, twenty-two years later, *A*'s first son might marry *W*. This would satisfy the condition subsequent beyond the perpetuities period, and *B*'s executory interest (now held by *B*'s daughter) would vest too late. Therefore, under the RAP the executory interest is void ab initio.

Special note on conditions: In this last example, since the language of condition ("but if") is conditional, the condition is also void, and *A* has a fee simple absolute at the time of the conveyance. If the language of condition in this conveyance had been durational, such as "to *A* and her heirs as long as *A*'s first son (as yet unborn) remains unmarried, then to *B*," the executory interest would still have been void, but the durational condition would have remained. *A* would have had a fee simple determinable. This distinction between estates determinable and estates subject to condition subsequent is important for determining what interests remain after the RAP has voided an interest.

Sometimes the measuring lives are specified in the conveyance. If they are, they must be reasonable in number.

> *Example:* Where *O* conveys "to *A* and his heirs as long as Blackacre is used as a farm, then to *B* if *X*, *Y*, or *Z* (three healthy children) is alive," *X*, *Y*, and *Z* are a reasonable number of measuring lives which ensure that *B*'s interest will not vest too remotely. The executory interest in *B* is valid under the RAP.

In the above example, there are two conditions precedent on *B*'s executory interest becoming a present interest: the failure to use Blackacre as a farm and the occurrence of this failure during the lifetimes of *X*, *Y*, and *Z*. If the condition precedent were only the failure to use Blackacre as a farm, *B*'s interest could vest beyond the perpetuities period because a holder of *B*'s interest who is not a life in being at the creation of the interest could take a present interest five hundred years from the time of the conveyance. Therefore, in this conveyance if it omits the phrase "if *X*, *Y*, or *Z*," the executory interest is void ab initio, and the conveyance is valid only as to *A*, giving *A* a present interest in fee simple determinable.

It should be apparent from this discussion that the focus of attention when applying the RAP is on the *interest* created in the conveyance and not on the *person* to whom it is conveyed. Once an interest is shown to be incapable of vesting beyond the period of the rule it does not matter who holds the interest nor for how long thereafter it is valid. Before an interest is vested, it does not matter that it is held at some point by a life in being; if it has the possibility of being held by a non-life in being and vesting beyond the perpetuities period, it is void ab initio.

B. A SYSTEM TO DETERMINE VALIDITY UNDER THE RAP

Validity of an interest under the RAP can be determined by asking four questions. If the answer to any of these questions is affirmative, the interest is valid. If not, the interest is most likely invalid and merely needs a hypothetical example of an invalid situation to prove it.

Question 1: Must the vesting events, if they happen, all happen within the period of the rule? A vesting event is an event that must occur before the interest can vest. It may be birth or ascertainment of the interest holder or the occurrence of an event specified in a condition precedent. Where *O* conveys "to *A*, but if the Dolphins win a football game, then to *A*'s first child," and *A* has no children at the time of the conveyance, the executory interest in *A*'s first child is void ab initio because one of the vesting events might occur beyond the period of the rule. The vesting events are the birth of *A*'s first child and the Dolphins winning a football game. Although the first event will happen within the perpetuities period, if it happens at all, the second event may happen beyond the perpetuities period.

Question 2: Must the interest terminate within the period? A life estate measured by a life in being at the time of the conveyance must terminate within the period because the twenty-one years cannot start to run until the life estate is over. Where *O* conveys "to *A*, but if the Dolphins win a football game, then to *B* for life," the executory interest in *B* is valid. Although the Dolphins may not win a football game within the period of the rule, it is not possible for the executory interest in *B* to vest beyond the rule because it can only vest, if it does vest, during the lifetime of *B*, a life in being at the creation of the interest. On *B*'s death, *B*'s life estate terminates.

Question 3: If the Destructibility Rule is in operation within the jurisdiction, does the interest as a legal contingent remainder, not in a class nor transformable into an executory interest, follow only prior life estates that are measured by lives in being? Such a contingent remainder is destroyed by the Destructibility of Contingent Remainders Rule if it does not vest on or before the termination of the prior life estates. Therefore, it cannot vest beyond the perpetuities period. Where *O* conveys "to *A* for life, then to *B* for life, then to *C*'s first grandchild," and *C* has no children at the time of the conveyance, there is a valid contingent remainder in *C*'s first grandchild. This remainder must vest, if it vests at all, by the time *A* and *B*, who are lives in being, die, or it will be destroyed by the Destructibility Rule.

Question 4: In the case of a class gift, must the class close and the interests of every member of the class vest, if at all, within the period of the rule? Where *O* conveys "to *A* for life, then to the children of *A*'s first-born son who reach age fifteen" and *A* has no children at the time of the conveyance, the interest in the children of *A*'s first-born son is valid. If no children of *A*'s first-born son are born by the time *A*'s life estate terminates, the children's interest will be destroyed by the Destructibility Rule. If a child is born to *A*'s first-born son, that child (or representative) will become entitled to distribution no later than the death of *A*, thus closing the class on or before the death of all lives in being. No child of *A*'s first-born son would be able to take a vested interest more than fifteen years (plus any actual period of gestation) later.

Note that in Question 3, the Destructibility Rule will not guarantee validity in the case of a class gift. For example, *O*'s conveyance when *A* has no children "to A for life, then to the children of A who reach the age of fifty" creates an invalid (and therefore no) interest in the children. The hypothetical situation that proves the invalidity of the children's contingent remainder is that the first child of A might reach fifty when the second child is twenty (transforming the first child's interest into a vested remainder subject to open and the second child's interest into an executory interest), and then A and all lives in being at the time of the conveyance might die at this time and thirty years later the second child might reach fifty causing her interest to vest beyond the period of the rule.

Also the Destructibility Rule will not guarantee validity in the case of a contingent remainder transformable into an executory interest, such as O's conveyance when A has no children "to A for life, and then to the first child of A, but if that child is not born or does not reach fifty, then to B." B has an invalid (and therefore no) interest. Without applying the RAP at the time of the conveyance, B and the unborn first child of A would have had alternative contingent remainders. The hypothetical situation that proves the invalidity of B's interest is that the first child might be born (transforming that child's interest into a vested remainder in fee simple subject to executory limitation and transforming B's interest into an executory interest); then A, B, and all lives in being at the time of the conveyance might die at this time; and then thirty years later the first child of A might die, causing B's interest (now held by his heirs) to vest beyond the period of the rule.

Problem Set VI

The problems in this section ask for a description of an interest or an estate. The answers for interest are:

    A. present interest
    B. executory interest
    C. reversion
    D. contingent remainder
    E. right of reentry
    F. vested remainder
    G. possibility of reverter
    H. vested remainder subject to open
    I. none
    J. none of the above is correct

The answers for estate are:

    A. term of years
    B. term of years determinable
    C. life estate
    D. life estate pur autre vie
    E. life estate determinable
    F. life estate subject to condition subsequent
    G. life estate subject to executory limitation

H. fee simple absolute
I. fee simple determinable
J. fee simple subject to condition subsequent
K. fee simple subject to executory limitation
L. none
M. none of the above is correct

Problems

O conveys "to *A* and his heirs, but if the property ceases to be used for agricultural purposes, to *B* and his heirs."

501. What is *A*'s estate?

O conveys "to *A* for life, then to *A*'s children for the life of the survivor, then to their children for the life of their survivor, then to *B* and his heirs." *A*'s first child, *X*, is born two years after *O*'s conveyance. Then *O* dies.

502. What is *A*'s unborn children's interest?
503. What is *A*'s unborn grandchildren's interest?
504. What is *B*'s interest?

O conveys "to *A* and his heirs for as long as the property is used as a tavern, then to *B* and her heirs." *O* then conveys all remaining interest that he has in the property "to *C* and his heirs."

505. What is *A*'s estate?
506. What is *C*'s interest?

O conveys "to my children who reach twenty-one and their heirs." *O* has no children at the time of the conveyance. Thirty years later he marries a bride who is eighteen years old, and he then dies two months later with his wife pregnant with his only child. The child, *B*, is born ten months later and reaches age twenty-one.

507. What is *B*'s estate?

O conveys "to the children of *A* who reach thirty." *A* is dead at the time of the conveyance and his children are ages three and twenty-nine.

508. What is *A*'s children's interest?

O conveys "to the children of *A* who reach thirty." *A* is alive at the time of the conveyance and has two children ages twenty-five and twenty-nine.

509. What is *A*'s children's interest?

O conveys "to the children of *A* who reach thirty." *A* is alive at the time of the conveyance and has two children, *X*, age twenty-five, and *Y*, age thirty-two.

510.   What is X's interest?

O devises Blackacre "to my great-grandchildren when my first grandchild reaches twenty-one." At O's death, O's wife is pregnant with his first and only child, A, who is born four months later and dies at the age of thirty, leaving his twenty-five-year-old wife pregnant with their only child, B, who is born five months later and subsequently, at age eighteen, bears a son, C. C's mother, B, reaches twenty-one.

511.   What is C's estate?

O conveys "to all my grandchildren who shall be born in the next thirty years." O has no grandchildren at this time.

512.   What is the unborn grandchildren's interest?

O devises "to all my grandchildren who shall be born in the next thirty years." The grandchildren of O are as yet unborn.

513.   What is the unborn grandchildren's interest?

O devises "to my great-grandchildren who reach the age of twenty-one and their heirs." O's children all die before O's death. O dies leaving two grand-children, A and B.

514.   What is the great-grandchildren's interest?
515.   What is O's heirs' interest?

O conveys "to A for life, then to A's widow for life, then to A's children then living and their heirs." A is married at the time of the conveyance.

516.   What is A's widow's interest?
517.   What is A's children's interest?

O conveys "to A and his heirs as long as Blackacre is used as a farm." O then conveys any interest he has remaining in Blackacre "to B and his heirs."

518.   What is A's estate?
519.   What is B's interest?

O conveys Blackacre "to my wife, A, for life, then to my niece, B, for the life of X, and if X dies, to the daughters of John and Elizabeth Jay." John and Elizabeth Jay are each ninety years old. One year later, O dies. Two years later A dies, leaving the Jays, their two fifty-year-old daughters, and B surviving her. B does not have children.

520.   What is the interest of the two living daughters?
521.   What is O's heirs' interest?

O conveys "to my wife, A, for life, then to my niece, B, and her heirs, and if she dies without issue, to the then living daughters of John and Elizabeth

Jay." John and Elizabeth Jay are each ninety years old. One year later, *O* dies. Two years later, *A* dies, leaving the Jays, their two fifty-year-old daughters, and *B* surviving her. *B* does not have children.

522.   What is the interest of the two living daughters?

O conveys "to my wife, *A*, for life, then to my niece, *B*, for the life of the survivor of *B* or *B*'s children, then to the then living daughters of John and Elizabeth Jay." John and Elizabeth Jay are each ninety years old. One year later, *O* dies. Two years later, *A* dies, leaving the Jays, their two fifty-year-old daughters, and *B* surviving her. *B* does not have children.

523.   What is the interest of the two living daughters?

O conveys "to my wife, *A*, for life, then to my niece, *B*, and her heirs, and if she dies without issue, to the daughters of John and Elizabeth Jay." John and Elizabeth Jay are each ninety years old. One year later, *O* dies. Two years later, *A* dies, leaving the Jays, their two fifty-year-old daughters, and *B* surviving her. *B* does not have children.

524.   What is the interest of the two living daughters?

O conveys "to *A* and his heirs, but if the property is ever used as a bar, to *X* for life."

525.   What is *X*'s interest?

O has one child, *A*, but no grandchildren living at her death. *O* devises Blackacre "to my grandchildren."

526.   What is the unborn grandchildren's interest?

O has one child, *A*, but no grandchildren living. *O* conveys Blackacre "to my grandchildren."

527.   What is the unborn grandchildren's interest?

O has one child, *A*, and two grandchildren, *X* and *Y*, living. *O* conveys Blackacre "to my grandchildren."

528.   What is the interest of *X* and *Y*?

O devises Blackacre "to *A* for life and then to *A*'s children who shall reach the age of thirty." At the time of *O*'s death, *A* has one two-year-old child, *X*.

529.   What is *X*'s interest?

O conveys "to *A* and his heirs." *A* then conveys "to *B* and her heirs as long as the property is used as a farm."

530.   What is *A*'s interest?

O conveys "to the children of *A* who are living when the next president of the United States will be elected."

531.   What is the interest of the children of *A*?

O conveys "to *A* for life, then, one day later, to the children of *A* who reach thirty." *A* is alive at the time of the conveyance and has two children, *M* and *N*, ages seven and thirty-one, respectively.

532.   What is *N*'s interest?

O conveys "to *A* for life, then to the great-grandchildren of *B*." *B* has two children, *X* and *Y*, and one great-grandchild, *Z*.

533.   What is *Z*'s interest?

O conveys "to *A* and his heirs as long as the property is used for purposes other than the selling of alcohol; otherwise to *A*'s heirs."

534.   What is *A*'s estate?

O devises Blackacre "to *A* for life, then to *A*'s children who shall reach the age of twenty-five." When *O* dies, *A* is ninety-four years old and has four living children, *W*, *X*, *Y*, and *Z*, all of whom are over thirty.

535.   What is the interest of the four children?

O conveys "to *A* for life, then to such and only such of *A*'s children as shall attain the age of thirty and their heirs, then to *C* and his heirs." At the time of the conveyance, *B* is *A*'s only child and is nineteen years old.

536.   What is *C*'s interest?

O plans to retire with his wife. His children, with the exception of one who has died, all are grown and making their own way. Some of them have given him grandchildren, but none of the grandchildren has reached eighteen. *O* then conveys "to my wife, *A*, for life, then to my children for the life of their survivor, then to my grandchildren who reach eighteen and their heirs."

537.   What is the living grandchildren's interest?

O conveys "to *A* and his heirs to have until twenty-one years and one day after *A*'s death, then to *B* and his heirs."

538.   What is *B*'s interest?

O conveys Blackacre "to *A* for twenty years, then to *B* for life, then to the heirs of *B*, but if the land is ever used to sell alcohol as a commercial enterprise, to *C* and his heirs."

539.   What is *B*'s estate?

O conveys "to *A*'s grandchildren who shall be living twenty-one years after the deaths of Alice and Mary."

540.   What is the interest of *A*'s grandchildren?

O devises "to my grandchildren." At the time of his death, *O*'s wife is pregnant with their only child, who is born four months later.

541.   What is the interest of *O*'s grandchildren?

O conveys "to *A* for life, then at least one year later to *B*'s grandchildren." *B* has one child, *X*, and no grandchildren at the time of the conveyance.

542.   What is the interest of *B*'s grandchildren?

O conveys "to *A* for life, then at least one year later to *B*'s children." *B* has no children at the time of the conveyance.

543.   What is the interest of *B*'s children?

O devises "to *A* for life, then at least one year later to my grandchildren who reach twenty-five." *O* has one child, *X*, and no grandchildren at the time of the conveyance.

544.   What is the interest of *O*'s grandchildren?

O conveys "to *A* for life, then at least one year later to *B*'s grandchildren for the life of *B*." *B* has no descendants.

545.   What is the interest of *B*'s grandchildren?

O conveys "to *A* for life, then one year later to *B*'s children as long as the land is used as a farm." *B* has no children at the time of the conveyance.

546.   What is the interest of *B*'s children?

O conveys "to *A*'s grandchildren, no matter when they should be born." *A* has two grandchildren, *X* and *Y*.

547.   What is the interest of *X* and *Y*?

O conveys "to *A* for life, then to *B* for life, then, if the old oak tree falls, to *C* and her heirs."

548.   What is *C*'s interest?

O conveys Blackacre "to *A* and *B* as tenants in common." *A* then conveys "to *X* until Blackacre is used as a tavern, and then to *Y*." *B* then conveys "to *Y* and his heirs." *Y* then conveys "to *X* until Blackacre is used as a tavern."

These conveyances all take place within the span of one year, and in the following year Blackacre is used as a tavern.

549.   What is *X*'s interest?

O conveys "to *A* for life, then to *A*'s children for the life of their survivor, then to *B* if *B* is then alive, and to *B*'s heirs if *B* is not then alive." *A* has no children.

550.   What is the interest of *B*'s heirs?

O devises Blackacre "to such of my descendants as shall be living twenty-one years and two months after my death." *O* dies leaving two children, *A* and *B*, as his only descendants and heirs. *A* has a child, *C*, and then dies five years later, devising all her property "to my friend, *X*." *B*, *C*, and *X* are all alive twenty-one years and two months after the death of *O*.

551.   What is *B*'s interest twenty-one years and two months after *O*'s death?

O conveys "to *A* for life, then to *B*'s first son for life, then, if *B*'s first son gets married, to *C* and her heirs." *B*'s first son, *X*, is born three years later.

552.   What is *C*'s interest?

O conveys "to *A* for life, then to the grandchildren of *B*." At the time of the conveyance, *B* has one child, *C*, who has no children. Two years later, *C* bears a child, *X*. Then *A* dies. Then two years later, *C* bears another child, *Y*. Then *B* dies. Then *C* bears another child, *Z*.

553.   What is *Y*'s interest?

O conveys "to *A* for life and then, one day later, to *B* for the life of *X*, then, if *X* dies in fewer than thirty years after the time of the conveyance, to *C*."

554.   What is *C*'s estate?
555.   What is *B*'s interest?

O conveys "to *A* for life, then to *A*'s widow for life, then twenty-five years after the termination of the life estates in *A* and *A*'s widow, to *B* for life."

556.   What is *B*'s interest?

O conveys "to *A* for twenty-five years, then to *B* as long as he does not use Blackacre as a farm; otherwise to *C*."

557.   What is *B*'s estate?

O devises "to *A* for life, then to *A*'s first son for life, then to *C* and his heirs if my first grandchild is a girl." *O* has one child, *X*, but *A* has no children at the time of the devise.

558. What is *C*'s interest?

O conveys "to *A* for life, then five years later to *B* for life as long as Blackacre is used as a farm, then to *C* and her heirs."

559. What is *B*'s estate?
560. What is *C*'s interest?

O conveys "to *A* for ten years, then to *B* and his heirs when St. Thomas University or Chapman University wins its next football game."

561. What is *B*'s estate?

O conveys "to *A* and her heirs, and if *A* dies, then to *B* and his heirs, and if *B* dies without issue, then to *C* and her heirs." At the time of the conveyance, *A*, *B*, and *C* each have a grandson, *X*, *Y*, and *Z*, respectively. One year later, *A*, *B*, and *C* each die in a car crash, leaving their grandsons as their only heirs.

562. What is *X*'s interest?
563. What is *Y*'s interest?
564. What is *Z*'s interest?

The day before *B*'s thirtieth birthday, *O* conveys "to *A*'s children who reach the age of thirty." *A* is impotent and on his deathbed. *B* is *A*'s only child. The next day, *B* reaches thirty. Then *A* dies.

565. What is *B*'s interest?

O conveys "to *A* for life, then to the children of *B* who reach twenty-two for the life of the survivor, then to the heirs of *A*." *B* has two children, *X* and *Y*, ages eighteen and twenty, respectively. Three years later *A* dies, leaving *Z* as her only heir.

566. What is *Y*'s interest?

O conveys "to *A* for life, then to the first child of *A* if that child reaches twenty-five, but if that child does not reach twenty-five, then to *C*." At the time of the conveyance, *A* has never had children. Five years later, *A* has her first child, *X*. Then *C* dies, leaving *Y* as her only heir. Then *O* dies, leaving *Z* as his only heir.

567. What is *X*'s estate?
568. What is *Z*'s interest?

O conveys "to *A* for the life of *M*, but if *A* dies without issue, then to the children of *B*." *B* dies two years later giving birth to her first child, *X*. One year after *X*'s birth, *A* dies, leaving his son, *H*, as his only heir.

569. What is *H*'s estate?

O conveys "to *A* and her heirs, but if *A* dies before *B*, then to *B* for life, then to the first child of *B* for life, then to the first grandchild of *B*." At the time of the conveyance, *B* has never had children. Two years later, *B* bears a daughter, *X*. Twenty years later, *X* bears a daughter, *D*.

570.   What is *D*'s interest?

O conveys "to *A* for life, then to the children of *A* for their joint lives, then to the issue of *B* then living for their joint lives, then to *B*'s widow for life, then to *C* and his heirs." At the time of the conveyance, *A* has one child in gestation. *A*'s child in gestation dies before birth. Two years later *A* successfully bears a child, *X*.

571.   What is *X*'s interest?
572.   What is *B*'s issue's interest?
573.   What is *B*'s widow's interest?
574.   What is *C*'s interest?

O conveys "to *A* for life, then to *B* for life, then twenty-two years after the death of *B*, to *C* if *C* is surviving."

575.   What is *C*'s interest?

O conveys "to *A* for life, then to *B* for life, then twenty-two years after the death of *B*, to *C*." One year later, *B* dies. Twenty-five years later, *C* conveys her interest "to *A*."

576.   What is *A*'s estate?

O conveys "to *A* for life, then for life to the first child of *A* to graduate from law school, then to *B* for life, then to *C* if the first child of *A* to graduate from law school does so before the age of twenty."

577.   What is *C*'s interest?

O conveys "to *A* for life, then, if *B*'s eldest son gets married, both to *B* for life and then to *C*, but, if *B*'s eldest son does not get married, to *D*." *B* has no children at the time of the conveyance.

578.   What is *C*'s interest?

O devises "to *A* for life, then to my children for the life of the survivor, then to my grandchildren." At the time of the devise, *O* has one child, *X*, and two grandchildren, *G* and *H*. Three years later, *X* has twins, *I* and *J*. Then *A* dies.

579.   What is *I*'s interest?

O conveys Blackacre "to *A* when Blackacre will be used as a farm." One year later, *O* uses Blackacre as a farm. Then *O* conveys any remaining interest she has in Blackacre "to *B*."

580.   What is *B*'s interest?

O conveys "to *A* for life, then to *B*'s eldest son for life, but if *B*'s eldest son gets married, then to *A*'s heirs instead of *B*'s eldest son." One year later, *B* bears her first son, *Y*. Two years later, *A* dies.

581.   What is *Y*'s estate?

O conveys Blackacre "to *A* for life, remainder to *A*'s children for the life of the survivor; otherwise to *A*'s heirs." *A* has no children at the time of the conveyance. One year later, *A* bears a son, *B*. Then *A* sells all her interest in Blackacre "to *X*."

582.   What is *X*'s interest?

O conveys "to *A* for life, then to *A*'s first son for life, then one year later to *A*'s first grandson for life, then to *B* for the life of *X*, then to *C* for life." *A*'s first son, *S*, is born two years after the conveyance, and *A*'s first grandson, *T*, is born eighteen years later.

583.   What is *T*'s interest?
584.   What is *B*'s interest?
585.   What is *C*'s interest?

O conveys "to *A* for life, then to *A*'s heirs for the life of the survivor, then to *B* for life, then to *B*'s heirs for the life of the survivor."

586.   What is the interest in *A*'s heirs?
587.   What is the interest in *B*'s heirs?

O conveys "to *A* for life, then to *A*'s heirs for the life of the survivor, then to *B* for life, then to *B*'s children who survive the termination of the preceding estates." At the time of the conveyance, *B* has one child, *X*. *B* dies one year later. Then *A* dies, leaving all interest in the property by will "to *X*." *A* has one intestate heir, *H*.

588.   What is *X*'s interest?

O conveys "to *A* for the life of *X*, and, if *X* dies, then to *B* for as long as *B* is alive, then to *C* if *C* gets married, but, if *C* divorces, then to *D* instead of *C*."

589.   What is *C*'s interest?

O devises Blackacre "to *A* and his heirs as long as *A* does not have a grandson, then to *B* for life, then to *C*." *O* leaves *L* as his only heir of the rest of his interest in Blackacre. Then *B* dies.

590.   What is *A*'s estate?
591.   What is *L*'s interest?

O conveys "to *A* for life, then to *B*'s children, but, if no child of *B* reaches twenty-five, then to *C*." *B* has no children at the time of the conveyance.

    592.   What is *C*'s interest?

O conveys "to *A* for the life of *X*, then to *B*'s children for the life of *B*, then, if Blackacre is ever used as a farm, both to *C* for life and then to *D*." *B* has no children.

    593.   What is the estate in *B*'s children?
    594.   What is *D*'s interest?

O conveys Blackacre "to the heirs of *A*'s first child." Two years later, *A* bears her first child, *X*. Then *O* conveys all remaining interest he has in Blackacre "to *X*."

    595.   What is *X*'s estate?

O devises "to my grandchildren." *O* has two children, *X* and *Y*, but no grandchildren. Two years later, *X* bears a son, *S*. Then four years later, *Y* bears a daughter, *D*. *O*'s heir is *H*.

    596.   What is *D*'s estate?

O conveys "to *A*'s first son, but, if *A*'s first son dies without issue, then to the now living daughters of *B*." At the time of the conveyance, *B* has two daughters, *X* and *Y*. Two years later, *A* bears her first son, *S*.

    597.   What is *S*'s estate?
    598.   What is *X*'s interest?

O conveys Blackacre "to *A* and his heirs." *A* dies leaving *S* as the only heir to his property but devising all his interest in Blackacre "to *B*."

    599.   What is *S*'s interest?

O conveys "to *A* for life, then to *A*'s children for the life of the survivor, then to *A*'s grandchildren for the life of the survivor, then to *A*'s heirs." *A* has one child, *S*. *S* has one child, *G*.

    600.   What is *G*'s interest?

Answers

    501.   *H. Fee simple absolute.* The condition subsequent may happen more than twenty-one years after *A*, *B*, and every other life in being are dead. *A* and *B* may have children, *X* and *Y*, respectively. All lives in being may die. *X* and *Y* would take their interests. The property may no longer be used for agricultural purposes more than twenty-one years later. At that point, *B*'s interest (now held

by *Y*) would vest too late. *B*'s interest is void under the RAP. *A* has a fee simple absolute since the condition is also eliminated with the invalidation of *B*'s interest.

502.   *B. Executory interest* in a life estate pur autre vie. On *O*'s conveyance, before application of the RAP, *A* has a present interest in a life estate, *A*'s children have a contingent remainder in a life estate pur autre vie (for the life of the survivor of the children), *A*'s grandchildren have a contingent remainder in a life estate pur autre vie, and *B* has a vested remainder in fee simple absolute. *A* is a measuring life since *A*'s children must take a vested interest by being born to *A*, if at all, within the lifetime of *A*, a life in being at the time of *O*'s conveyance. Therefore, the interest of this class is good under the RAP. On *X*'s birth, *X* takes a vested remainder subject to open in a life estate pur autre vie subject to executory limitation.

503.   *I. None.* What would be the contingent remainder of the grandchildren would vest when they are born. This could happen beyond the perpetuities period since they are not born to lives in being at the time of *O*'s conveyance: *A*'s child, *X*, and *B*'s child, *Y*, could be born after *O*'s conveyance. All lives in being at the time of the conveyance could die. *X* would hold a present interest in a life estate, and *Y* would inherit *B*'s vested remainder in fee simple absolute. The unborn grandchildren would continue to have a contingent remainder in a life estate pur autre vie. Then, more than twenty-one years later, *A*'s grandchild, *Z*, could be born. At this point, *Z*'s interest would vest too late.

504.   *F. Vested remainder* in fee simple. *B*'s interest vests at the time of the conveyance.

505.   *I. Fee simple determinable.* *B*'s interest is void under the RAP: After *O*'s attempted conveyance of an executory interest to *B* in fee simple absolute, *X* and *Y* could be born to *A* and *B* respectively. Then all lives in being at the time of the conveyance could die, and *X* and *Y* would take *A*'s and *B*'s interests. The property may cease to be used as a tavern more than twenty-one years later, causing *Y*'s interest to vest too late. Since the language of condition is durational, the condition subsequent is not invalidated, and *O* has a possibility of reverter.

506.   *G. Possibility of reverter* in fee simple absolute. *O*'s possibility of reverter does not change in nature when he conveys it. Note that it is vested from the beginning. Effectively, *C* gets the same interest as *B*, except that it is valid by being created first as a possibility of reverter.

507.   *H. Fee simple absolute.* *O* is the measuring life to ensure that his children's executory interest vests within the perpetuities period. We may hypothesize that *B*, a child in gestation, may conceivably take beyond an actual twenty-one years from *O*'s death. His mother may not be a life in being, and when his father dies all lives in being may be dead. Although *B*'s interest might not vest until twenty-one years and ten months later, the ten months would be an actual period of gestation and, therefore, the interest is valid under the RAP.

508. *B. Executory interest* in fee simple absolute. There will be no more children born; therefore, the children now alive are their own measuring lives.

509. *I. None. O* attempted to convey an executory interest. It is invalid under the RAP: The two living children may die before reaching thirty. *A* may have another child and *O* may have a child, and then all lives in being at the time of the conveyance, including *O* and *A*, may die, *O*'s child would inherit her parent's interest. Then *A*'s child would reach thirty more than twenty-one years later. The last child would take beyond the perpetuities period.

510. *B. Executory interest* in fee simple absolute. This executory interest is subject to the condition precedent that the child reach thirty. Since the older child, *Y*, is entitled to distribution at the time of the conveyance, the class is closed and the only child who has an executory interest is the younger child, *X*, who will take, if at all, within the perpetuities period.

511. *L. None.* If *O*'s first grandchild reaches twenty-one before there are any great-grandchildren, there are no members of the class at the time designated for distribution and the class of great-grandchildren remains open until the deaths of all the grandchildren. Since a grandchild who is not a life in being at the time of *O*'s death may have a child more than twenty-one years after the death of every life in being, that child's interest would vest beyond the perpetuities period. Therefore, the devise to the great-grandchildren is void under the RAP. To demonstrate, let us assume that *A* is born, then *A*'s child is born, then *A*, *O*, and all lives in being die, then *A* has a child (*O*'s grandchild) who reaches twenty-one before any of *O*'s great-grandchildren are born, and then *O*'s first great-grandchild is born more than twenty-one years after the death of all lives in being. At this point, the first great-grandchild's interest would vest too late.

    Since the Rule of Convenience, which regulates class closings, is only a rule of construction that gives way to a contrary intent in the grantor, a devise by *O*, to his great-grandchildren when his first grandchild reaches twenty-one *and no later*, would be valid. By this devise *O* would exclude all great-grandchildren born after the designated time. The designated time is no more than twenty-one years (plus any actual period of gestation) after the death of a child of *O*, and every child of *O* is a life in being. *O*'s child, *A*, born four months after *O*'s death, is considered a life in being. The first grandchild would not be able to reach twenty-one more than twenty-one years after the death of this child (except for a gestation period, which is permitted). All great-grandchildren born before this time would have an executory interest in fee simple that would vest in possession at the time the first grandchild reaches twenty-one, which is within the perpetuities period.

512. *I. None. O* might have children; all the lives in being, including *O*, might die; then *O*'s children might inherit *O*'s present interest in fee simple subject to executory limitation; then *O*'s children who were not alive at the time of the conveyance might give birth to *O*'s grandchildren twenty-two years later within the thirty-year

period of the conveyance. The grandchildren's interest would vest beyond the perpetuities period and would therefore be void under the RAP.

513. *B. Executory interest* in fee simple absolute. *O* cannot have any more children. He is dead. Therefore, the children are the measuring lives of any grandchildren who are born—that is, a grandchild cannot be born more than twenty-one years after the death of all lives in being because a grandchild will be born to a life in being.

514. *B. Executory interest* in fee simple absolute. *A* and *B* are the measuring lives since no great-grandchild can be born after they are dead and, therefore, no great-grandchild can reach twenty-one more than twenty-one years (plus any actual period of gestation) after the death of all lives in being.

515. *A. Present interest* in fee simple subject to executory limitation to fill the gap before the great-grandchildren take. This interest remains in *O* when the devise becomes effective at the moment of her death and is at that moment inherited from her by her heirs at her death. The heirs take by inheritance, not by devise.

516. *D. Contingent remainder* in a life estate. Since *A* may lose or divorce his present wife and remarry, his widow is presently unascertained.

517. *I. None.* This is an example of what is called the "unborn widow" rule. The attempted conveyance of a contingent remainder in fee simple absolute to the children is invalid because, after the conveyance, *A* and *O* may have children and *A*'s widow may be born and marry *A*, then *A* and all lives in being at the creation of the interest may die and *A*'s widow may hold a present interest in a life estate for twenty-two years, while *A*'s children continue to hold a contingent remainder (condition precedent is survival of the widow) and *O*'s children inherit and hold *O*'s reversion in fee simple absolute, and then *A*'s widow may die and the children's interest would vest after the perpetuities period is over. Their interest is thus void under the RAP.

518. *I. Fee simple determinable.* The RAP does not prevent interests from extending indefinitely into the future. It merely prevents them from vesting too remotely.

519. *G. Possibility of reverter* in fee simple absolute. *O* retains a possibility of reverter in himself in the first conveyance and transfers it to *B* in the second. If *O* had attempted to create a future interest (executory interest) in *B* in the same conveyance to *A*, *B*'s interest would have been void under the RAP. The possibility of reverter, on the other hand, is always vested for purposes of the RAP.

520. *H. Vested remainder subject to open* in a fee simple subject to executory limitation. At the time of the conveyance, *A* has a life estate. *B* has a vested remainder in a life estate pur autre vie. The words "if *X* dies" are superfluous since they merely refer to the ending of the preceding estate. Therefore, the daughters of the Jays who are living take a vested remainder subject to open in a fee simple subject to executory limitation. It is subject to open because we must accept the fiction under the RAP that the Jays may have more children (fertile octogenarian rule). Unborn daughters have an

executory interest in fee simple absolute. The vested remainder subject to open is valid under the RAP because the class closes and vests in all its members no later than the death of Elizabeth Jay, who was a life in being at the time of O's conveyance. Taking into consideration the events that have occurred since the time of the conveyance, B and the Jays are still alive, and therefore the daughters still have a vested remainder subject to open.

521. *I. None.* There is no reversionary interest in O in the conveyance and therefore no interest to pass to O's heirs by inheritance.

522. *B. Executory interest* in fee simple absolute. At the time of the conveyance, A has a present interest in a life estate. B has a vested remainder in fee simple subject to executory limitation (condition subsequent being the death of B without issue). The daughters of the Jays have an executory interest subject to two conditions: the death of B without issue at that time and the survival of the daughter(s) to that time. Since these conditions cannot be satisfied beyond the death of B, who is a life in being at the time of O's conveyance, the executory interest in the daughters is valid under the RAP. If both conditions are satisfied, the interest in the daughter(s) will immediately vest (in possession if A is dead and as a vested remainder if A is alive). The interest in the daughters is not changed by the events subsequent to the conveyance. On A's death, B's interest becomes a present interest in fee simple subject to executory limitation.

523. *I. None.* On O's conveyance, A has a life estate, B has a vested remainder in a life estate pur autre vie, and O has a reversion in fee simple absolute. Before applying the RAP, the daughters of the Jays have a contingent remainder subject to the condition precedent that they be living at the time the life estate pur autre vie terminates. This interest is invalid under the RAP because after the conveyance B may have children, the Jays may have more daughters (according to the legal fiction), and O may have a child. Then all the lives in being at the time of the conveyance may die, B's children may hold the life estate pur autre vie and O's child may inherit and hold O's reversion for more than twenty-one years, and then the life estate pur autre vie may terminate, giving the daughters of the Jays who may then be living a present interest in fee simple absolute too late. Therefore, the interest of the daughters is invalid under the RAP.

524. *B. Executory interest* in fee simple absolute. At the time of the conveyance, A has a life estate, B has a vested remainder in fee simple subject to executory limitation, and the daughters have an executory interest. The daughters of the Jays have an executory interest that must vest, if at all, at the death of B. The class closes at that time if not before. Therefore, the executory interest is valid under the RAP.

525. *B. Executory interest* in a life estate. A has a fee simple subject to executory limitation. X's executory interest is valid under the RAP because it must vest, if at all, in X's lifetime. X's life estate is followed by a possibility of reverter in O.

526. *B. Executory interest* in fee simple absolute. There are no grand-
      children at the time of the devise when the interest is ready for
      distribution. Therefore, the class of grandchildren will close only
      on the death of *A*, *O*'s only child. The executory interest of each
      grandchild is valid under the RAP because it must vest in posses-
      sion, if at all, no later than the death (plus any actual period of
      gestation) of *A*, a life in being at the creation of the executory
      interest. Since the conveyance is a devise, no other children of
      O will be born.

527. *I. None.* The class of grandchildren may include any grandchild
      born to *O*. *O* may have another child, *B*. Then all lives in being at
      the time of the conveyance may die, and *B* may inherit *O*'s present
      interest in fee simple subject to executory limitation, and then
      more than twenty-one years later *B* may have a child whose inter-
      est would vest too late under the RAP. Therefore, *O*'s conveyance
      is invalid. *O* is left with his original interest, a present interest in
      fee simple absolute.

528. *A. Present interest* in fee simple absolute. The class of grandchil-
      dren is closed at the time of the conveyance because *X* and *Y* are
      born and entitled to distribution. *X* and *Y* take a present interest in
      fee simple absolute, sharing undivided half interests as tenants in
      common.

529. *I. None. A* takes a present interest in a life estate and *O*'s heir
      inherits *O*'s reversion in fee simple absolute. Before applying
      the RAP, *X* has a contingent remainder (conditional on *X* reach-
      ing thirty). *A*'s unborn children also have this contingent remain-
      der conditional on their being born and reaching thirty. *X*'s inter-
      est is invalid under the RAP because a member of the class of
      A's children may take a vested interest beyond the perpetuities
      period: *X* may reach thirty at which time his interest would trans-
      form into a vested remainder subject to open in a fee simple sub-
      ject to executory limitation and the unborn children's interest
      would transform into an executory interest in fee simple absolute;
      then *A* may have another child, *Z*, and *X* may have a child, *Y*; then
      all lives in being at the time of the conveyance may die, including
      A and *X*, with *Y* inheriting *X*'s interest that is now a present inter-
      est subject to open in a fee simple subject to executory limitation
      and with *Z* retaining an executory interest in fee simple absolute;
      then more than twenty-one years may pass before *Z* reaches thirty,
      at which time his interest would vest too late. Therefore, *A*'s chil-
      dren, including *X*, have nothing.

530. *G. Possibility of reverter* in fee simple absolute. It is prepared to cut
      short *B*'s fee simple determinable. The possibility of reverter is
      vested for purposes of the RAP. If *O* had conveyed "to *B* and
      her heirs as long as the property is used as a farm, then to *A*
      and his heirs," *A*'s executory interest would have been invalid
      under the RAP. The conveyance from *O* to *A* and then from *A*
      to *B* in this problem avoids such invalidity.

531. *I. None.* Since it is possible, even though very unlikely, that the
      next president will not be elected until more than twenty-one
      years after the death of every life in being at the creation of the

interest, the interest is void under the RAP: *O* and *A* may have children after *O*'s conveyance, then *O*, *A*, and all lives in being may die, and *O*'s child may inherit *O*'s present interest in fee simple subject to executory limitation, and then the next president may be elected more than twenty-one years later.

532. *I. None.* The attempted conveyance of an executory interest to *A*'s children is invalid under the RAP. The older child, *N*, would be capable of taking a present interest subject to open whenever the life estate in *A* terminates and one day passes. Until that time, when he would be entitled to distribution, however, the class of children is open to admit other children born after the conveyance. *A*'s child, *X*, might be born. *N* might have a child. Then *A* might die and the class would close. Then one day after *A*'s death, *N* would take a present interest subject to open, and *M* and *X* would have an executory interest. Then all lives in being at the creation of the interest might die. *N*'s child might inherit *N*'s present interest, and *X* would continue to have an executory interest. Then *X* might live to age thirty at which time his interest would vest beyond the perpetuities period. Therefore, the interest in all the children, including the older child, *N*, is void under the RAP.

533. *H. Vested remainder subject to open* in a fee simple absolute. Unborn great-grandchildren have an executory interest, but none will receive a vested present interest beyond the death of *A* (except for an actual period of gestation) because the Rule of Convenience closes the class at the time designated in the conveyance for great-grandchildren to take distribution, since *Z* or someone who holds his interest will be able to take distribution at that time. The time for distribution is at the death of *A*, a life in being; only great-grandchildren alive at or before this time (or in gestation and later born alive) will be included in the class, and only their interests will take at this time.

534. *I. Fee simple determinable. O* attempts to convey an executory inter-est to *A*'s heirs. The Rule in Shelley's Case does not apply, but the RAP does. Following the conveyance, one may hypothesize that *X*, a stranger, and *Y* and *Z*, *A*'s future heirs, may be born. *A* may sell her interest to *X*. Then *A*, *O*, and all lives in being may die. *Y* and *Z* would have an executory interest until alcohol might be sold on the property more than twenty-one years later. At this point, the executory interest would become a vested present inter-est too late. Therefore, the executory interest is void, leaving *A* with a fee simple determinable. The condition subsequent has durational language and therefore remains.

535. *I. None. A* has a present interest in a life estate and *O* has a rever-sion in fee simple absolute. Before applying the RAP, *A*'s born children have a vested remainder subject to open in a fee simple subject to executory limitation since they have already reached thirty. Their interest is invalid under the RAP because *A* may have another child (remember the fertile octogenarian rule) and the heirs of *W*, *X*, *Y*, and *Z* may be born; then all lives in being at the time of the conveyance may die and the heirs of *W*, *X*, *Y*, and *Z* may inherit their interests as a present interest subject to open in a

fee simple subject to executory limitation, with *A*'s afterborn child holding an executory interest in fee simple absolute; then the after-born child's executory interest, contingent on reaching twenty-five, may vest more than twenty-one years later, beyond the perpetuities period. Therefore, *A*'s children have nothing.

536. *F. Vested remainder* in fee simple absolute. Before applying the RAP, *A* has a present interest in a life estate, *A*'s children, including *B*, have a remainder in fee simple absolute contingent on their reaching thirty, *C* has an alternative contingent remainder (remember the Contingent Remainder Cannot Divest a Vested Remainder Rule) in fee simple absolute (subject to the implied condition that *A*'s children not reach thirty), and *O* has a reversion in fee simple absolute. The RAP invalidates the interest in *A*'s children because *B* may reach thirty and the interest in *A*'s children who have not reached thirty will transform into an executory interest at that time. *A* and *B* then may have children and die along with all other lives in being at the creation of the interest. *B*'s child would inherit a present interest subject to open in a fee simple subject to executory limitation, and *A*'s child would have an executory interest in fee simple absolute. *A*'s child then would reach thirty more than twenty-one years later and take a vested interest too late. Therefore, *C*'s interest (no longer forced to be a contingent remainder because of the existence of the interest in *A*'s children) is a vested remainder in fee simple absolute following *A*'s life estate.

537. *I. None. A* has a present interest in a life estate, *O*'s born children have a vested remainder subject to open in a life estate pur autre vie (for the life of the survivor of the children) subject to executory limitation, *O*'s unborn children have an executory interest in fee simple absolute, and *O* has a reversion in fee simple absolute. The attempted conveyance to *O*'s grandchildren, before application of the RAP, is a contingent remainder following (not cutting short) the life estate pur autre vie subject to executory limitation in the children. This interest is invalid because *O* may have a child, *X*, fertile octogenarian that he is, and *O*'s future devisee, *Y*, also may be born; then all lives in being at the time of the conveyance may die, leaving *X* with a present interest in a life estate and *Y* taking *O*'s reversion by will; then *X* may bear *O*'s grandchild more than three years later; and then the grandchild's contingent remainder may vest beyond the perpetuities period. Therefore, the interest in the whole class of *O*'s grandchildren is void. (If *O* devises rather than conveys inter vivos, his children would all be lives in being at the time the devise becomes effective (*O*'s death), and the grandchildren's interest would not become vested more than eighteen years (plus any actual period of gestation) after the death of every life in being at the creation of the interest. In such a case the grandchildren's contingent remainder would have been valid.)

538. *I. None.* Before application of the RAP, *A* would have a fee simple subject to executory limitation, and *B* would have an executory interest (which may vest only in possession) in fee simple absolute. *B*'s interest is void under the RAP because it may vest one

day beyond the perpetuities period. One could hypothesize that one hour after *O*'s conveyance the future heirs of *A* and *B* may be born. Then, one hour later, all lives in being might die, and the executory interest now in *B*'s heir would vest twenty-two hours too late. Remember that it is *B*'s interest that is void; *B* need not be holding the interest at the time it would vest. Therefore, *A* has a present interest in fee simple determinable, and *O* has a possibility of reverter in fee simple absolute.

539. *H. Fee simple absolute.* The RAP voids the interest in *C* and removes the accompanying condition. *B* has a present interest in a life estate, and, before application of the Rule in Shelley's Case, *B*'s heirs have a contingent remainder. Under the Rule in Shelley's Case, *B* takes a vested remainder in lieu of the interest in the heirs. This vested remainder in fee simple merges with *B*'s life estate to give *B* a present interest in a fee simple absolute subject to a term in *A* (remember the Piggyback Rule).

540. *B. Executory interest* in fee simple absolute. *O* has a present interest in fee simple subject to executory limitation. The interest in *A*'s grandchildren is valid under the RAP because the survivor of Alice and Mary is the measuring life.

541. *B. Executory interest* in fee simple absolute. The interest is valid under the RAP because *O*'s child, being in gestation and later born alive, is considered a life in being at the creation of the interest. The grandchildren cannot take an interest beyond the date of death of this life in being, their parent, except for a period of gestation, which would also be permitted.

542. *I. None. A* receives a present interest in a life estate followed by a reversion in fee simple absolute in *O*. The attempted creation of an executory interest in *B*'s grandchildren is invalid under the RAP because *B* may have another child after the conveyance and *O*'s future heir may be born, then all lives in being may die and *O*'s heir would inherit *O*'s reversion in fee simple subject to executory limitation as a present interest, and then *B*'s first grandchild may be born more than twenty-one years later, causing the fee simple subject to executory limitation in *O*'s heir to be cut short in favor of a vested present interest in the grandchild too late.

543. *B. Executory interest* in fee simple absolute. *A* receives a present interest in a life estate, followed by a reversion in *O* in fee simple subject to executory limitation. Since vesting on or after one year following *A*'s death is dependent only on the birth of the interest holder to a parent, *B*, who is a life in being, the interest in *B*'s children is valid. Vesting cannot occur more than twenty-one years after the deaths of *A* and *B*.

544. *I. None. A* receives a present interest in a life estate followed by a reversion in fee simple absolute in *O*. The attempted conveyance of an executory interest to the grandchildren is invalid. Vesting in each grandchild on or after one year following *A*'s death is dependent on the grandchild being born and reaching twenty-five. Although each grandchild would be born to *O*'s child, who is a life in being at the time of *O*'s death, it is possible that the condition (reaching twenty-five) might occur more than twenty-one years

after the death of every life in being. *X* may bear *O*'s grandchild after the conveyance, *O*'s heir also may be born, all lives in being may die, leaving *O*'s heir with a present interest in fee simple subject to executory limitation and *O*'s grandchild with an executory interest in fee simple absolute, and then *O*'s grandchild would reach twenty-five more than twenty-one years later. At this point the executory interest in *O*'s grandchild would vest too late.

545. *B. Executory interest* in a life estate pur autre vie. Since the interest will terminate no later than the death of *B*, a life in being, vesting of the interest in any member of the class cannot take place too late. The interest is valid. *O* has a reversion in fee simple subject to executory limitation (following *A*'s life estate) and a possibility of reverter (following the life estate pur autre vie in the grandchildren).

546. *B. Executory interest* in fee simple determinable. Since vesting in each child on or after one year following *A*'s death is dependent only on the birth of a child to *B*, who is a life in being, the interest is valid. The condition subsequent on the children's estate has nothing to do with the vesting of their interest. It only determines the length of time during which the estate will last. *O* has a reversion in fee simple subject to executory limitation (following *A*'s life estate) and a possibility of reverter in fee simple absolute (prepared to cut short the fee simple determinable in the children).

547. *I. None.* The Rule of Convenience, which would ordinarily close the class of grandchildren at the time of the conveyance in this case (because *X* and *Y* are entitled to distribution), does not operate. It is a rule of construction that gives way to the contrary intent expressed by the grantor that all his grandchildren should share in the conveyance. Since a grandchild could be born more than twenty-one years after the death of all lives in being, the whole gift is invalid. More specifically, the attempted conveyance before application of the RAP is a present interest subject to open in a fee simple subject to executory limitation in *X* and *Y*, and an executory interest in fee simple absolute in the unborn grandchildren. One could hypothesize that another child of *A* and the heirs of *X* and *Y* may be born, then all lives in being may die, leaving the heirs of *X* and *Y* holding the present interest, and then another grandchild may be born more than twenty-one years later. This grandchild would take a vested interest too late.

548. *D. Contingent remainder* in fee simple absolute. *A* has a present interest in a life estate, *B* has a vested remainder in a life estate, and *O* has a reversion in fee simple absolute. *C*'s interest must vest, if at all, on or before the deaths of *A* and *B*, who are both lives in being. If *C*'s interest has not vested by that time, it is destroyed by the Destructibility of Contingent Remainders Rule.

549. *I. None. O* conveys a present interest in fee simple absolute to *A* and *B. A* conveys her undivided half interest to *X* in fee simple determinable, because the attempted conveyance of an executory interest to *Y* is void under the RAP. This leaves a possibility of reverter in an undivided half interest in *A* in fee simple absolute.

B conveys his undivided half interest to *Y* in fee simple absolute. *Y* conveys his undivided half interest to *X* in fee simple determinable, leaving a possibility of reverter in *Y*. The condition precedent, which is the same for both possibilities of reverter, occurs. *X*'s estate is cut short, and *A* and *Y* are left with undivided half interests as tenants in common in fee simple absolute.

550.   *D. Contingent remainder* in fee simple absolute. *A* has a present interest in a life estate. *A*'s children have a contingent remainder in a life estate for the life of their survivor. *B* has a contingent remainder in fee simple absolute that must vest, if at all, while *B* is alive (according to the condition precedent). *B*'s heirs have an alternative contingent remainder that must vest, if at all, on *B*'s death. At that time the heirs will be determined and the condition precedent (*B*'s death before the death of the last child of *A*) will also be determined. None of the interests is invalid under the RAP.

551.   *A. Present interest* in fee simple absolute shared as a one-half undivided interest in a tenancy in common. *O*'s devise is invalid under the RAP because the executory interest in *O*'s descendants may vest more than twenty-one years after the death of all who were alive at the time of the devise. One can hypothesize that one day after *O*'s death, *B* might conceive a son, *S*, who might be born a month and a half later. (Such facts are considered possible within the confines of the RAP.) *S* would have an executory interest subject to open in fee simple absolute. Then within two months of *O*'s death, every life in being at the time of *O*'s death (the time at which the devise is effective) may die. *B*'s son would not take a vested interest until more than twenty-one years later. At this point, the interest would vest too late. Therefore, Blackacre does not pass by devise on *O*'s death. It passes by descent to *O*'s children, *A* and *B*. *A* conveys to *X*. *B* and *X* share as tenants in common.

552.   *I. None. A* has a present interest in a life estate, *B*'s first son has a contingent remainder (condition being the birth of *B*'s first son) in a life estate, and *O* has a reversion in fee simple absolute. The attempted conveyance of a contingent remainder (following the life estate in *B*'s first son) to *C* in fee simple absolute is invalid because *B*'s first son and the heirs of *O* and *C* may be born; then all lives in being may die, leaving *B*'s son holding a present interest in a life estate, *O*'s heir holding *O*'s reversion, and *C*'s heir holding *C*'s contingent remainder; and then *B*'s son may marry more than twenty-one years later, causing *C*'s interest (held by her heir) to vest too late.

553.   *I. None.* The interest created by *O* in *B*'s grandchildren is valid since no grandchild can take a vested interest later than *A*'s death by operation of the Destructibility of Contingent Remainders Rule if there are no grandchildren or by operation of the Rule of Convenience to close the class if there are grandchildren. At the time of the conveyance, *A* has a present interest in a life estate, and *B*'s grandchildren have a contingent remainder in fee simple absolute. On *X*'s birth, *X* has a vested remainder subject to open, and *B*'s grandchildren have an executory interest in fee simple absolute. *A*'s death entitles *X* to distribution, and the Rule of

Convenience closes the class. Only grandchildren who are alive (or in gestation and later born alive) at that time are entitled to take. *X* has a present interest in fee simple absolute.

554. *H. Fee simple absolute. A* has a present interest in a life estate, *O* has a reversion in fee simple subject to executory limitation, *B* has a springing executory interest in a life estate pur autre vie, followed by a possibility of reverter in *O* in fee simple absolute, and *C* has an executory interest in a fee simple absolute. *C's* interest cannot vest too late under RAP because (a) *X* may die before one day after *A's* death and before thirty years after the conveyance, in which case *C's* interest will vest one day after *A's* death, or (b) *X* may die after one day after *A's* death and before thirty years after the convey- ance, in which case *C's* interest will vest upon *X's* death, or (c) *X* may die after thirty years after the conveyance, in which case *C's* interest will never vest. There is no possibility of *C's* interest vesting too late.

555. *B. Executory interest* in a life estate pur autre vie.

556. *B. Executory interest* in a life estate. *B's* estate for life ends no later than the death of *B*, a life in being. Therefore, it is valid under the RAP. *A* has a present interest in a life estate, *A's* widow has a contingent remainder in a life estate, *O* has reversion in fee simple subject to executory limitation and a possibility of reverter following *B's* executory interest in a life estate.

557. *K. Fee simple subject to executory limitation. A* has a term of years, *B* has a present interest in a fee simple subject to executory limita- tion, *C* has an executory interest in fee simple absolute. *C's* interest is valid because it must vest, if it vests at all, no later than *B's* death. (*B* can use Blackacre as a farm only during his lifetime.)

558. *D. Contingent remainder* in fee simple absolute. *A* has a present interest in a life estate, *O* has a reversion in fee simple absolute, *A's* first son has a contingent remainder (condition being the birth of *A's* first son) in a life estate. *C's* contingent remainder following *A's* first son's life estate is valid because it vests upon the happen- ing of *O's* first grandchild being a girl and, since *O's* only child after his death (when *O* can have no more children) is a life in being at the creation of the interest, no grandchild can be born more than twenty-one years after the deaths of all lives in being since the grandchild must be born, if at all, to *X*, a life in being.

559. *G. Life estate subject to executory limitation. A* has a present interest in a life estate. *O* retains a reversion in fee simple subject to execu- tory limitation. *B* has a springing executory interest. *C* has an executory interest that springs (together with *B's*) from *O's* fee simple. *C* also has an executory interest that shifts from *B's* life estate. *C's* interest is valid because it becomes vested no later than five years after *A's* death, either as a vested remainder (ready to follow *B's* present interest in a life estate if it does not sooner cut short the life estate) or as a present interest (if *B's* life estate is over).

560. *B. Executory interest* in fee simple absolute.

561. *L. None. A* has a term of years. *O* retains a present interest in fee simple absolute. *B's* executory interest is invalid under the RAP

because St. Thomas or Chapman may win its next football game more than twenty-one years after the death of all lives in being. One may hypothesize that the heirs of *A*, *B*, and *O* (*X*, *Y*, and *Z*, respectively) may be born after *O*'s conveyance, then all lives in being may die (leaving *X* to inherit the term of years, *Z* to inherit *O*'s present interest in fee simple subject to executory limitation, and *Y* to inherit *B*'s executory interest in fee simple absolute), and then St. Thomas or Chapman may win its next football game more than twenty-one years later. At this point, *C*'s executory interest (now held by *Y*) would vest as a present interest too late.

562. *I. None.* At the time of the conveyance, *A* has a present interest in a life estate since the words "and her heirs, and if *A* dies" are the words of limitation (Subsumption Rule). When *A* dies, *X* takes nothing because *A*'s life estate is over.

563. *A. Present interest* in fee simple absolute. At the time of the conveyance, *B* had a vested remainder in fee simple subject to executory limitation. With the death of *A* it became a present interest, and with the death of *B* with issue it became a fee simple absolute and was inherited by *Y*.

564. *I. None.* *C*'s executory interest is destroyed by the failure of the condition precedent that *B* die without issue. *Z* has nothing to inherit.

565. *I. None.* The RAP invalidates *B*'s interest (the interest of all *A*'s children) because it is an interest of a class, one member of which may take a vested interest too late. One may hypothesize that *B* may die before turning thirty, *A* may have another child, *O*'s heir may be born, and then all lives in being may die. At this point, *O*'s heir would inherit *O*'s present interest in fee simple subject to executory limitation, and *A*'s second child would have an executory interest in fee simple absolute. Then *A*'s child may reach the age of thirty more than twenty-one years later, and the executory interest would vest as a present interest too late. Therefore, *O*'s conveyance is invalid ab initio.

566. *I. None.* Before application of the RAP, *O*'s conveyance gives *A* a present interest in a life estate, *B*'s children a contingent remainder in a life estate pur autre vie, and *A* (by operation of the Rule in Shelley's Case) a vested remainder in fee simple absolute. There is no merger between *A*'s two vested interests despite the existence of an intervening contingent remainder because of the exception for simultaneous creation. It is possible for a child of *B* to take a vested interest beyond the perpetuities period, and therefore the interest in *B*'s children is void under the RAP. One might hypothesize that *Y* reaches age twenty-two (her interest becoming a vested remainder subject to open, followed by *A*'s vested remainder in fee simple absolute) and she conveys her interest to *S*, someone born after *O*'s conveyance. *B* may have another child, *M*. All lives in being at the time of *O*'s conveyance may die, leaving *S* with a vested remainder subject to open in a life estate pur autre vie, *M* with an executory interest in a life estate pur autre vie, and *A*'s heir, *R*, also born after *O*'s conveyance, with a vested remainder in fee simple absolute. *M*'s executory interest would become a

present interest too late (more than twenty-one years later, when *M* reaches twenty-two). Therefore, *O*'s conveyance creates a life estate in *A* and a vested remainder in fee simple absolute in *A*. These interests merge to give *A* a present interest in fee simple absolute. When *A* dies, *Z* takes her interest.

567.   *H. Fee simple absolute.* At the time of the conveyance, the first child of *A* is unborn. Therefore, before application of the RAP, *A* has a present interest in a life estate, *O* has a reversion in fee simple absolute. *A*'s first child has a contingent remainder in fee simple subject to executory limitation, and *C* has an alternative contingent remainder (condition precedent being the failure of *A* to have a child) in fee simple absolute. If a child is born to *A*, that child's interest becomes a vested remainder in fee simple subject to executory limitation, and *C*'s interest (before application of the RAP) transforms into an executory interest in fee simple absolute. This classification is due to the Preference for Vesting Exception. The first child of *A* has a valid interest under the RAP because its interest can never vest later than its birth to a life in being. However, *C*'s interest is invalid under the RAP because *C*'s heir (*Y*) and *A*'s first child (*X*) may be born; then all lives in being may die, leaving *A*'s child with a present interest in fee simple subject to executory limitation and *C*'s heir with an executory interest in fee simple absolute; and then *A*'s first child may live more than twenty-one years after the death of every life in being and die before age twenty-five, causing *C*'s interest (now in *Y*) to vest too late. Since the language of condition ("if that child reaches twenty-five, but if that child does not reach twenty-five") is conditional, the condition is also eliminated. (Remember: words of condition are eliminated; words of duration remain.) *A*'s first child has a contingent remainder in fee simple absolute, and *O* has a reversion in fee simple absolute following *A*'s present interest in a life estate. When *X* is born, *X* takes a vested remainder in fee simple absolute, divesting *O*'s reversion.

568.   *I. None.* When *O*'s reversion is divested, there is nothing for *Z* to inherit.

569.   *D. Life estate pur autre vie.* On *O*'s conveyance, *A* has a present interest in a life estate pur autre vie determinable (condition subsequent being the death of *A* without issue), *O* has a possibility of reverter in fee simple subject to executory limitation (condition subsequent being the birth of a child to *B*), the children of *B* have an executory interest in fee simple absolute, and *O* has a reversion (following *A*'s life estate pur autre vie) in fee simple absolute. The executory interest is valid under the RAP because it will vest, if at all, no later than the death of *A* or *B*, lives in being. When *B* gives birth to a child, *O*'s fee simple (in the possibility of reverter) is cut short and *A*'s life estate pur autre vie determinable is transformed into a life estate pur autre vie subject to executory limitation. When *B* dies, the class of *B*'s children closes. When *A* dies, the executory interest in *X* is destroyed by the failure of the condition subsequent to occur. *A*'s life estate pur autre vie

determinable transforms into a life estate pur autre vie and descends by inheritance to *H*.

570. *I. None.* On *O*'s conveyance, *A* has a present interest in a fee simple subject to executory limitation, *B* has an executory interest in a life estate, *O* has a possibility of reverter (following *B*'s life estate) in fee simple absolute, and the first child of *B* has an executory interest (following *B*'s life estate) in a life estate. The interest of the first grandchild of *B* is invalid under the RAP because it could vest too late. In order to show the invalidity, one could start with the premise that the grandchild has an interest and hypothesize that *B* may have a child, *X*, and *O*'s heir also may be born. *X* would have an executory interest in a life estate, following *B*'s life estate and followed by *O*'s possibility of reverter. *B*'s first grandchild would have an executory interest following *X*'s life estate. Then all lives in being may die with *A* dying before *B*. At this point, *X* would have a present interest in a life estate, *O*'s heir would take *O*'s possibility of reverter now transformed into a reversion, and *B*'s first grandchild would have a contingent remainder in fee simple absolute. Then *X* may bear *B*'s grandchild more than twenty-one years later, after the perpetuities period has run. This would vest the interest in *B*'s grandchild too late, thus making the interest invalid at the time of the conveyance.

571. *H. Vested remainder subject to open* in a life estate pur autre vie subject to executory limitation (condition subsequent that partially divests the estate is the birth of another child). On *O*'s conveyance, *A* has a present interest in a life estate, *C* has a vested remainder (following *A*'s life estate) in fee simple absolute, *A*'s children have a contingent remainder (following *A*'s life estate) in a life estate pur autre vie (life of the first to die), and *B*'s widow has a contingent remainder (following *A*'s children's life estate) in a life estate. When *X* is born, his interest vests subject to open in favor of other children who might be born up until the termination of *A*'s life estate. The unborn children have an executory interest after *X*'s birth. The life that determines the length of *X*'s estate is that of the first child to die, since the estate is for joint lives. *X*'s interest is valid under the RAP because the interest of every member of the class must vest, if at all, on or before the death of *A*.

572. *I. None.* The interest is invalid under the RAP. One might hypothesize that, after *O*'s conveyance, *A* may have a child, *B* may have a child, *B*'s future widow may be born, and *C*'s heir may be born. Then all lives in being may die, leaving *A*'s child with a present interest in a life estate, *B*'s child with a contingent remainder in a life estate, *B*'s widow with a vested remainder in a life estate, and *C*'s heir with a vested remainder in fee simple absolute. *B*'s child would have a contingent remainder because she must survive the termination of *X*'s life estate in order to take a vested interest. The death of *A*'s child more than twenty-one years later would cause the interest in *B*'s child to vest too late.

573. *D. Contingent remainder* in a life estate. *B*'s widow is unascertained and may even be unborn at the time of *O*'s conveyance. However, *B*'s widow, if any, is ascertained on *B*'s death, at which time her

interest would become vested. *B*'s widow's interest is valid under the RAP.

574. *F. Vested remainder* in fee simple absolute. *C*'s interest is vested at the time of the conveyance and thus valid under the RAP.

575. *B. Executory interest* in fee simple absolute. On *O*'s conveyance, *A* has a present in a life estate, *B* has a vested remainder in a life estate, and *O* has a reversion in fee simple subject to executory limitation. The conditions subsequent, both of which must be satisfied to vest *C*'s executory interest, are the passage of twenty-two years from the death of *B* and the survival of *C*. The latter condition ensures that *C*'s interest will become vested, if at all, during the life of *C*, a life in being.

576. *C. Life estate*. On *O*'s conveyance, *A* has a present interest in a life estate, *B* has a vested remainder in a life estate, and *O* has a reversion in fee simple absolute. Before applying the RAP, *O* would have had a reversion in fee simple subject to executory limitation, and *C* would have had an executory interest in fee simple absolute. The condition subsequent that would have had to be satisfied to vest *C*'s executory interest would have been the passage of twenty-two years from the death of *B*. *C*'s interest is invalid under the RAP. We may hypothesize that *O* and *C* may each bear a child, *X* and *Y*, respectively. Then all lives in being, including *A*, *B*, and *C*, may die. At this point, *X* would have a present interest in fee simple subject to executory limitation and *Y* would have an executory interest in fee simple absolute. Twenty-two years would pass, and then *C*'s interest (now held by *Y*) would vest too late. Therefore, when *C* conveys her interest to *A*, there is nothing to convey.

577. *D. Contingent remainder* in fee simple absolute. *A* has a present interest in a life estate. The first child of *A* to graduate from law school is unascertained and therefore has a contingent remainder in a life estate. *B* has a vested remainder in a life estate. *C*'s interest is subject to a condition precedent. This condition precedent must take place, if at all, within twenty-one years of *A*'s death. Therefore, *C*'s interest is valid under the RAP. *O* has a reversion in fee simple absolute.

578. *D. Contingent remainder* in fee simple absolute. *A* has a present interest in a life estate, *B* has a contingent remainder (following *A*'s life estate) in a life estate, *C* has a contingent remainder (following *B*'s life estate) in a life estate, *D* has a contingent remainder (following *A*'s life estate) in a fee simple absolute, and *O* has a reversion (following *A*'s life estate and supporting the contingent remainders under the Backup Rule) in a fee simple absolute. The interests of *B* and *C* are both contingent on *B*'s eldest son being born and getting married. *B*'s contingent remainder must vest, if at all, on or before the termination of *A*'s life estate or it will never vest. The Destructibility of Contingent Remainders Rule destroys any contingent remainder that has failed to vest on or before the termination of the preceding estates. Likewise, *C*'s interest must vest, if at all, on or before the termination of *A*'s and *B*'s estates. Since *A*'s estate and *B*'s estate can terminate only on or before their

deaths and they are lives in being, *B*'s and *C*'s interests are valid under the RAP.

579. *H. Vested remainder subject to open* in fee simple subject to executory limitation (condition subsequent being the birth of another grandchild) shared as a tenancy in common with the other living grandchildren. At the time of the conveyance, *A* has a present interest in a life estate, *X* has a vested remainder in a life estate, the living grandchildren have a vested remainder subject to open in a fee simple subject to executory limitation, and the unborn grandchildren have an executory interest in fee simple absolute until they are born. The vested remainder subject to open in the living grandchildren opens to receive *I* and *J* when they are born. The class will close so as to eliminate the executory interest when *X* dies. Therefore, no grandchild in the class may take a vested interest after the death of all lives in being (except for a possible period of gestation, which is permitted under the RAP), and the vested remainder in the living grandchildren is valid under the RAP. When *A* dies, *X*'s interests transforms into a present interest in a life estate.

580. *A. Present interest* in fee simple absolute. *O*'s attempted conveyance of an executory interest to *A* is invalid under the RAP because Blackacre may be used as a farm more than twenty-one years after the death of every life in being at the creation of the interest. One may hypothesize that, after *O*'s conveyance, *O*'s future heir, *X*, is born, and *A*'s future heir, *Y*, is born. Then all lives in being may die, leaving *X* with *O*'s present interest and *Y* with *A*'s executory interest. Then Blackacre may be used as a farm more than twenty-one years later. At this point, *A*'s interest (now held by *Y*) would vest too late. Therefore, *O*'s second conveyance to *B* is the entire present interest in fee simple absolute.

581. *C. Life estate.* On *O*'s conveyance, *A* has a present interest in a life estate, *B*'s eldest son, who is unborn, has a contingent remainder in a life estate, and *O* has a reversion in fee simple absolute. The attempted creation of an executory interest in *A*'s heirs is invalid under the RAP. To demonstrate this invalidity, one might hypothesize that *B*'s son, *Y*, and *A*'s future heir, *H*, and *O*'s future heir, *P*, may be born; all lives in being may die, leaving *Y* with a present interest in a life estate subject to executory limitation, *H* with an executory interest, and *P* with the reversion; and then *B*'s son would marry more than twenty-one years later, allowing *A*'s heir to take a vested present interest beyond the perpetuities period. This interest is void ab initio. Therefore, when *Y* is actually born, his interest becomes a vested remainder in a life estate, and when *A* dies, it becomes a present interest in a life estate, followed by a reversion in fee simple absolute in *O*.

582. *J. None of the above is correct.* On *O*'s conveyance, before application of the Rule in Shelley's Case, *A* has a present interest in a life estate, *A*'s children (yet unborn) have a contingent remainder (following *A*'s life estate and with a condition precedent of birth) in a life estate pur autre vie, and *A*'s heirs have a contingent remainder (following *A*'s life estate and with a condition precedent of ascertainment) in fee simple absolute. The Rule in Shelley's

Case transforms the heirs' remainder into a remainder in *A*. Therefore, *A* has a vested remainder (following *A*'s life estate) in fee simple absolute. There is no merger of *A*'s two ownerships because of the exception to the Merger Rule. The interest in *A*'s children is valid under the RAP because it vests in each on birth (to a life in being). When *A* bears a child, *B*, that child's contingent remainder transforms into a vested remainder subject to open in a life estate pur autre vie subject to executory limitation, and the contingent remainder of the unborn children transforms into an executory interest in a life estate pur autre vie. *B*'s vested remainder pushes *A*'s vested remainder further along to follow *B*'s life estate pur autre vie. When *A* sells her interest in Blackacre to *X*, *X* has a present interest in a life estate and a vested remainder in fee simple absolute.

583. *I. None.* Before application of the RAP, at the time of the conveyance, *A* has a present interest in a life estate, *A*'s first son has a contingent remainder (following *A*'s life estate) in a life estate, *O* has a reversion (following *A*'s life estate) in fee simple subject to executory limitation, *A*'s first grandson has an executory interest (conditions subsequent that must be satisfied in order for it to vest are birth and the passage of one year from termination of the preceding estates) in a life estate, *B* has an executory interest (following *A*'s grandson's life estate) in a life estate pur autre vie, *C* has an executory interest (following *B*'s life estate pur autre vie) in a life estate, and *O* has a possibility of reverter (following *C*'s life estate) in fee simple absolute. The interest of *A*'s first grandson is invalid under the RAP. One may hypothesize that *A* may have a first son, *M*, and that *O*'s future heir, *H*, may be born. Then all lives in being may die, leaving *M* with a present interest in a life estate, *H* with a reversion in fee simple subject to executory limitation, *A*'s first grandson (unborn) with an executory interest in a life estate, and *H* with a possibility of reverter in fee simple absolute. Then more than twenty-one years later *M*'s wife may bear *A*'s first grandson, *G*, and *M* may die, and one year later, *G* would take a vested present interest too late.

584. *B. Executory interest* in a life estate pur autre vie. Since the interest in *A*'s first grandson is void under the RAP, *A* has a present interest in a life estate, *S* has a vested remainder in a life estate, *O* has a reversion in fee simple subject to executory limitation, *B* has an executory interest (condition subsequent that must be satisfied for it to vest is the passage of one year after the termination of the estates in *A* and *S*) in a life estate pur autre vie, *C* has an executory interest (following *B*'s life estate pur autre vie) in a life estate, and *O* has a possibility of reverter (following *C*'s life estate) in fee simple absolute. *B*'s interest is valid because it vests, if at all, no later than the death of *X*, a life in being at the creation of the interest.

585. *B. Executory interest* in a life estate. *C*'s interest is valid because it vests, if at all, no later than the death of *C*, a life in being.

586. *D. Contingent remainder* in a life estate pur autre vie. *A* has a present interest in a life estate. *B* has a vested remainder (following

A's life estate) in a life estate, and *O* has a reversion (following *B*'s life estate) in fee simple absolute. *A*'s heirs have a contingent remainder (following *A*'s life estate) in a life estate pur autre vie, and *B*'s heirs have a contingent remainder (following *B*'s life estate) in a life estate pur autre vie. The Rule in Shelley's Case does not apply when the estate of the heirs is a life estate. *A*'s heirs are determined at the time of *A*'s death, at which time they take a vested present interest (or nothing if there are no heirs or *A*'s life estate has terminated by forfeiture before *A*'s death). Therefore, the interest in *A*'s heirs is valid under the RAP because it must vest, if at all, on the death of a life in being.

587. *D. Contingent remainder* in a life estate pur autre vie. *B*'s heirs are determined at the time of *B*'s death, at which time they take either a present interest or a vested remainder (or nothing if there are no heirs or the preceding life estates have terminated before *B*'s death). Therefore, their interest is valid under the RAP.

588. *I. None. X*'s interest is void under the RAP. On *O*'s conveyance, *A* has a present interest in a life estate, *A*'s heirs have a contingent remainder in a life estate pur autre vie, *B* has a vested remainder in a life estate, and *O* has a reversion in fee simple absolute. On *A*'s death, *H* takes a present interest in a life estate and *O* has a reversion in fee simple absolute. Before application of the RAP, *B*'s children would have had a contingent remainder in fee simple absolute on *O*'s conveyance. One might hypothesize that *A*'s future heir, *F*, and *B*'s child, *G*, and *O*'s future heir, *J*, then may be born; all lives in being may die, leaving *F* with a present interest in a life estate, *J* with the reversion in fee simple absolute, and *G* with the contingent remainder in fee simple absolute; then *F* may die more than twenty-one years later, giving *G* a vested present interest too late. Therefore, the interest in *B*'s children is invalid at the time of the conveyance.

589. *D. Contingent remainder* in fee simple subject to executory limitation. *A* has a present interest in a life estate pur autre vie. The condition "if *X* dies" is superfluous because it merely restates how *A*'s life estate pur autre vie ends. Therefore, *B* has a vested remainder. *B*'s estate is a life estate because the words "for as long as *B* is alive" define the limits of a life estate. *C*'s contingent remainder in fee simple subject to executory limitation has a condition precedent to *C*'s interest (*C*'s marriage) and a condition subsequent to *C*'s estate (*C*'s divorce). *D* has an executory interest in fee simple absolute. *O* has a reversion (following *B*'s life estate) in fee simple absolute.

590. *I. Fee simple determinable.* On *O*'s conveyance, *A* has a present interest in fee simple subject to executory limitation, *B* has an executory interest in a life estate, *C*'s interest is invalid under the RAP, and *L* (inheriting from *O*) has a possibility of reverter in fee simple absolute. *B*'s interest is valid under the RAP because it must vest before *B*, a life in being, dies (or else *B*'s interest is over). When *B* dies, *A*'s estate transforms into a fee simple determinable, and *L* has a possibility of reverter in fee simple absolute. The attempted conveyance of an executory interest in fee simple absolute to *C* is invalid

under the RAP because one might hypothesize that *A*'s child and heir, *X*, and *C*'s heir, *H*, may be born; then all lives in being may die, leaving *X* with the present interest in fee simple subject to executory limitation and *H* with *C*'s executory interest in fee simple absolute; then *X* may have *A*'s first grandson, *G*, more than twenty-one years later, allowing *C*'s heir, *H*, to take a vested interest too late.

591. *G. Possibility of reverter* in fee simple absolute.

592. *I. None. B*'s children are unborn. Before application of the RAP, their interest would be a contingent remainder in fee simple subject to executory limitation. *C* would have an alternative contingent remainder in fee simple absolute that would stand ready to take whenever *A*'s life estate terminated subject to the condition precedent that no child of *B* be born. If *B* were to bear a child, *X*, that child would have a vested remainder subject to open (for future-born children) in a fee simple subject to executory limitation. *B*'s unborn children would have an executory interest in fee simple absolute. *C*'s remainder would transform into an executory interest dependent on the condition (subsequent to the estate in *B*'s child, *X*) that *B* and all his children die without any child of *B* reaching twenty-five. *C*'s interest is invalid under the RAP because one might then hypothesize that *C*'s future heir, *H*, may be born; then all lives in being may die, leaving *X* with a present interest in fee simple subject to executory limitation, and *H* with an executory interest in fee simple absolute; and then *X* may die before reaching twenty-five but more than twenty-one years later, at which time *H*, holding *C*'s interest, would take a vested interest too late. Therefore, at the time of *O*'s conveyance, *A* has a present interest in a life estate, *O* has a reversion in fee simple absolute, and *B*'s children have a contingent remainder in fee simple absolute. The condition subsequent on the interest of *B*'s children uses conditional language and is considered void along with *C*'s interest. (Note that before application of the RAP, *C*'s interest is a contingent remainder that may take on the termination of the preceding life estate in *A*, a life in being, but the Destructibility of Contingent Remainders Rule does not ensure that *C*'s interest is valid on application of the RAP. *C*'s interest may transform into an executory interest here, and it is invalid under the RAP because it may vest not merely on the termination of the preceding life estate but also by cutting short an estate in fee simple beyond the perpetuities period.)

593. *D. Life estate pur autre vie.* On *O*'s conveyance, *A* has a present interest in a life estate pur autre vie, following which *B*'s children have a contingent remainder in a life estate measured by the life of *B*, following which *C* has a contingent remainder in a life estate, following which *D* has a contingent remainder in fee simple absolute, and following *A*'s life estate pur autre vie, *O* has a reversion in fee simple absolute. The remainder in *B*'s children is contingent on birth to *B*, a life in being, and is therefore valid under the RAP.

594. *D. Contingent remainder* in fee simple absolute. The contingent remainders in *C* and *D* are contingent on Blackacre's use as a

farm, a condition precedent that may occur more than twenty-one years after the death of every life in being. These remainders are valid, however, because they cannot vest more than twenty-one years after X's and B's death since the Destructibility of Contingent Remainders Rule requires vesting, if at all, on or before the deaths of X and B or else the remainders will be destroyed.

595. *H. Fee simple absolute.* O's first attempted conveyance of an executory interest in fee simple absolute to the heirs of A's first child is invalid under the RAP. One may hypothesize that A's first child, X, and O's heir, H, and X's future heir, T, may be born; then all lives in being may die, leaving H with O's present interest in fee simple subject to executory limitation; and then A's first child may live for more than twenty-one years after the death of all lives in being and then die, leaving T to take a vested present interest too late. Therefore, O has a present interest in fee simple absolute after his first invalid conveyance. He conveys this interest to X.

596. *K. Fee simple subject to executory limitation.* The devise to the grandchildren is valid under the RAP. The grandchildren have an executory interest in fee simple absolute until they are born, at which time they take a present interest subject to open in a fee simple subject to executory limitation. The interest of each grandchild vests no later than birth to a life in being, X or Y, because there can be no more children born to O, who is dead. The class closes naturally with the death of X and Y.

597. *H. Fee simple absolute.* At the time of O's conveyance, A's first son (being unborn) has an executory interest. Before application of the RAP, the estate of A's first son would be a fee simple subject to executory limitation. The condition subsequent would be the death of A's first son without issue living at his death. X and Y would share as tenants in common in an executory interest in fee simple absolute. This executory interest is invalid under the RAP. One might hypothesize that A's son, G, and the heirs of X and Y may be born; all lives in being may die, leaving G with a present interest in fee simple subject to executory limitation, and the heirs of X and Y with their executory interest in fee simple absolute; and then G may live for more than twenty-one years and die without issue, allowing the interest of the heirs of X and Y to vest too late. Since the interest of X and Y is invalid, and the condition subsequent on the estate of A's first son ("but if A's first son dies without issue") uses conditional language, the condition subsequent is also invalid. O's conveyance gives A's first son an executory interest in fee simple absolute, which becomes a present interest in S on S's birth.

598. *I. None.*

599. *I. None.* O's conveyance gives A a present interest in fee simple absolute. On A's death, B takes this interest by will. S never receives anything.

600. *I. None.* On O's conveyance, A has a present interest in a life estate, S has a vested remainder subject to open in a life estate pur autre vie subject to executory limitation, and the unborn children have an executory interest in a life estate pur autre vie. The interest in

A's heirs is an interest in *A* under the Rule in Shelley's Case. Therefore, *A* also has a vested remainder in fee simple absolute. The interest in *A*'s grandchildren (including *G*) is invalid under the RAP. Before application of the RAP, *G* would have had a vested remainder subject to open in a life estate pur autre vie subject to executory limitation (following *S*'s life estate pur autre vie subject to executory limitation), and *A*'s unborn grandchildren would have had an executory interest in a life estate pur autre vie. One might hypothesize that *A* may have another child, *T*, and that *G*'s future heir, *R*, and *A*'s future devisee, *V*, may be born; then all lives in being may die, leaving *T* with a present interest in a life estate, *R* with a vested remainder subject to open in a life estate pur autre vie subject to executory limitation, *A*'s unborn grandchildren with an executory interest in a life estate pur autre vie, and *V* with a vested remainder in fee simple absolute; and then *T* may have a child, *Z*, more than twenty-one years later, allowing *Z* to take a vested interest too late under the RAP.